Building Effective Project Teams

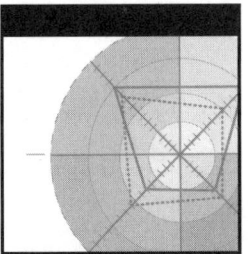

Building Effective Project Teams

Robert K. Wysocki

Wiley Computer Publishing

John Wiley & Sons, Inc.
NEW YORK • CHICHESTER • WEINHEIM • BRISBANE • SINGAPORE • TORONTO

Publisher: Robert Ipsen
Editor: Theresa Hudson
Developmental Editor: Kathryn A. Malm
Managing Editor: Angela Smith
Associate New Media Editor: Brian Snapp
Text Design & Composition: Publishers' Design and Production Services, Inc.

Designations used by companies to distinguish their products are often claimed as trademarks. In all instances where John Wiley & Sons, Inc., is aware of a claim, the product names appear in initial capital or ALL CAPITAL LETTERS. Readers, however, should contact the appropriate companies for more complete information regarding trademarks and registration.

This book is printed on acid-free paper. ∞

Copyright © 2002 by Robert K. Wysocki. All rights reserved.

Published by John Wiley & Sons, Inc., New York

Published simultaneously in Canada.

No part of this publication may be reproduced, stored in a retrieval system or transmitted in any form or by any means, electronic, mechanical, photocopying, recording, scanning or otherwise, except as permitted under Sections 107 or 108 of the 1976 United States Copyright Act, without either the prior written permission of the Publisher, or authorization through payment of the appropriate per-copy fee to the Copyright Clearance Center, 222 Rosewood Drive, Danvers, MA 01923, (978) 750-8400, fax (978) 750-4744. Requests to the Publisher for permission should be addressed to the Permissions Department, John Wiley & Sons, Inc., 605 Third Avenue, New York, NY 10158-0012, (212) 850-6011, fax (212) 850-6008, E-Mail: PERMREQ @ WILEY.COM.

This publication is designed to provide accurate and authoritative information in regard to the subject matter covered. It is sold with the understanding that the publisher is not engaged in professional services. If professional advice or other expert assistance is required, the services of a competent professional person should be sought.

The Interaction Triangle reproduced in Figures 8.2 through 8.9, 11.1, 11.10, and 13.3 is reproduced by special permission from the Strength Deployment Inventory, copyright 1972, 2000 by Personal Strengths Publishing. Further reproduction is prohibited without the prior written consent of the Publisher, Personal Strengths Publishing.

SDI, Strength Deployment Inventory, and the Interaction Triangle are registered trademarks of Personal Strengths Publishing.

Library of Congress Cataloging-in-Publication Data:

Wysocki, Robert K.
    Building effective project teams / Robert K. Wysocki.
       p. cm.
    Includes bibliographical references and index.
    ISBN 0-471-01392-7 (pbk. : alk. paper)
    1. Teams in the workplace. 2. Project management. I. Title
HD66 .W96   2001
658.4'02—dc21
                                                2001045454

Printed in the United States of America.

10 9 8 7 6 5 4 3 2 1

To Mom and Dad, who taught me to love learning and reading and to always be inquisitive. I owe them more than I could ever thank them for. Dad, you are up there watching and I know you are proud.

To Nancy, my wife, companion, and friend for more than 37 years. Your support and encouragement of my aggressive and over-demanding working habits are a constant source of strength to me. Thanks for being there and staying there.

Contents

Introduction		**xiii**
Acknowledgments		**xxiii**
About the Author		**xxv**
Part One	**The Background**	**1**
Chapter 1	**The Successful Project**	**3**
	Our Environment	4
	Project Support Environment	5
	Enterprise Environment	6
	Business Environment	6
	Project/Team Environment	8
	Why So Many Projects Fail	8
	Inadequate Communication	9
	Ineffective Use of the Project Team	10
	Inappropriate Project Management Process	11
	Project Critical Success Factors	11
	User Involvement	11
	Clear Requirements Statement	12
	Proper Planning	12
	Competent Staff	13

	Clear Vision and Objectives	14
	Hard-Working and Focused Staff	14
	Project Team Critical Success Factors	15
	A Balanced Problem-Solving Capability	15
	A Balanced Decision-Making Capability	16
	A Balanced Conflict Management Capability	16
	A Balanced Skill Profile	17
	Characteristics of Successful Project Teams	17
	Putting It All Together	18
Chapter 2	**The Project Environment**	**19**
	Project Classes	20
	Value of Project Classes for Team Formation	21
	Value of Project Classes for Methodology Selection	21
	Project Complexity Model	22
	Project Classification Rules	25
	Project Templates	26
	Organizational Structures	26
	Functional	27
	Matrix	28
	Projectized	32
	Team Leadership Models	34
	Deciding Which Model to Use	37
	Environmental Considerations	37
	Dispersed versus Co-located	39
	Temporary versus Permanent	39
	Putting It All Together	40
Chapter 3	**Team Models**	**41**
	Belbin Team Role Model	42
	Margerison and McCann Team Management Wheel	44
	DISC System	47
	Shortcomings	50
	Putting It All Together	52

Chapter 4	**Project/Team Alignment Model**	**53**
	The Basis of the Model	54
	P4 System	57
	Project Scope	58
	Project Profile	59
	Team Profile	59
	Project Management Process	59
	Project Management Life Cycle	60
	Initiating Phase	60
	Planning Phase	61
	Launching Phase	63
	Monitoring Phase	63
	Closing Phase	64
	Team Life Cycle	65
	Creating an Effective Project Team	66
	Assessment Stage	66
	Formation Stage	67
	Development Stage	68
	Deployment Stage	68
	The Project/Team Alignment Model	68
	Putting It All Together	73
Part Two	**Assessment**	**75**
Chapter 5	**The Case Study**	**77**
	The O'Neill and Preigh Business Situation	78
	The Gold Medallion Organ Project	79
	The Gold Medallion Organ Project Team	80
	Project Manager	81
	Project Administrator	81
	Manager of Applications Development	81
	Programmer	82
	Systems Analyst	83
	Manufacturing Engineer	83
	Mechanical Engineer	83
	Organization of the Gold Team	84
	Putting It All Together	84

Chapter 6   Thinking Styles — 87

Herrmann Brain Dominance Instrument — 88
   Thinking Styles — 89
   Double, Triple, and Quadruple Profiles — 92
   Test-Retest Reliability — 96
Candidate Pool Members' HBDI Data — 97
Putting It All Together — 102

Chapter 7   Problem-Solving and Decision-Making Styles — 105

How We Learn — 106
Learning Styles Inventory — 107
   Individual Learning Style Types — 109
LSI and the Problem-Solving Process — 112
   Problem-Solving Model — 112
   Problem Solving and the LSI — 115
LSI and the Decision-Making Process — 115
   Decision Styles — 116
   Decision Making and the LSI — 117
Candidate Pool Members' LSI Data — 120
Putting It All Together — 123

Chapter 8   Conflict Management Styles and Strategies — 125

Conflict Management — 126
Conflict Management Styles — 127
Strength Deployment Inventory — 129
   Motivational Values — 130
   Test-Retest Reliability — 133
   SDI and Conflict Management Strategies — 133
   Relationship between the Strategies and the SDI — 137
Candidate Pool Members' SDI Profiles — 138
Putting It All Together — 143

Chapter 9   Project Management Skills and Competencies — 145

Project Manager Skill Assessment — 146
   Skills — 146
   Measuring Skill Proficiency Levels — 148

What Does Your Skill Profile Tell You?	151
Candidate Pool Members' PMSA	155
Project Manager Competency Assessment	160
Candidate Pool Members' PMCA	161
Putting It All Together	165

Part Three Formation — 167

Chapter 10 Establishing the Profile of the Project — 169

Every Project Has a Profile	171
Profiling the Phases of a Project	175
Creating the HBDI Profile of the Gold Project	177
Putting It All Together	181

Chapter 11 Establishing the Profile of the Project Team — 183

Analyzing the Candidate Pool	184
Candidate Pool HBDI Profile	184
Candidate Pool LSI Profile	191
Candidate Pool SDI Profile	193
Candidate Pool Skills Profile	194
Steps to Forming a Project Team	199
Populating the Project Team	199
Building Effective Project Teams	201
Putting It All Together	215

Chapter 12 Assessing Team Alignment and Balance — 217

Team-to-Project Alignment	218
Definition of an Alignment Gap	219
Interpreting Alignment Gaps	219
Assessing a Project Team	221
Team Alpha Assessment	223
Team Beta Assessment	223
Team Gamma Assessment	226
Team Delta Assessment	226
Team Epsilon Assessment	230
PMSA Assessment for All Five Teams	230

	Putting It All Together	233
Part Four	**Development and Deployment**	**235**
Chapter 13	**Developing and Deploying the Project Team**	**237**
	General Strategies	238
	Strengths	238
	Weaknesses	239
	Opportunities	240
	Threats	240
	SWOT Analysis of the Gold Team	241
	PMSA Team Profile	241
	HBDI Profile of the Gold Team	245
	SDI Profile of the Gold Team	245
	LSI Profile of the Gold Team	246
	SWOT Summary	248
	Project Change Management	250
	Project Scope Management	251
	Project Team Change Management	251
	Putting It All Together	252
Appendix A	**References and Reading List**	**255**
Appendix B	**Sources of Information**	**261**
Appendix C	**How to Get TeamArchitect Tools**	**263**
Appendix D	**The Companion CD-ROM**	**265**
Index		**267**

Introduction

Of all the variables that contribute to the success or failure of projects, the one that is most neglected, and in need of the most attention, is the project team itself. Yes, there are hundreds of books on building high-performance teams, but a closer look reveals that the project itself is hardly ever discussed as a factor to be considered in building high-performance teams. One might erroneously conclude that a team is a team is a team and that it really doesn't make any difference what the project is, team effectiveness and performance are invariant to the project.

After more than 35 years of practicing, training, and consulting in project management, I have reached the conclusion that that belief is just blatantly incorrect. In the chapters of this book I hope to share with you not only why I feel justified in making such a bold statement but also a set of tools that everyone should be using to improve team effectiveness as a function of the project. Positioning the project team to be more effective is a project-driven and project-dependent activity.

It's time we adopted a killer instinct and did something innovative to attack the reasons for project failures. We all know that project failure rates are unacceptably high. Surveys of IT managers conducted throughout the 1990s report failure rates ranging from 50 to 80 percent or more. Regardless of the type of business you are in, that failure rate is unacceptable. Equally unacceptable is the fact that many of the managers who were surveyed were not surprised by the reasons for those project failures. They readily admitted that they had not been very effective in taking corrective steps to reduce the incidence of project failure.

Over 50 percent of the failures that occur are due, at least in part, to the behavioral characteristics of the project team itself. I am not referring to the behavioral characteristics of any individual team member but rather to the collective behavioral characteristics of the team. For example, suppose that the team was composed of very analytic members and that the project they were working on required a great deal of creativity. What do you think would happen? You probably wouldn't get the results you were expecting. Conversely, suppose that the team was composed of all creative people and that the project required the implementation of a new computer system. What do you think would happen? Again, you might be disappointed because the creative energies of the team will somehow find a way into the project, and that is definitely not what you want to have happen. Implementation requires following a well-defined procedure, and that doesn't leave much room for creativity. Such a team would be frustrated to the point where the risk of failure would be very high.

I find it very interesting that we go to extreme lengths to build the best professional sports team but put almost no effort into building the best project team. Take baseball, for example. Compare the effort that goes into building a winning baseball team to what we do to build a project team. Players demonstrate their ability through the actions they take and the decisions they make when presented with actual game situations. This is how their coaches and managers assess them. Project team members, on the other hand, rarely are evaluated or assessed as to how they make decisions, solve problems, or resolve conflicts. Their managers seldom have an opportunity to observe performance in any of these areas. Teams are formed with little or no consideration for these less obvious, but oh so important, traits and skills.

How do you build your project team? It probably goes something like this: Harry just came off an implementation project. He's a database architect. We need a database architect on the new design project, so let's put him on the team. To form your team as casually as this is asking for trouble. There is a lot more than a person's availability to consider when forming a successful project team. You probably have guessed that technical skills are a requirement. Of course, they are, but there is more—much more. I am going to supplement your practices with a whole new set of ideas—things you may have never thought about before. If you follow my lead, you will be more successful with your projects.

As I conducted my own study of the published research on team effectiveness and the tools that are commercially available to achieve it, it was quite clear that there was no "how to" book on building effective project teams. In addition, I was unable to find a single publication that drew all of this information together in a way that the practitioner could use it.

My book will teach you several practical team assessment, formation, development, and deployment strategies that you can use to reduce project failure rates significantly. I'll show you how to use existing tools to form a balanced team that is designed to be effective and how to assess the strengths and weaknesses of an existing team and build strategies to take advantage of its strengths and mitigate its weaknesses.

One concept that I develop in this book is that the project, the project team, and the project management process form a system. I can't claim to be the first person on the planet to come to that conclusion, but I found no mention of that idea in any of the project management books I had read. This system relationship is significant. In order for a system to work, all of its parts must perform their function. In order to perform their function, all the parts must be integrated into a functioning whole. Furthermore, the parts, when integrated and functioning according to their purpose, will create a synergy—the whole is greater than the sum of the parts. Sounds good so far. You might now be asking: "So, how do we know if the parts can be integrated?" Or, perhaps for the practitioner, the more relevant question is: "How do we make the parts so that they can be integrated?"

Integrating the three parts—the project, the project team, and the project management process—is the central theme of this book. Much of what I cover in this book is not new. What is new is the way in which I have integrated these three parts into a system. In so doing I have built a working model with the tools to support it.

What Is Not in This Book

This is not a book about project management methods. I will introduce and briefly discuss a robust five-phase project management life cycle, which is an essential part of the project team life cycle model introduced in Chapter 3, "Team Models." Other than a few comments on methods scattered elsewhere, that is all you will find about project management methods in this book. My previous book, *Effective Project Management, 2nd Edition* (Wysocki et al., Wiley, 2000), covers project management methods in more detail. You will find the ideas and concepts expressed here to be entirely consistent with that book.

This book will not cover how to improve an individual's performance as a member of your team. I am pleased to be able to refer you to a book that

I wrote with my good friend Jim Lewis and that was recently published. It is called *The World-Class Project Manager: A Professional Development Guide* (Wysocki & Lewis, Perseus Books, 2001). In that book you will find a completely developed strategy for defining your project manager career goals and building a professional development plan to achieve them. The focus of that book is the individual. The focus of this book is the project team. In this book, the only discussion of an individual's skills, competencies, and behavioral characteristics is in relation to their contribution to the team.

This book also does not cover how to build high-performance teams. Appendix A, "References and Reading List," contains a listing of some of the better-known books on the topic. The hundreds of books on building high-performance teams focus on the general characteristics of teams regardless of the work to be assigned to the team. Most of those books assume that the team is co-located and working on one assignment at a time. While there are examples of such teams, in today's contemporary world that is not a very likely situation. Team members work on several projects simultaneously and are often geographically dispersed. That radically changes the strategy one might choose for building project teams. Contemporary project teams cannot expect to spend a lot of time together (that is a prerequisite for high-performance teams).

You may be familiar with the stages of team development (forming, storming, norming, and performing). Although these are valid stages, frankly they generally won't occur in most cases because of the constraints that are placed on teams by today's business environment. We live and work in a fast-paced, fast-change, and high-demand environment. Projects tend to be of short duration. Contemporary project team membership can change at the drop of a hat. High-performance team building strategies fall apart under those conditions. It is my experience that project change is constant and can affect the characteristics of the project; hence, it can radically affect the effectiveness of the team. Only by recognizing these facts and quantifying them can we hope to build teams that can perform to expectations.

Who Should Read This Book

If you are involved in the assessment, formation, development, and deployment of project teams for mission-critical or troubled projects, you need this book. I will cover two situations. The first and most likely situation occurs when the project manager inherits a team whose membership has already been determined. There is little or no flexibility to replace any of the members. This book can help by showing the project manager how to assess the behavioral characteristics of the team using commercially available tools. This book will also show project managers how to deploy the team most effectively based on those characteristics. It will help the project manager visualize team strengths and weaknesses and recommend assignments as well as training needs.

The second and least likely situation occurs when the project manager can recruit team members and form the entire project team. This will happen in projectized organizations. In this case, this book can help project managers by providing a decision support system. It provides the capacity for "what if" scenarios so that the project manager can examine and analyze the consequences of alternative team composition.

Once the team is formed and work on the project begins, you'll find additional uses for this book. Project phases and milestones represent major shifts in project focus and can have an impact on team member deployment. Changes could be customer initiated or market driven. A change in project scope may alter the alignment between the project and the project team, which may require an adjustment in deployment strategy or a change in team membership. The loss of one or more team members will require a replacement. This book can help the project manager evaluate alternative choices for replacing the lost member(s).

How Is This Book Organized?

This book consists of this Introduction, 13 chapters arranged in 4 parts, and 3 appendices.

Part One, The Background, consists of four chapters that provide the background and infrastructure for our journey to effective project teams.

Chapter 1, "The Successful Project," summarizes the most recent study on project failures and identifies not only the critical success factors for projects but also the critical success factors for project teams. That will lead us to consider the characteristics of successful project teams.

Chapter 2, "The Project Environment" also examines the environments in which projects are undertaken. That involves a discussion of organizational structures and team structures with reference to how they help or hinder the project team. Many of the tools discussed in this book are effective or not depending on the environment in which they are used.

We need to understand that environment in order to apply the tools effectively.

Chapter 3, "Team Models," contains brief overviews of three approaches to team role models. These represent the current thinking regarding team structure, independent of the nature of the work the team will be charged to complete. This will help the reader understand how teams have been analyzed in the past and why these models are not sufficient for today's project environment.

In Chapter 4, "Project/Team Alignment Model," I introduce my concept of the project-driven team structure that I believe addresses team effectiveness much better than the generic models in Chapter 3. I introduce my own life cycle model for describing the project team and integrate it with a robust project management life cycle. The result is a paradigm shift in thinking about the whole development process of teams that can be more effective. Let me assure you that I have not taken a radical approach to this notion but rather incorporated the best from the existing research on creating high-performance teams and merely factored the project into the models.

In addition to skill and competency assessments, which may have been done to form the initial project team, a number of other assessments are needed in order to determine the likely effectiveness of the project team. While some of these assessments may be used to further adjust team membership, the more likely scenario is to use them to formulate strategies as to how to use the existing team most effectively. *Part Two, Assessment,* covers the assessment process and introduces four tools that provide the data on which TeamArchitect depends.

Chapter 5, "The Case Study," is a brief introduction to the case study, O'Neill & Preigh Church Equipment Manufacturers. It includes a description of the business situation facing them, the project they have commissioned to build a touch-screen organ called the Gold Medallion Organ, and the candidate pool of 16 potential team members from which a project team will be formed. The next four chapters discuss the behavioral characteristics of the project team members.

In Chapter 6, "Thinking Styles," we discuss assessing the thinking styles of the project team members using the Herrmann Brain Dominance Instrument (HBDI) from Herrmann International. The HBDI is a 120-question instrument that measures the extent to which each of the four thinking styles (right-brain, left-brain, cerebral, limbic) is preferred by an individual.

Chapter 7, "Problem-Solving and Decision-Making Styles," assesses problem-solving and decision-making styles using the Learning Styles Inventory (LSI) from Hay McBer Training Resources Group. The LSI is a 12-question instrument that measures the extent to which each of the four learning styles (assimilator, diverger, accommodator, and converger) are preferred by an individual.

Chapter 8, "Conflict Management Styles and Strategies," discusses assessing conflict management styles and strategies using the Strength Deployment Inventory (SDI) from Personal Strengths Publishing. The SDI is a 20-question instrument that measures the extent to which each of the three major value-relating styles (altruistic-nurturing, assertive-directing, and analytic-autonomizing) are preferred by an individual and the sequence of strategies they can be expected to follow in conflict situations.

Chapter 9, "Project Management Skills and Competencies," introduces the Project Manager Skill Assessment (PMSA) and the Project Manager Competency Assessment (PMCA), both available from Enterprise Information Insights. The PMSA is a 54-skill inventory based on Bloom's Taxonomy of Cognitive Learning. The PMCA is a 72-question survey that utilizes a 360-type assessment to measure the observed behavior of an individual in 18 areas involving business, personal, interpersonal, and management competencies. These five assessment tools (HBDI, LSI, SDI, PMSA, and PMCA) form the database on which TeamArchitect depends.

In choosing these assessment instruments, I tried to pick tools that did not require a specially trained consultant to interpret the results. The Learning Styles Inventory (Chapter 7) and the Strength Deployment Inventory (Chapter 8) met this criterion. Furthermore, they are both self-scoring, paper-based instruments although through this book you have access to TeamArchitect and can administer these at a password-protected Web site. The skill and competency assessments (Chapter 9) are also self-scoring, but in the case of the competency assessment, that data must be analyzed by computer to produce the necessary reports. Web-based versions of both of these instruments are available, and the reports that are automatically produced do not require a consultant for interpretation. The Herrmann Brain Dominance Instrument is different. It is not self-scoring, and it does require a certified professional to fully interpret the results. To the extent possible I will try to provide sufficient detail in Chapter 6 and all of Part Three to overcome some of that need.

The Gold Team data is included in all four chapters with interpretations provided. Also, you will have the opportunity to further assess the team members at a password-protected Web site available to you. Based on material presented in these chapters you will be able to interpret the results. This preparation will be needed in Part Three where we extend the analysis to the project team.

Formation encompasses two separate but interdependent activities: profiling the project and profiling the project team. In Part One, I advanced the notion that team effectiveness results from having configured the team around the characteristics of the project. We already configure the team to ensure that the team has the necessary technical skills and competencies required by the project. That is, of course, necessary but by no means sufficient to ensure the formation of an effective team. More is required. To peel back the onion and better understand the relationship between project and team I developed an innovative application of a commercially available survey instrument (the HBDI) that measures the project and the team on the same set of characteristics. By applying this to the project and the project team we will be able to visualize and discuss the degree to which the project and the project team are in alignment with one another as well as proscribe strategies to account for any observed misalignment. This is the only tool that I know of that has that property.

Part Three, Formation, takes the information you compiled in Part Two and shows how the five assessment tools are used to profile a project and a project team. It consists of three chapters.

Chapter 10, "Establishing the Profile of the Project," shows how the HBDI can be used to create the profile of a project by using a modified version of the HBDI. The project profile is superimposed on the same four thinking styles as the original HBDI. We will look at several examples of the application of this pro forma capability to information technology projects. This is a new application of the HBDI and is introduced for the first time in this book.

Chapter 11, "Establishing the Profile of the Project Team," shows a number of ways we can use the individual HBDI profiles to summarize up to the project team level and represent the HBDI profile of the project team.

Chapter 12, "Assessing Team Alignment and Balance," combines the HBDI project profile with the HBDI project team profile and the other assessment reports to show overall team alignment and balance. The result is a display of the gap that exists between the two. This is also a new application of the HBDI and is introduced for the first time in this book. The analysis presented in this chapter is the basis for the team formation capabilities of TeamArchitect.

Part Four, Development and Deployment, shows how the results from Part Three are used to develop strategies for making the final team alignment decisions and how to sustain that alignment over the life of the project.

Chapter 13, "Developing and Deploying the Project Team," shows by example how alignment is enhanced through team development and through assignments of team members to specific tasks over the life of the project.

TeamArchitect

TeamArchitect is a totally new concept for project managers. It is a decision support system for the project manager. It is a comprehensive system for assessing, forming, developing, and deploying effective project teams. In its present form TeamArchitect consists of this book, an accompanying CD-ROM, and a password-protected Web site called www.teamarchitect.com.

This book introduces the concept, model, and application of TeamArchitect. For those who choose to implement TeamArchitect in their companies, this book will be an indispensable reference. It will show, by way of example, how to present and interpret team assessment data and how to develop and deploy team members to the tasks of the project. Use this book as you take on the responsibility for a project and are forming the project team with which you will want to work. This book should be your companion throughout the entire life cycle of the project. Use it to help form your team, to assess the strengths and weaknesses of your team, to develop strategies for using your team members in the most effective way possible, and to adjust team membership in the likely event of a project change.

The CD-ROM that accompanies this book has all of the data used in the case study that I developed to illustrate the full range of capabilities of TeamArchitect. Ninety-two graphic reports were generated for this case at the TeamArchitect Web site. These reports contain the assessment of a 16-person candidate pool of potential team members, the assessments of 5 different teams that were formed from the candidate pool, and the assessment data of each individual in the candidate pool. You will find this to be a rich source of data for further analysis that you may conduct on your own as you hone your TeamArchitect skills. That information is indexed for easy retrieval and analysis. The CD-ROM also contains a searchable version of the book.

And, finally, the third component of TeamArchitect is www.teamarchitect.com. For those who would like to experience, first hand, the analysis of the case study data, you can try TeamArchitect on the raw case study data. You can create your own teams, analyze the data, and make decisions on development and deployment. By working with the case study data in this fashion you will be experiencing the look and feel of TeamArchitect. If you would like to obtain TeamArchitect for your own company, you can find the details in Appendix C, "How to Get TeamArchitect Tools."

TeamArchitect is a work in progress. I am currently using TeamArchitect and have been using many of its tools for several years. The results are very encouraging. I have been able to produce good value for my clients in what is presented here. But there is much more. I continue to work with several colleagues who share my desire and approach to improving team effectiveness. I assure you that we are only beginning a great journey. And that great journey will produce a number of significant boundary-stretching tools and techniques for improving team effectiveness. I hope to affect your approach to building project teams and show you how TeamArchitect can make a measurable bottom-line impact on the business of your company.

You will undoubtedly form opinions about what I have presented and will have thoughts and ideas of your own as to how it could have been done better. If that is the case, I want to hear from you. If we can collaborate and share ideas, we can have a positive effect on project success. I want to hear from you!

Bob Wysocki
rkw@eiicorp.com

Acknowledgments

There are a number of very special people in every person's life to whom he owes a debt of gratitude and special thanks. It's hard to remember all of them, but I have a special place in my heart for my EII colleagues, especially Beth Agostino and Honorine Misner. Their support and encouragement of this project have been a source of strength for me, especially during the hard times. Beth is totally responsible for the Web site development and for bringing the simulated case to life. Her positive attitude and "can do" approach are her strengths. Honorine has been a colleague and fellow worker for more than seven years. I have worked with her on a number of projects and have always valued her candor and professional approach to her responsibilities. I truly value their friendship and contribution to the TeamArchitect concept.

There have been so many peers who have contributed to the formation and development of my approach to team formation, assessment, development, and deployment that it is impossible to list them all here. Special mention is due to Jim Lewis, a friend, colleague, and co-author. His advice and ideas regarding TeamArchitect have helped me make several improvements to earlier models. Thanks also to Ann and Pat Herrmann for their willingness to listen to new applications of the Herrmann Brain Dominance Instrument and to their father, Ned Herrmann, who passed away recently but was a source of inspiration and encouragement to me during the formative years of the TeamArchitect model. Tim Scudder, CEO of Personal Strengths Publishing, offered food for thought as I began to incorporate the Strength Deployment Inventory into my team assessment model. Similarly, Ginny Flynn, at the Hay McBer Training Resources Group, offered her willingness to support the inclusion of the Learning Styles Instrument into my team assessment model.

Finally, to Terri Hudson, my editor, and to Kathryn Malm, my developmental editor on this project, I owe special thanks and recognition. This is the third project that the three of us have worked on together, and each one has been a productive and rewarding experience for me, personally and professionally. They have listened to my ideas, which I truly appreciate, especially when my ideas were at times somewhat unusual. We have always been able to create a better product as a result. I hope that there are many more to come.

About the Author

Robert K. Wysocki, Ph.D., has over 35 years experience as a project management consultant and trainer, information systems manager, systems and management consultant, author, training developer and provider. He has written ten books on project management and information systems management. He has over 30 publications and presentations in professional and trade journals and has made more than 100 presentations at professional and trade conferences and meetings.

In February 2001 he joined the Sapient Corporation in Cambridge, Massachusetts, where he is Director of Program Management. His responsibilities include project/program management methodology development, integration and deployment, project manager professional development and certification and project management tool evaluation, acquisition and integration. Sapient was founded in 1991 and has grown to become a leading business consulting, systems design and development, and systems integration company with offices throughout North America, Europe, and Asia.

In 1990 he founded Enterprise Information Insights, Inc. (EII), a project management consulting and training practice specializing in project management methodology design and integration, project support office establishment, the development of training curriculum, and the development of a portfolio of assessment tools focused on organizations, project teams, and individuals.

He is a member of the ProjectWorld Executive Advisory Board, the Project Management Institute, the American Society of Training & Development, and the Society of Human Resource Management. He is past Association Vice President of AITP (formerly DPMA). He earned a BA in Mathematics from the University of Dallas, and an MS and Ph.D. in Mathematical Statistics from Southern Methodist University.

The Background

CHAPTER 1

The Successful Project

The environment in which the project is undertaken contains the key to our understanding of how to increase the likelihood of project success. There are three parts to that environment: the project support environment, the enterprise environment, and the business environment. These environments are not static but are constantly changing. As they change they affect the project, the project manager, and the project team. Therefore, as any one of these environments changes, the project manager must be able to respond with strategies and action plans to accommodate those changes. This book provides the tools to build those strategies and action plans.

In this chapter, we are going to do a little homework to lay the foundation for learning those tools and how to use them effectively. We begin by describing the three components of the environment and how they can affect the project.

The project world in which we live is fast paced, dynamic, challenging, confusing, frustrating, and ever changing. Unfortunately, it has also been marked by a less-than-acceptable track record. The most recent comprehensive survey, which was published in 1995 by the Standish Group (see www.standishgroup.com and the two reports, *Chaos* and *Unfinished*

Voyages), reports failure rates to be 70 percent and higher. By anyone's standards, that is unacceptable.

Before we can improve this situation, we must have a clear and shared understanding of the difficult project world in which we live. Understanding the root causes of project failure will give us a starting point from which we can begin to improve our track record. After you have an understanding of the three parts to our project environment, I will turn to the causes of project failure and discover what lies beneath them. I made that discovery some years ago and share it with you now. It is what gave me the impetus to write this book.

Our Environment

Three interdependent environments influence the construct formed by a project and its project team, as shown in Figure 1.1:

- Project support environment
- Enterprise environment
- Business environment

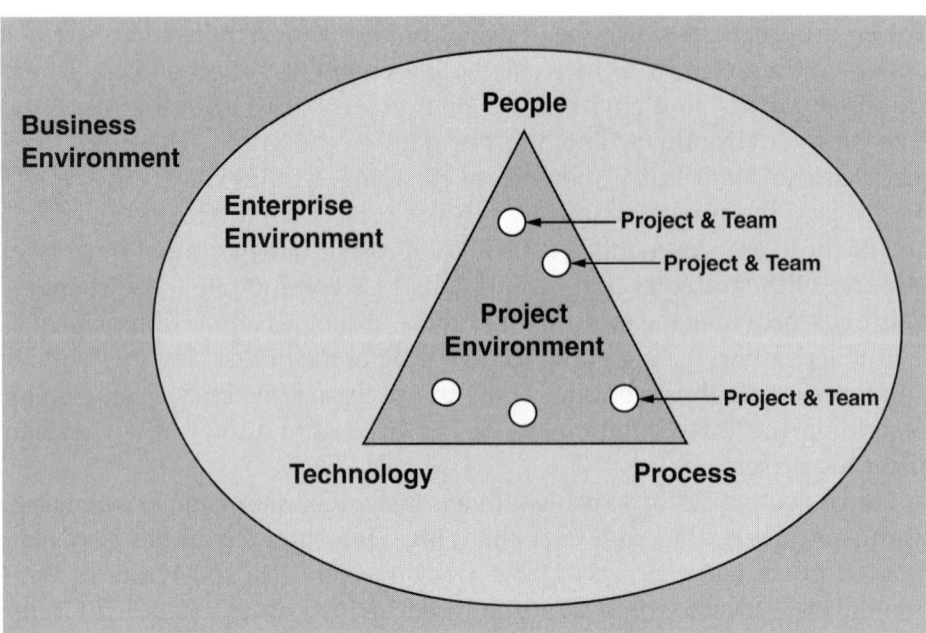

Figure 1.1 The project/team environment.

These environments always seem to be in a state of turmoil—each one makes it difficult for the project team to meet its objectives and function smoothly. Let's take a brief look at the dynamics at play here.

Project Support Environment

The project environment can be defined by three parameters: people, process, and technology. These parameters form a *system*, or a necessary set of conditions, that must be in harmony with one another in order for the project support environment to function effectively.

The first parameter is that there must be a sufficiently skilled workforce to meet the project staffing requirements of the current and planned projects in the enterprise's portfolio. In the technology world this is difficult to attain. Turnover and a short supply of talent are the realities with which we all have to live.

Second, a *process* or a project management methodology must be defined and integrated into the enterprise. This process must be adaptive; it must adjust to the type of project. To insist on a "one size fits all" approach is self-defeating. Furthermore, all managers (senior, business, resource, and project), as well as professional staff, must understand their roles and responsibilities in the process. In addition to having a process, there must be a commitment to use the process. How often have you heard the comment from your manager? "I don't care if your plan says you will come in late and that you need more staff, I know you will find some way to get the job done. You'll just have to be a little more creative." You most likely walk away scratching your head and hope for a revelation.

Finally, the technology infrastructure must support the people and process appropriately. For me the operative word in this last sentence is "appropriately." The project management software packages available today give us more functionality than we typically require. That's better than not having enough functionality, but the trap here is that we stop thinking about what we are doing and allow the software to do our thinking for us.

All of this is very easy to say but is so difficult to do. Enlightened organizations understand that an effective project management environment is a critical success factor, but few have been able to achieve it to their satisfaction.

At the most granular level of the system are the projects and project teams. These two entities also form a subsystem. The project and the project team must be in balance with one another if the project is to have a chance to be successful.

Enterprise Environment

The enterprise provides the set of necessary conditions for project success. It provides the people, technology, and process that are required to support an effective project management environment. The extent to which that has happened in our enterprises is a mixed bag. A few enterprises have done a good job of providing and nurturing that environment, and their numbers are increasing; others have done so only to some extent, and their numbers are also increasing; and the majority have done so marginally or not at all, and their numbers are decreasing. In fairness to all of these organizations, however, keep in mind that many of their options are compromised because of these factors:

- Unemployment is at record lows and turnover at a record high.
- The demand for skilled technical professionals far outstrips the supply, and the situation is getting worse.
- Technology is changing at lightning pace, and the pace of change is increasing.
- Keeping the technology aligned with the business presents management with a bewildering array of choices and no clear evidence of the best choices or even of the acceptable choices.
- Outsourcing, facilities management, Application Service Providers (ASP), virtual organizations, the Internet, and dispersed teams contribute even more confusion to an already confusing business environment.

The bottom line is that stability no longer exists. Change is constant, and to ignore it is to court disaster. Do more with less, and do it faster. Customers expect immediate gratification. If you don't give it to them, they will find someone who will. All of these factors fly in the face of traditional project management practices. The challenge for project managers is to be adaptive and to find ways to be successful in this turbulent environment. To fit into this environment and to be successful, project teams must be able to embrace change rather than avoid change. What is best for the customer should drive all project-related decisions.

Business Environment

Isn't it great to be alive and working in the twenty-first century! Only our own creativity and initiative limit what we can accomplish. There are so many opportunities that the largest and even the smallest of our organizations can position themselves to take advantage of them. The Internet has leveled the playing field. That's the good news.

The bad news is that survival depends on the enterprise's ability to constantly change and discover new opportunities before someone else does. The agile organization is the organization that will survive. For the project manager this new business environment challenges the very foundations of project management. All of the things the project manager has counted on (a well-defined goal, a customer who knows what he or she wants, a fixed deadline, skilled and available resources, and a stable enterprise environment) are no longer expected. In their place are vague or even undefined goals. Customers never seem to know what they want and are always changing their minds. Deadlines are in a constant state of flux because market conditions have determined a new set of rules. The needs of the customer can change without notice; competitors can enter and leave the market as well as reposition themselves within the market. The winners are going to be those organizations that can quickly adjust deliverable dates, and that means adjusting project schedules. Resources are in short supply, and the few we have are overcommitted to projects. Finally, reorganization, rightsizing, outsourcing, mergers, and acquisitions result in confusion and delays for the project manager.

Add to these the fact that the Web and e-business applications are quickly becoming pervasive in the business world. Web-based application systems are being developed under a new set of rules called *complex adaptive systems development*. This development process is similar to prototyping but with the added feature that the customers aren't telling the developers what they want. For the most part, the customers don't know what they want, but they'll know it when they see it. Traditional project managers are confused.

Traditional project management practices will not work under the new rules of *extreme projects*. That is the reality of today's business environment, and unfortunately, it is not likely to revert to the way it used to be in the good old days. Project managers must adapt their processes accordingly. The traditional project manager may see this business environment as a threat; the progressive project manager sees it as an opportunity. In either case, there is great risk. As project managers, we must do whatever we can to mitigate that risk. This book will help with one of the risk factors—properly configured project teams.

FURTHER READING For more information on extreme projects, read *The World-Class Project Manager: A Professional Development Guide* by Robert K. Wysocki and James L. Lewis (Perseus Books, 2001), *Extreme Programming*

Explained by Kent Beck (Addison Wesley, 2000), or *Planning Extreme Programming* by Kent Beck and Martin Fowler (Addison Wesley, 2001).

Project/Team Environment

So what does this changing environment mean to the project team? The team will have to possess the characteristics that will allow it to function effectively in its environment. That list of characteristics includes these traits—adaptable, analytical, strategic, creative, process-oriented, organized, strong personal and interpersonal skills, and leadership—and these roles—decision-makers, problem-solvers, and negotiators. Although these characteristics generally are attributed to individuals, this book will examine them in a team context. No individual will have all of these credentials. For the team to have a characteristic, someone on the team must possess that characteristic or some part of that characteristic. The goals are to leverage the characteristics of all the team members to create a balanced team and to build a strategy to mitigate against the risks that arise from a team that is not balanced and cannot be balanced.

Some authors claim that balance is a robust concept. They would argue that balance is the same for all teams and therefore is independent of the project. I argue that the characteristics of the project suggest the characteristics required of the project team to achieve that balance. Balance is defined in terms of the project, rather than as some general notion of balance, which is considered independently of the project. There will be some characteristics that are common to all teams. I discuss these, but I emphasize that there will also be some characteristics that are unique to the project.

Why So Many Projects Fail

In 1995, the Standish Group reported the results of an extensive survey of IT executives. The survey attempted to identify the reasons for the high incidence of IT project failure. Their sample of 365 respondents was stratified into three groups: large, medium, and small companies. Only 9.0 percent, 16.2 percent, and 28.0 percent of all IT projects undertaken were successful, respectively, in these three groups. If you do a little analysis of the data they report, you uncover some rather remarkable results. For example, the expected loss per IT project is $119,714.00. Wow! An interesting question to ask is "What would you be willing to spend per project to reduce the expected loss by 50 percent? Or how about by 20 percent?" Or just 10 percent? A 10 percent savings would be $11,971.40, and that's per

CRITICAL SUCCESS FACTORS	COMMUNICATIONS	TEAM	PROCESS
User Involvement	X	X	X
Executive Management Support	X	.	.
Clear Statement of Requirements	X	.	X
Proper Planning	X	X	X
Realistic Expectations	X	.	.
Smaller Project Milestones	X	.	X
Competent Staff	.	X	.
Ownership	X	X	.
Clear Vision & Objectives	X	X	.
Hard-Working, Focused Staff	.	X	.
	8	6	4

Figure 1.2 Project critical success factors.

Adapted from: Standish Group, the *Chaos Report* (1995).

project! Suppose your company does only 100 IT projects per year. That's an annual cost avoidance of over $1 million per year. Wow! Sooner or later this adds up to real money.

The survey also reports project critical success factors, shown in Figure 1.2 in ranked order with user involvement as the most important and hard-working and focused staff as the least important. Remember that these are the top 10 success factors; they are all important.

Let's take a step back from this list and look at it from a higher-level perspective to see if we can discover more fundamental causes of project failure. I did that, and I found what I believe are the major root causes of project failure. There are three:

- Inadequate communication
- Ineffective use of the project team
- Inappropriate project management processes

In my mind these major reasons are related to the 10 critical success factors shown in Figure 1.2.

Inadequate Communication

I don't think anyone would be surprised by the fact that 8 of the 10 critical success factors are related to person-to-person communications. Doesn't it seem that we should be able to communicate effectively? Truth be known, we can't, or at least we haven't. There are probably many reasons for this, but a few stand out in my mind as appropriate to mention here:

- Inability to identify what information needs to be communicated
- No verification that the message sent is the same as the message received
- Not knowing the best format in which to communicate the information
- Not knowing to whom and how often the information should be communicated
- Not knowing what kind of feedback should be sought

Further discussion of these reasons is the topic of another book and is not directly referenced here. Effective communications management is important, however. As we consider project team membership, keep these reasons for communication failure in mind. You need to assess whether your project manager and team members can correctly assess the communications needs of their project and implement the appropriate communications programs. If they can't, you have a problem that you must address. I will show you how to make those assessments and how to use them to improve team effectiveness.

FURTHER READING   If you are interested in more information on how to improve project communications, refer to the discussion of Conditions of Satisfaction in *Effective Project Management, 2nd Edition* by Wysocki et al. (Wiley 2000). See also the Project Environment section of Appendix A.

Ineffective Use of the Project Team

As you saw in Figure 1.2, team composition is directly related to 6 of the 10 critical success factors. Team formation and deployment are explored in detail throughout this book. I will show you how team formation and deployment are a function of the characteristics of the project and how to assess the extent to which the team is aligned and in balance with the project. For now, it is sufficient to recognize that the development and deployment of the team are important considerations as you try to increase the probability of project success. You may not have the luxury of choosing the team members, but you are still responsible for understanding the team you do have and for knowing how prepared it is to take on the work of the project effectively. In other words, forewarned is forearmed. The alternative is to proceed blindly, and that doesn't seem like a smart choice to me.

Inappropriate Project Management Process

While the project management process is related to only 4 of the 10 critical success factors, as shown in Figure 1.2, it is related to 4 of the top 6 critical success factors. I maintain that a "one size fits all" mentality to your project management methodology plants the seeds for project failure. The project manager and the project team must view the project management process as a value-add. On the contrary, the rigid enforcement of a standard methodology will often be viewed as a burden and not a value-add. For example, suppose the methodology calls for a formal project planning session with all affected parties represented. If the project were mission critical, most people would agree to the formal planning session. But what if the project was small and not at all mission critical? It would seem that a formal planning session would be overkill and more likely to be seen as a burden by the team. On the other hand, a less formal—perhaps even informal—planning session would be seen in a positive light.

Project Critical Success Factors

Because we are focusing on project team effectiveness, I would like to spend a few lines on each of the critical success factors that are relevant to the project team. From Figure 1.2 they are:

- User involvement
- Clear requirements statement
- Proper planning
- Competent staff
- Clear vision and objectives
- Hard-working and focused staff

User Involvement

Some projects will require greater user involvement than others. This is clearly the case in the information technology industry when we compare user involvement in design projects with user involvement in development projects and in implementation projects. With some exceptions, direct user involvement is greatest in implementation projects, somewhat lesser in design projects, and least in development projects.

Because user involvement is so important to project success, it only makes sense that the team should possess characteristics that support and encourage meaningful user involvement. For example, does the team encourage open discussion of alternatives? Does the team have strong interpersonal skills? Does the team seek and respond to meaningful feedback, and does the team appreciate different points of view? These are but a few of the characteristics that the team must possess if it is to have meaningful user involvement. We'll explore this factor in more detail later in the book.

Furthermore, the interpersonal characteristics required of the team will vary depending on the type of project or project phase being undertaken. For example, in projects where the project goal is less clearly understood, the importance of meaningful user involvement increases. That happens because the team becomes more dependent on the user for clarity of vision, for direction, and for timely change requests.

Clear Requirements Statement

The need for effective communications between the customer and the project team is really put to the test when drafting the requirements statement. I have noticed in project after project that whenever there was not a clear statement of requirements, scope creep was more pronounced. In addition, the projects tended to miss deadlines and exceed budgets more than those cases where there was a clear statement of requirements. In other words, scope creep is the result of a poor attempt to define requirements clearly.

The problem begins when the difference between needs and wants is overlooked. We all expect that customers will tell us what they want. A problem will arise if what customers really need is different from what they tell us they want. If this gap between wants and needs is not removed, the project is heading for serious difficulty. I believe it is the responsibility of the project manager to convince customers that what they have said they want is not really what they need. And then convince them to want what they really do need. This will not be easy, but it is well worth the investment of time to make sure you get it right.

Ensuring that the team is delivering needs and not simply wants places a heavy demand on the interpersonal, personal, and business skills of the project manager. To further complicate the situation, the skill profile required of the team will vary as a function of the type of project and the phase of the project. I will have more to say about this relationship in Part Two, "Assessment."

Proper Planning

Why so many managers view planning as a waste of time has always confused me. They are more interested in having the team get to work on the project than in having the team plan the work of the project. We seem to be able to find time to repeat poor or incorrect work that could have been avoided had we planned properly from the start. The fact of the matter is, we didn't, and as a result we suffer added costs, inconveniences, and missed deadlines. I guess this phenomenon will go down in history as one of those great unsolved mysteries of project management. Let's agree that we won't do that; instead we will treat planning as a necessary part of good project management.

Being effective at planning will call on several personal and interpersonal skills of those who participate in the planning—specifically the project manager and certain members of the project team. Those skills include problem solving, creativity, decision making, conflict resolution, and thinking styles. I'll talk more about them in Chapter 10, "Establishing the Profile of the Project," in which I focus on profiling the project.

Competent Staff

Nothing new here—we always want a competent staff. But the twist in this book is that we want a competent *team*. Our unit of analysis will be the team and how it collectively possesses the needed competencies and skills to accomplish the work of the project. To illustrate my point, consider the problem-solving process. A typical problem-solving process might include the following steps:

1. Define the problem.
2. Analyze the possible causes.
3. Collect the necessary data.
4. Formulate alternative solutions.
5. Evaluate and prioritize the solutions.
6. Select the best solution.
7. Develop an action plan.
8. Implement the solution.
9. Evaluate the results.

Somewhere on the planet there may be an individual who possesses all the skills needed to complete all of these steps. Expecting to have this person on your project team may be wishful thinking, though. It is more realistic to expect your project team to possess all of the required skills. Each team member might perform a different step.

As you will learn in Part Two, "Assessment," the project team needs several types of skills and thinking styles if they are to be successful with the work of the project, and one person is unlikely to possess all of them. The job is to solve the problem—not to create heroes. Your job as project manager is to make sure that the team possesses the skills and can solve the problem efficiently and professionally. In this book, we will use some psychometric tools to establish whether that skill profile is present among the team members. If not, we will have to implement corrective action plans to adjust for the known deficiencies. We will discuss this in more detail in Chapter 11, "Establishing the Profile of the Project Team" and in Chapter 12, "Assessing Team Alignment and Balance."

Clear Vision and Objectives

Both the team and the customer must be able to clearly define and share the vision of the project. Everybody must be on the same page and committed to that vision. Beyond a shared vision, both the team and the customer must understand how that vision will be accomplished. That is embodied in the objectives, which are nothing more than a restatement of the vision in more detail. Developing clear vision and objectives will require the team to have skills in project planning, change management, consensus building, and more. Even though much of this is communications related, it will be important for the team to have this understanding. That will follow from open and frank discussions about how each team member understands the project. The dynamics and balance among the team will be critical if that common understanding is to emerge. This is not the place to have a team characterized by groupthink.

Hard-Working and Focused Staff

The team must understand the work of the whole, and each team member must understand his or her role in the whole. There is no room for rugged individualists on the effective project team. Each team member will be charged to produce specific deliverables by a specific date. A team that can maintain focus and direction is a team that increases its chances of a successful project. In the absence of focus, team members often take it on themselves to do project work they like to do, ignore project work they don't like to do, and do work on the project that is outside the scope of the project. The result is that they spend project time and dollars on work that has nothing to do with the project. The last thing the project manager wants is such surprises from the team.

Project Team Critical Success Factors

In addition to the project critical success factors, there are additional critical success factors that are specific to the project team. These critical success factors are as follows:

- A balanced problem-solving capability
- A balanced decision-making capability
- A balanced conflict management capability
- A balanced skill profile

And they lie at the core of every successful project team. Let's take a quick look at each of them.

A Balanced Problem-Solving Capability

Problems are constant in project work. They arise as a result of changes in the business climate, actions by competitors, and changes mandated by market intelligence, resource constraints, poor vendor performance, changing priorities, organizational learning, mistakes, misunderstandings, and a host of other reasons. Many of them will be solved only through the most creative, "outside of the box" thinking by the team.

This means that the team must have breadth and depth in a variety of areas. The problem might be of a technical or business nature and require that the team have analytical skills in both and be able to integrate both. The problem could be people related and involve issues within the team or between the team and its customers or vendors. That will call on a number of interpersonal skills. More generally, the team will have to possess a working knowledge of tools such as force-field analysis, cause-and-effect diagrams, affinity diagrams, decision trees, Pareto charts, and others.

The team also must have a diverse collection of members with different orientations and value systems. For example, some will need to be more people oriented, others more management oriented, and others more analytically oriented. Some will have to be focused on the needs of individuals, or of the team, or the customer and the company as well. Some will have to be more visionary, others more focused on the short term.

Sometimes a solution can come from a most unlikely source, but it won't come at all if that unlikely source is not represented on the team. In other words, the team must possess a balanced problem-solving capability.

A Balanced Decision-Making Capability

Along with identifying and presenting alternative solutions to problems, the team will also have to evaluate the consequences of taking alternative decisions to a number of situations. For example, one of the major problems with technical teams is their penchant for a rush to judgment. What I mean by that is that once a decision regarding some aspect of a problem has been proposed, the team tends to accept it without looking for an alternative. Such teams will need to have at least one member who reminds them to find at least one other approach and compare it to the first. Another example would be a systems development team whose members are all technical. With no one there to represent the customer or user of the deliverable, how would the team know that what they are designing is, in fact, what would be usable and acceptable?

Decision making is so important as a critical success factor that we will devote a considerable part of Chapter 7, "Problem-Solving and Decision-Making Styles," to examining how the team characteristics and skills need to cover all phases of the models that are used for problem solving and decision making.

A Balanced Conflict Management Capability

I like to think of conflict as the opposite of groupthink. Groupthink can be the fatal flaw in many teams because it stifles any chance of creativity among the team. When one team member suggests an approach everyone on the team nods in agreement whether they agree or not. That is what we mean by groupthink, and it is something that the team must avoid at all costs. That means that conflict can be a healthy pursuit in teams and that it is something that teams need to learn to handle constructively. Conflict can be hazardous to the health and well-being of the project, but it can also be a source of tremendous help.

I have never been on a project that did not have conflict—if I were, I would be concerned. Conflict is a great way to test an idea, an approach, or a strategy and to avoid having it shortchange the project team. The team that has adopted a healthy conflict management strategy is the team that encourages open discussion and the presentation of alternatives. It is the team whose members feel comfortable challenging the opinions of others without fear of retaliation or insult.

If you were to form a team in which the presence of conflict would be desirable, what would be the composition of the team? What characteristics would you expect to have in such a team? I don't expect you to answer these questions, at least not just yet. I will present some material in Chapter 8, "Conflict Management Styles and Strategies," that will help you do just that.

A Balanced Skill Profile

Every human being has a skill profile. The profile will include technical skills, business skills, management skills, personal skills, and interpersonal skills. Almost without exception, teams are formed based on the technical skills of their members. For example, the team needs an information architect. Harriett is an information architect, and Harriett is available. Put her on the team. While this is certainly expedient, it is by no means a sound practice. In forming their teams project managers too easily ignore the other skills. Maybe those other skills have never been formally assessed and the project manager is going on second-hand information about an individual's performance. How often have you heard statements like "Marvin understands finance, and he did a good job with the last financial systems project he was on. Let's put him on the team." That may be fine in some cases, but I submit that if it proves to be the correct staffing decision, it is more an accident than a planned result. In Chapter 9, "Project Management Skills and Competencies," I will show you a better approach to skill profiling and how it can be used to improve the selection of project managers as well as team members. We simply have to bring a halt to the practice of selecting team members based on two skills: technical and availability. Yes, in many companies it appears that availability is treated as a skill.

In this book the skill profile of a project manager or team member consists of 54 skills, only 18 of which are specific to project management. The other 36 are spread across personal, interpersonal, management, and business areas. I will have more to say on those later in Chapter 9. For now it is sufficient to know that there is more to a team member's skill profile than technical skills.

Characteristics of Successful Project Teams

As you might have guessed by now, every successful project team is a balanced team. The definition of balance in a specific situation is determined by several factors. The first is the project itself. As we will see in Part Three, "Formation," the characteristics of the project determine the definition of balance for the team that will work on that project. As the project changes, so does the definition of what it means for its team to be balanced.

This notion of a balanced team may be new to many of you. It is central to the approach I have taken in this book. Much of what we are going to learn in this book revolves around the idea of understanding the degree to which the team is out of balance (not aligned with the project) and what the project manager can do about it. I have compiled the tools to assess this alignment and take the appropriate corrective actions in a system called TeamArchitect.

Putting It All Together

In this chapter I hoped to raise some thoughts in your mind regarding the several factors that hinder or promote project success. Many of you were already aware of the conclusions from the Standish Group surveys and knew why many of your projects were failing. At the same time, many of you may have been surprised by how a focus on team balance with respect to decision making, problem solving, and conflict resolution can also contribute to project success. The bottom line is that we can positively affect project success by focusing on achieving that balance or mitigating the risks when that balance cannot be achieved. We spend the remaining chapters of this book building on that notion of balance and showing how it can be attained and dealt with effectively. There are still a few odds and ends to consider in fully understanding the project environment; these are discussed in the next chapter.

CHAPTER 2

The Project Environment

There are three other aspects of the project environment that will help or hinder project success: project classes, organizational structures, and team leadership models. Rather than treating all projects as equal for the purposes of team formation and choice of methodologies to use and leadership models to employ, we will see how recognizing that projects are different—and basing team formation and choice of methodologies and leadership models on those differences—can lead to improved success rates. The organizational structure is fixed, at least in the short run, and the team must understand how that structure can help or hinder project success and act accordingly. Finally, the nature of the project will suggest which team leadership models will work best.

This chapter describes these parts of the project environment and suggests strategies to follow. It sets the stage for a refreshing, exciting, and different way of thinking about projects, teams, and processes. Understanding these three aspects is critical to understanding the rationale behind the new models that are introduced in Chapter 4, "Project/Team Alignment Model." Let's get going!

Project Classes

Every project is different and unique. It has never been done before, at least not under the same set of circumstances, and it will never be done again, at least not under the same set of circumstances. How the project team is formed and how the project team will plan and execute are determined by the characteristics of the project that give it its uniqueness. The project support environment must give the project manager some guidance and advice about how to best respond to that uniqueness. The best way to do that is to define broad groupings of projects based on their similarity to one another. We call these groupings *project classes*. As you will learn in this section, there are many ways to define project classes.

Books on team building typically do not account for the fact that differences between projects can have an effect on team formation and development. Instead, they treat all projects as though they were alike. The discussions of team formation and development leave the characteristics of the project out of the equation. These books needlessly oversimplify the situation and can, in fact, be misleading. I agree that there are some characteristics that the team must possess that are independent of the project type, but there are also characteristics that *depend* on the project type. Curious? Let me explain.

Let me illustrate using one of my clients as an example. My client builds systems for large retail financial institutions in the United States. It is working on three projects:

- Design a customer support system
- Build the customer support system
- Implement the customer support system

You may argue that this could just as easily have been one project, and I won't take issue with you. The reason for commissioning three projects is very simple. First, the client wasn't exactly sure what it wanted, so senior management decided to charter the design project first in order to give the customer a chance to get a better idea of what was wanted. At the same time, this would allow senior management to get a better idea of the time and cost requirements for the development and implementation of the entire system. The build project would probably be assigned to the applications development group. An internal team formed by the vendor and with representatives from the client bank's retail locations would handle the implementation project.

Value of Project Classes for Team Formation

Apart from the requirements, are the characteristics or the "personality" of these three projects different? Yes, they are. The design project is a creative project and will involve significant interaction with the client through the design stages. The build project is technical and will require less client interaction than the design project, but it will require a team that has strong analytical and process skills. The implement project is procedural and will require heavy client involvement as the system is brought into production at the client site and will require a team that can follow established process and procedure. Are those differences significant enough to say that the characteristics of each of the project teams, apart from their technical skills, will also need to be different?

The answer to both questions is yes. At a general level, the differences between the three project teams have to do with the analytical, organizational, interpersonal, and conceptual characteristics of each team. At a more specific level, the differences have to do with creativity, problem solving, human interface, and people skills, to name a few. The traits for each project differ, and, as a result, each team will have to have more or less of each of the traits to be successful. Even if the application were put into a single project, these observations would be the same. As the project goes through each phase, the team composition, or at least the deployment of the team to project activities, would have to change in order to meet the needs of the project at each phase.

If you agree that knowing the type of project would help you select a more appropriate team and hence improve the likelihood of project success, then you would agree that creating project classes makes perfect sense.

Value of Project Classes for Methodology Selection

One size does not fit all. We've heard that expression many times, and it drives an important message home about project management methodologies. Let me clarify with an example from one of my recent client engagements. Several years before I became involved with my client the company had hired a consultant to design and implement a project management methodology for use across the corporation. The client insisted that there be one methodology and that everyone would learn it and use it for every project. The consultant delivered what the client had asked for, and the project was deemed a success—at least that's what everyone thought on the day that the methodology went live. Two years later I got a call from the CEO. "Bob, we need some help. We had this great methodology developed for us, and now only a few people are using it. All I seem to hear are grumblings and complaints. Most people are saying that it is nothing more than busy work and doesn't add any value. What should I do?" It didn't take long for me to find the root cause of the client's problem and put a fix in place. The details are not important, but let me tell you the lesson my client learned: A methodology is going to be used and accepted if and only if the people who are affected by it find value in its use.

Obviously, the people in my client company didn't find value in its use. If one size does not fit all, how many sizes are needed? Project classes are those sizes. Each project class has associated with it some variation of the methodology. For example, projects greater than six months' calendar duration require network scheduling; projects less than six months' calendar duration require Gantt chart scheduling. Or, projects greater than six months' calendar duration require a joint planning session with all major stakeholders represented; projects less than six months' calendar duration require a planning session with all core team members present. In other words, calendar duration is one determinant of project class. There are many other determinants that could be used, as discussed in the text that follows. In the next section, there are additional examples of project classification rules.

If you agree that knowing the type of project will help you tailor the methodology to more appropriately fit the project situation, then you would agree that creating project classes makes perfect sense. The question to be answered then is how to create these project classes. There are three ways, which are discussed next.

Project Complexity Model

The *Project Complexity Model* is a project classification rule developed by the Center for Project Management, a project management consulting and training company headquartered in San Ramon, California. It defines four classes of project using two variables: organizational complexity and technical complexity. Each of these variables is measured using a proprietary survey instrument created by the Center. The survey is used to measure the complexity of the project and place the project into one of four classes. Each class has associated with it a specific project management approach and team formation strategy. Simpler projects require a less rigorous methodology; the most complex projects require the most comprehensive methodology. In other words, one size does not fit all. The Center has had excellent results using this approach to project classification. If you are interested in obtaining more information on the Project Complexity Model from the Center for Project Management, see Appendix B, "Sources of Information." The four classes are described in the following sections.

Simple

Simple projects can be defined by one of several characteristics. There may have been several very similar projects that were done in the past. There are no longer any surprises with these projects, and many of the people who worked on prior projects are available for this one. Because projects in this class have been done several times, their templates may be available for use. Simple projects will use well-established technologies, have lower risk, be of short duration, and have adequate available resources. There are not a lot of open issues regarding this project, and most people are ready to take on the new deliverables. For example, a project to install a computer network in a regional field office would be a simple project. It would have been done several times before and probably would use well-defined templates and procedures for its implementation. All of the project tasks would be known and understood.

Projects in this class are good starting projects for those new to project management. A good candidate for project manager for a simple project is someone who has been a successful team leader within an area of specialization in a few projects and is ready to move to an assignment that has a little more scope and responsibility. He or she will have limited experience with project management skills and may need some formal training in planning and control.

FURTHER READING If you are interested in how projects can be used for professional and career development, consult *The World-Class Project Manager: A Professional Development Guide* by Wysocki and Lewis (Perseus Books, 2001).

Technically Complex

The next class of projects in the Project Complexity Model is the *technically complex* class. Projects in this class typically use a technology that is new to the organization or an old technology in a new and innovative way. In either case, problems are expected. Projects also fall into this class because they will require considerable creativity in addition to the technology to solve a difficult problem for the enterprise. For example, a project to convert to a new network architecture would be in this class. Because the architecture is new, the skill and experience of the technical support staff will be limited. There are likely to be problems and surprises.

A project manager who has been successful with simple projects will be a good candidate to manage technically complex projects if he or she has the specialized technical knowledge to manage specialists in that area of technology. He or she may be doing some of the technical work but more likely will be managing others. He or she will be assigned these projects based more on his or her ability at problem solving and creativity than for technical prowess.

Organizationally Complex

Projects are categorized as *organizationally complex* if they involve significant change for the enterprise or are enterprise-wide in scope. Problems are expected as the project deliverables are implemented across a wide range of managers with diverse opinions. Turf wars are likely as well. To the extent that change is threatening to many, additional integration problems will be expected as these projects near completion. For example, the acquisition of another company and the merging of its information systems into those of the acquiring company would be an organizationally complex project. Differences in business rules, databases, software infrastructures, and more would be present and would need to be resolved.

A project manager who has successfully managed simple projects and has demonstrated strong interpersonal skills is a good candidate for managing these projects. He or she will draw heavily on his or her leadership skills and can expect challenging situations that will tax his or her skills of diplomacy, interpersonal behavior, conflict management, and negotiations.

Critical Mission

Critical mission projects have all of the characteristics of the technically and organizationally complex projects. Furthermore, they have high visibility in the organization. Senior management may be betting the future of the company on the success of these projects. For example, the conversion of Egghead Software to a Web-only retail operation or the development of the staples.com Web site would fall into this project class.

Projects in this class are for the most senior project managers or program managers. These candidates are in a position where project success depends more on their general business and management skills than on any technical skills they may have. They will not be involved in doing any of the activity work on the project and may well have, at least for the large projects, project managers accountable to them as part of their team.

Project Classification Rules

Another approach to creating project classes is through the development of a classification rule. The rule itself defines the project classes, as the following example illustrates. I have had the opportunity to implement several such rules in my client organizations. They are all based on using several critical variables, such as duration, risk, cost, technology, and number of departments affected, to characterize projects and to define project class boundaries.

Table 2.1 is an example of a classification rule based on critical variables. To determine the class of a newly proposed project, the manager first considers Type A. If the project meets any of the criteria at that level, it is classified as a Type A project. If not, the project manager will consider each type in turn until the current project meets the specified criteria.

Some organizations will link project manager types to project classifications as a way of assigning project managers to projects that match their experiences and skills. The same mapping can be used for career planning and professional development of project managers. For example, let's say that the company has defined a career path for project managers using the four positions: associate project manager, project manager, senior project manager, and program manager. To each of these positions is attached a skill profile that must be achieved by anyone who aspires to that position. Furthermore, these positions are mapped to the project classes as follows: to manage a Type D project the person must be at least at the Associate Project Manager level; to manage a Type C project the person must be at least at the Project Manager level; to manage a Type B project the person must be at least at the Senior Project Manager level, and finally, to manage a Type A project the person must be at least at the Program Manager level. A similar mapping might be constructed using the Project Complexity Model discussed earlier.

Table 2.1 Project Classification Rule

CLASS	DURATION (IN MONTHS)	RISK	COMPLEXITY	TECHNOLOGY	PROBABILITY OF PROBLEMS
Type A	>18	High	High	Breakthrough	Certain
Type B	9–18	Medium	Medium	Current	Likely
Type C	3–9	Low	Low	Best of breed	Some
Type D	<3	Very low	Very low	Practical	None

Project Templates

In some organizations projects or parts of projects are repeated. The field office network installation example used previously in this chapter is an example of a project that is repeated. The design, development, and deployment of a training course is another example of a project that is repeated. In both of these examples a sequence of tasks is repeated over and over again; this sequence is the same from project to project. Repeated projects can form a project class of their own, and each project class can have its own template defined by the sequences of tasks. For the previous examples, one class of project would be field office network installation projects; another class would be training course development projects.

Here is an example from one of my recent client engagements. My client was a software developer that built customer support systems for use in large financial institutions. Its customers were not happy with the time that was required to install their systems, and my client approached me with this question: Could a project management process be developed and integrated into its system installation process with the purpose of reducing install time? After some preliminary data gathering and analysis I developed a set of templates for each type of systems installation project the client encountered. The client actually had seven types of installations that ranged in complexity from off-the-shelf to those that required reengineering one or more processes or departments. Each type followed a set procedure, from which a template work breakdown structure and network schedule were developed. The template approach was successful in meeting the client's goal of reducing installation time. As an added benefit, it created a learning environment through the lessons learned on each type of product installation project. That afforded an opportunity for a continuous quality improvement program that further contributed to the effectiveness of the client's installation projects.

Organizational Structures

The type of organizational structure within which the project resides can either help or hinder team effectiveness. For example, a completely projectized organizational structure is most supportive of team effectiveness initiatives because the team is a recognized unit in the organization and can develop its own culture, mores, and patterns of operation. On the other hand, a matrixed organization is generally associated with individuals having concurrent multiple project assignments and offers fewer opportunities for team effectiveness initiatives. We explore these two structures as well as the functional organization structure next and show how they either help or hinder team effectiveness. If we are serious about improving team effectiveness, we need to be aware of how those differences might affect our project.

Functional

A *functional organizational structure*, also known as a *stovepipe organization*, is archetypal of the industrial age. We don't see too many of these organizational structures in today's business world. Most have been replaced either partially or totally by other, more resource-efficient or customer-focused structures, such as a matrix, projectized, or other hybrid form.

A functional organization divides responsibility along the business functions, as shown in Figure 2.1. Each business function has departments and is staffed by managers, professionals, and administrative personnel whose business skills are limited to those skills that are directly related to the business function that defines their unit. Projects have little visibility in these organizations. Someone in each functional area may manage a given project during the time that his unit is working on the project. As a result, no one really understands the entire project, and the whole process of completing a project takes too long. The staff in the business function understands the work they have to do on a project but has little understanding of the project beyond the boundaries of the business discipline. The risk of project failure is very high.

On the positive side, the functional structure uses resources very efficiently. These organizations generally are good at producing products and providing services but traditionally are not good at solving enterprise-wide problems. The only projects that work in these structures are single-department projects or projects that can be decomposed into subprojects that require little integration or cross-department collaboration.

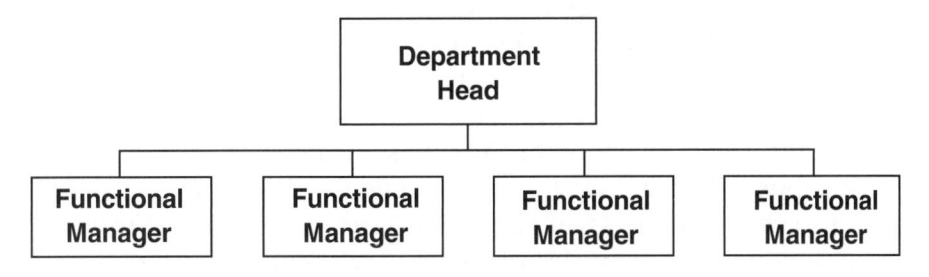

Figure 2.1 Functional organization structure.

Despite the fact that the functional structure is not very supportive of project management, it is a good environment for team effectiveness. Projects, at least those undertakings that are recognized as projects, live within a single business function. There is no such thing as a cross-functional project. This truly is rare in today's business environment, which may be one of the reasons why the purely functional organization is going the way of the dinosaur. In this environment, projects also are very narrowly defined in the sense that the project requires a limited set of specialized skills that exist among the staff who are assigned to that function.

Projects tend to be repetitive. For example, let's suppose that you work at McDonald's in the Pickle Department (a business function) of the Big Mac Assembly Division. Your job is to put three pickles on each Big Mac. That is all you do. You receive your input—a bottom bun with a hamburger patty on it. You add the three pickles, being careful to ensure that they are distributed symmetrically on the patty, and then pass the partially assembled burger to the Condiment Department (another business function). You will have to grant me the right to call pickle putting a project (it's really a process). Your department is staffed with people who have the skills to put pickles on Big Macs. They have developed these skills over the years. There are no surprises. They know exactly what they should be receiving for input, and if they don't get it they send it back from whence it came. They know exactly what they have to do with it—there is no scope creep or need for change management procedures. They know where to send their output and how it should look—they know what their customer expects. They have worked together as a team on several such projects and know each other's working styles. This is an effective team, and it got that way by repetition within clearly defined boundaries.

Matrix

A *matrix organization* divides responsibility along two lines: business functions and projects. Your first reaction should be: "Doesn't that leave room for politics and power struggles?" And your second question should be: "Won't I be caught in the middle?" The answer to both questions is "It depends," but there is good news in the answer.

In general, the matrix structure has a professional staff reporting to a business unit. The business unit is usually a business function at a department or subdepartment level, but it also could be a Center of Excellence or other resource unit. Project managers draw their team members from these units. Individual professional staff usually are assigned to more than one project at a time. While the project manager does not have line authority over the team members, he or she is responsible for getting the work of the project done through the team members. Doing so will draw more on the leadership skills of the project manager than his or her people management skills. It might help to think of the business function manager as being responsible for managing the person and the project manager as responsible for managing the work that the person does.

Almost every organization has some vestiges of a matrix structure, but hardly any organizations are pure matrix structure throughout. That is important to know because it will have an effect on efforts to improve project team effectiveness. Simply put, the matrix structure is the result of superimposing projects across a functional structure. It is also important to know that projects come and go, but functions always remain. That definitely will have an impact on team effectiveness because the power base and leverage in the organization are already firmly established in the business functions; changing that will not be met with open arms by the functional managers.

Matrix structures come in three different flavors: weak, balanced, and strong. The flavor references the leverage that projects have with respect to the rest of the organization. These are discussed in detail in the sections that follow. Each brings a different set of challenges and opportunities for you as project manager. The flavors arise when we change the power base from functions (weak matrix structure) to neutral (balanced matrix structure) to projects (strong matrix structure). All three variations could exist simultaneously in one organization. Which form of the matrix structure is used, may, in fact, be determined by the importance of the project to the organization or the importance of the project as compared to the importance of the business functions. Let's take a look at each one and see how it helps or hinders the project manager's efforts to improve project team effectiveness.

Weak Matrix

The *weak matrix,* shown in Figure 2.2, is common in today's organizations. It is a functional organization that has recognized the importance of cross-functional project management and has superimposed projects across the functional areas. At heart, it is still a functional structure because the functional managers control what projects will be supported and to what extent they will be supported. In many cases the project manager simply ships the project work and expected deliverables at an agreed-on time to the appropriate functional area. At one extreme, the project manager will not know who has been assigned to do the work of the project. That is the decision of

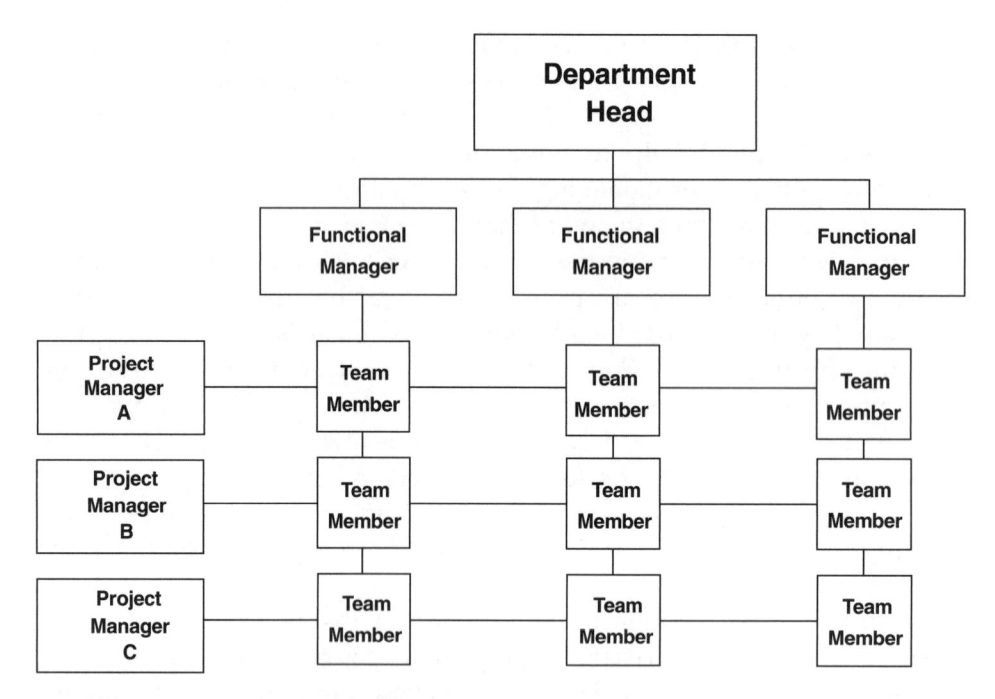

Figure 2.2 The weak matrix structure.

the functional manager and in no way affects the flow of work. At the other extreme, the project manager will know, but the person assigned to do the work will not be a true "team member" because he or she is not directly associated with the project and may not even have any knowledge of the project. That person is simply performing a task assigned by his or her manager.

Regardless of which situation the project manager faces, the means of improving team effectiveness are obviously quite limited. The project team is not much more than a loose federation of independent workers. Furthermore, the individual who is assigned the work clearly owes allegiance to his or her functional manager and may, in fact, have little commitment to or even knowledge of the project from which the work assignment has come.

Balanced Matrix

As the successful completion of projects becomes more important in the organization, the weak matrix structure may give way to a *balanced matrix structure,* shown in Figure 2.3. This is good news to the project manager because he or she now has a level playing field. The line manager is the same person to whom the functional managers report. The project

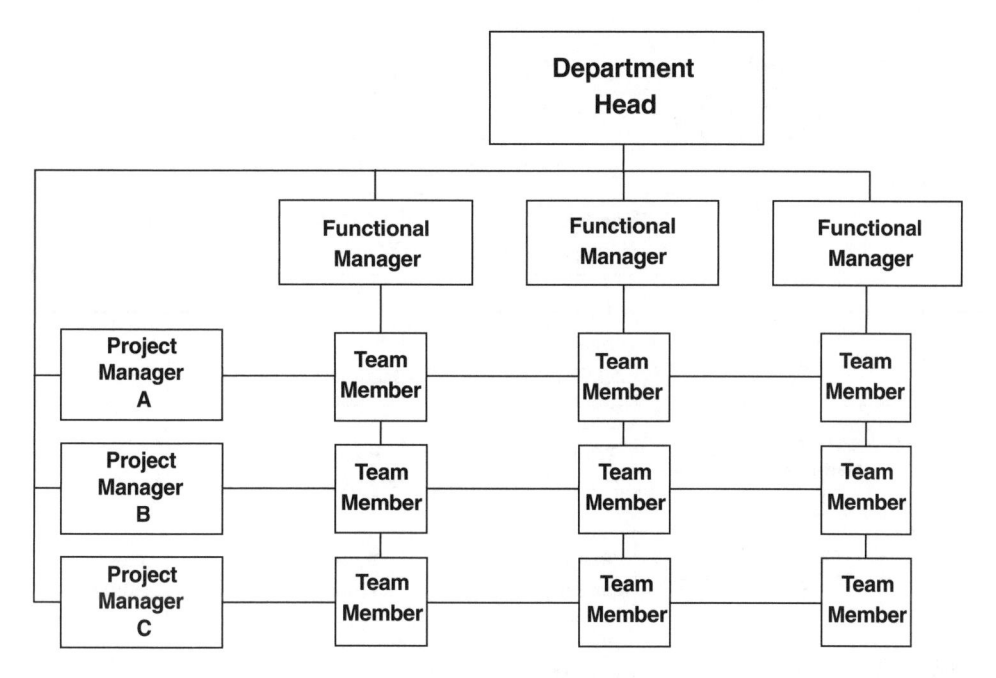

Figure 2.3 The balanced matrix structure.

manager can negotiate with the functional managers to have specific staff assigned to the projects and can use the manager's office as the place to go when resource contention problems need to be mediated. The balanced matrix structure is fraught with politics and power struggles between the project managers and the business function managers. You get what you get, and you will have to make the best of it. To the extent that you have a good relationship with one of these functional managers, you might try to negotiate and trade to improve your team's effectiveness.

The balanced matrix structure is an easier structure in which to improve team effectiveness as opposed to the weak matrix structure. Team members from the functional area have a greater commitment to the project than they would have in the weak matrix variation. They attend team meetings and bring issues and schedule problems back to their functional manager for advice and perhaps resolution. Part of their performance evaluation includes input from the project managers for whom they worked.

Strong Matrix

In the *strong matrix structure*, shown in Figure 2.4, senior management has recognized that increasing the project success rate is a critical success factor for the enterprise. The project manager is in a position of power. The

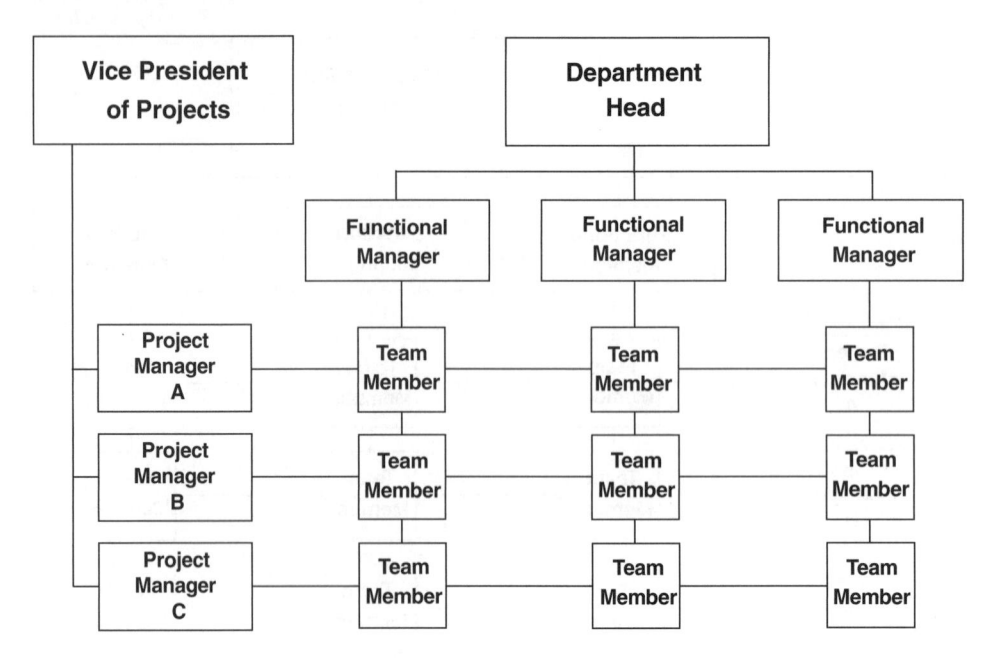

Figure 2.4 The strong matrix structure.

functional manager's role has become reactive. He or she focuses on the need for certain skills through staff training and development programs, and he or she deploys staff to projects based on specified staffing needs and staff skills. The political environment is not as highly charged as it is in the balanced matrix structure. In the strong matrix structure, the project manager's line manager is at the same organizational level as the functional manager's manager. VP of Projects is a common position title for the manager of project managers.

The strong matrix structure is the best situation regarding improving team effectiveness. The project manager has greater influence over who is assigned to his or her project. The project manager is still in a negotiating position, however. He or she may be able to use non-critical path activities in projects, such as on-the-job training for junior staff, as a trade for assigning more senior level staff to critical path activities. The project manager has more leverage in the strong matrix structure than in either the balanced or weak matrix forms.

Projectized

The third type of organizational structure is the *projectized structure*. In this structure, shown in Figure 2.5, the project manager has line authority over the team members. Team members are assigned to a single project and

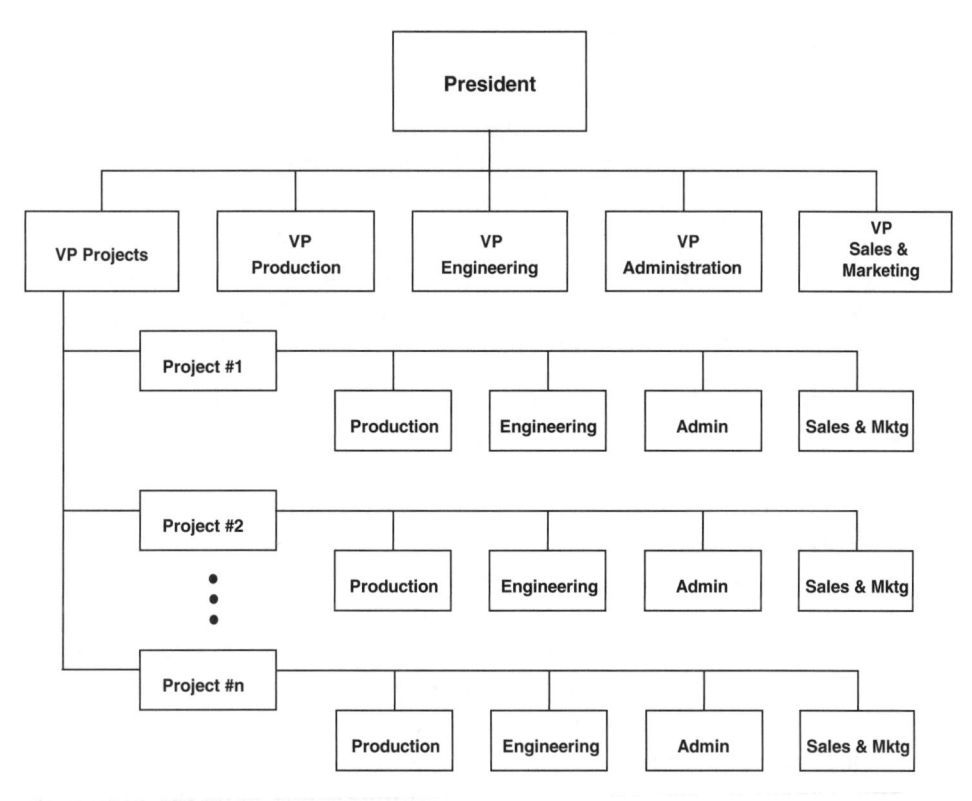

Figure 2.5 The projectized structure.

remain with it until it is finished. Once the project has been completed the team is usually disbanded and its members reassigned elsewhere. There will be cases where the team remains intact and is assigned to another project. In cases where the project is repetitive, such as a product installation project, a team can be expected to remain as a unit. In both cases, the project team becomes an island unto itself and is expected to have all of the skills it needs to accomplish its mission. In these situations improving team effectiveness is a high priority for the project manager.

Hybrids of the projectized structure are found in e-business companies that are developing applications for the Web. Also known as B2B, B2C, and E2E companies, they work in the world of complex adaptive systems development. These development projects are characterized by rapid development, unclear and shifting goals, and constant change. Managers of such projects rarely have more than one project active at a time. Team members also often are assigned to one project at a time. All of this follows from a need to get the application done ASAP. And that means having resources totally devoted to a single project until it is complete.

Team Leadership Models

An important part of aligning the team to the project is the choice of leadership model. One size does not fit all. In other words, the type of project will have something to do with the choice of leadership model.

Regardless of the organizational environment in which projects exist, decisions need to be made on how the project team will be organized and how it will function from a leadership perspective. There are five models to consider. They are shown in Figure 2.6.

Hierarchical. The *hierarchical leadership model* has its roots in the industrial age. Projects are decomposed into functions, similar to how a business is decomposed into business functions, such as R&D, engineering, manufacturing, marketing, sales, distribution, accounting, and finance, with all functions reporting to the same executive. One person, the project manager, is responsible for the project, and all team members are directly accountable to him or her. The project manager makes all decisions, and everything must receive his or her approval.

In this model there is little meaningful interaction between team members. Everything is under the control of the project manager. The project manager makes the decisions, and the decisions are final. The atmosphere is very much one of command and control, similar to the model that is used in the military and in conducting an orchestra.

Even as the project grows in size, and as midlevel or subproject managers are used, the top-down control and decision-making author-

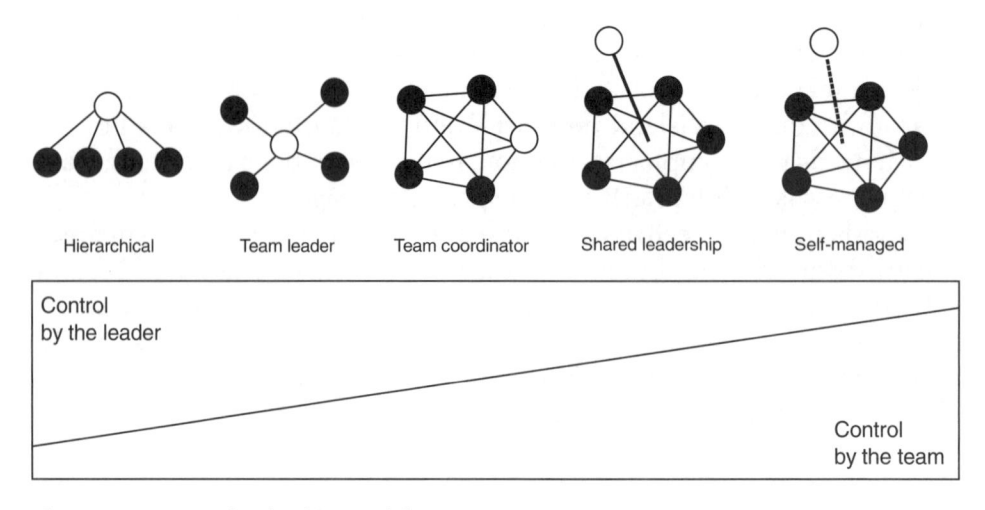

Figure 2.6 Team leadership models.

ity persists. You can see that for very large projects this becomes cumbersome and, in fact, can become dysfunctional. The model breaks down, and some of the authority must be delegated. Despite the delegation, decisions are still made in a very structured and well-defined environment. Nothing is left to chance.

This approach has both advantages and disadvantages. Because decision making is held by one person, decisions can be made quickly, and projects or situations that require quick decisive action will benefit. Unfortunately, it can work to the detriment of the project if that decision maker is not decisive and quick to act. In that case, the individual becomes a bottleneck and will actually slow project progress. On the other hand, because one person is making the decision it is possible that important information will not be on his or her radar screen, and bad decisions will result. As project complexity increases, the hierarchical model becomes dysfunctional.

Team leader. The *team leader model* is the simplest form of non-hierarchical leadership. In this model, all members of the team are treated as equals, with one person appointed to serve as the group leader. As in the hierarchical model, all team members in the team leader model are accountable to one person, the group leader, and there is little interaction between members.

The group leader is expected to work on the project activities just like any other team member. The group leader is also responsible for representing the group to outside constituencies and higher-level managers. In this capacity, the leader will communicate project progress, problem situations, and other relevant information. He or she will also receive change requests and priority adjustments and pass schedule changes to the project team. The group leader is responsible for all decisions but requests input from the team prior to making such decisions.

This approach has both advantages and disadvantages. Compared to the hierarchical model, this model will require more time to make decisions, but it reduces the risk of a bad decision considerably. The team leader will get input from the team (that takes time), but it is unlikely that relevant information will be overlooked.

Team coordinator. The *team coordinator model* is similar to the team leader model in that the leader and the coordinator are both members of the team and both represent the team to outside constituencies. This model differs from the team leader model in only one way: In this model team members have to interact with one another to carry out their assigned tasks. That is not the case in the team leader model, where the only interaction is with the team leader and not with one another. Because direct interaction is allowed between team members there will be situations that are outside the direct view of the team coordinator. The coordinator relies on status reporting and informal communications links to each team member to manage the team. The team coordinator thus has all of the duties of the team leader with the added responsibility of making sure that all work involving interactions between members is facilitated and completed as required.

This approach has both advantages and disadvantages. Because of the interactions the team is less likely to overlook anything that might be helpful to it. The model supports good communications practices within the team. The only disadvantage is that the coordinator can lose control of the project if communications channels do not operate effectively.

Shared leadership. In the *shared leadership model* the responsibility for leadership is shared across the team and is based on the expertise of the team member. In other words, a specific team member assumes the role of leader when the situation involves his or her area of expertise. All team members are fully engaged in decision making and problem resolution. The manager is not a working member of the team. Instead, he or she proactively defines the boundaries or expectations of the team and leaves it to the team to decide the best way to accomplish its charter.

This approach has both advantages and disadvantages. It provides flexibility in choosing leaders when leaders are needed and empowering team members when empowerment is called for. Problems arise in this approach when members of the team are not able to accept empowerment and be responsible for their own output.

Self-managed. *Self-managed teams* are fully responsible for completing the project to which they have been assigned. Their manager is external to the team and acts as a resource to the team at its request. That is, the manager is reactive, as opposed to proactive. The team is authorized to select and remove its own team members. If they do not have a particular skill that is needed, they may hire from outside the team or train one of their own members, as they deem appropriate. In some organizations self-managed teams also have profit-and-loss responsibility, which means they plan and manage their own budgets.

This approach has both advantages and disadvantages. It recognizes the individual team members and fully empowers them to make management decisions. It fosters commitment to the project because of that empowerment. The downside is that it is not for everyone, and discerning when it is appropriate to use may be difficult.

Deciding Which Model to Use

All five of the team leadership models are appropriate for projects. But not every project must use the same leadership model. Depending on the enterprise constraints, at any point in time all models may be active in an organization.

How do you choose which is appropriate for a given project? Table 2.2 lists the criteria that can be used to make that determination. The first column is the leadership model that is appropriate for projects whose characteristics are shown in the second through fifth column. Identify your project in terms of the nature of project activities, the type of team member interaction required, the types of problems and decision-making situations expected in the project, and finally the types of conflict situations the project is likely to encounter. Where your project falls in the second through fifth columns determines the type of leadership model you should use. For example, a simple project (based on the Project Complexity Model) will have activities that are well documented and repetitive and for which no problems are expected and no conflicts are likely to arise. That suggests the use of a hierarchical leadership model.

Environmental Considerations

I am going to complicate the situation a bit by throwing in a dose of reality. While we might like our project team members to be housed in one physical location and always accessible to one another, that simply isn't going to happen very often. Teams are frequently distributed across geographies and multiple time zones. Video conferencing and email have replaced face-to-face interactions. People are reassigned from project to project as priorities change.

Furthermore, teams are typically temporary entities that come and go for a variety of reasons. As projects are completed team members are reassigned to other projects, and any progress that might have been made to make them a high-performance team will have been lost due to the reassignment.

Table 2.2 Project Leadership Model Characteristics

LEADERSHIP MODEL	NATURE OF ACTIVITIES	TEAM MEMBER INTERACTION	PROBLEM SOLVING AND DECISION MAKING	CONFLICT MANAGEMENT
Hierarchical	• Simple • Routine • Well documented • Repetitive • Reasonably independent	Expects to work independently of one another	No problems expected	No conflicts expected
Group leader	• Interdependent and moderately complex activities • Requires communications among team members	Requires minimal help from one another	Moderately complex problems that require team involvement to solve	Minor conflicts that require participation from selected team members
Team coordinator	• Highly dependent and complex activities • Requires collaboration among team members	Must support one another	Complex problems that require creative involvement of selected team members	Serious conflicts that require involvement of selected members
Shared leadership	• Very complex activities • Requires full participation of all team members	Must function as a true team	Complex problems that require creative involvement of the full team	Serious conflicts that require extensive effort from the full team
Self-managed	• Very complex and perhaps unfamiliar activities • Requires total commitment of all team members	Must function as a high-performance team	Complex problems that require creative involvement of full team	Serious conflicts that require extensive effort of the full team

These two observations complicate our efforts to build high-performance teams, but they can be neutralized to some extent. Let's take a closer look at both situations.

Dispersed versus Co-located

A *dispersed* or *virtual* team is a team whose members are geographically dispersed to the extent that they may be in several different time zones. They have little chance of ever physically coming together in one place and may, in fact, have never met one another before. They work together via email and telephone conference calls. If they are fortunate, team members may enjoy video conferences once in while so at least they can put a face with a voice. These time and distance barriers will have an effect on any attempts to build "team."

The *co-located* team, on the other hand, is physically located in one office area or are at least close enough so that frequent face-to-face meetings can be arranged. Co-located teams would seem to have an advantage over dispersed teams in that they can spend quality time with one another both on the job and off the job—something a dispersed team cannot do.

If your project is going to be staffed by a dispersed team, what can you do to improve the effectiveness of the team? For one thing, you can pick team members who do not need the social environment that a co-located team provides. The Internet has become pervasive and can be used in a number of ways to replace face-to-face contact and interaction. Web-based project tools are available. The cost of video conferencing has come down and may be an affordable alternative.

Temporary versus Permanent

Most project teams are usually embedded in some form of matrix organization. The team member is often assigned to more than one project at a time, and projects tend to come and go for reasons that are not always obvious. If the organization is a weak matrix organization, the team member's allegiance will be to his or her functional manager rather than to the project manager. In this highly volatile environment the team is often loosely knit and more like a group than a team.

If the project team is a permanent structure, the situation is quite different. Here the team may have line responsibility to the project manager and will probably be full-time on only one project. They remain with the project until it is finished and then move on to another project assignment.

Putting It All Together

Project classes, organizational structures, and team leadership models integrate and interact with one another to form a complex environment within which the project manager must perform. When project managers take a close look at their teams and the extent to which they are positioned to be effective, they will have to consider this total environment. For example, if the team leadership model is hierarchical, the team's decision-making capabilities are not all that important because the project manager makes all the decisions. On the other hand, if the organizational structure is the balanced matrix form, the project manager's and project team members' skills at negotiation and conflict management are critical. These are but a few of the many factors that the project manager and team will have to take into account as they consider team effectiveness and how to improve it.

Now that we understand the environment in which projects are undertaken we can turn our attention to the models that have been used to describe how teams function in this environment. In the next chapter we will present three models that have been used to describe the roles that should be present if the team expects to be effective.

CHAPTER 3

Team Models

Every successful project team has a set of necessary characteristics—that is, characteristics that the team *must* possess, regardless of the nature of the project to which they have been assigned. Three models have been developed to define a team's necessary characteristics:

- Belbin Team Role Model
- Margerison and McCann Team Management Wheel
- DISC System

All three models lack one important feature: None of them considers the team's assigned project as a relevant factor in determining a successful team. The project to which a team is assigned defines an additional set of characteristics that a project team must possess in order to be effective. These characteristics, when combined with the necessary team characteristics described in the three models listed here, form the necessary and sufficient set of characteristics that the team must possess in order to position itself for success. This chapter introduces these three team models in detail.

Belbin Team Role Model

The earliest and most definitive work was written by R. Meredith Belbin. Published in 1981, *Management Teams: Why They Succeed or Fail* (Butterworth–Heinemann) reported the results of several years of experimentation on what makes a successful team. His later works, *Team Roles at Work* (Butterworth–Heinemann, 1993) and *Changing the Way We Work* (Butterworth–Heinemann, 1997) further expanded the ideas presented in the original book.

Belbin reports on two major research experiments conducted over a period of nine years under the guidance of the Administrative Staff College at Henley in Cambridge, England. The result was the identification of nine team-roles that the researchers contend must be present on every team that expects to be successful. These nine roles must be present regardless of team size. In many cases one team member will support more than one role.

Belbin's nine roles are as follows:

- **Plant.** A creative role. The incumbent is expected to bring new ideas and breakthrough thinking on major problems and issues the team is facing.
- **Resource investigator.** A link to external sources of ideas, developments, and resources that may be useful to the team.
- **Coordinator.** A leadership role, also called *Chairman*. The incumbent is responsible for keeping the work of the team moving forward by taking advantage of team strengths and avoiding team weaknesses. The coordinator makes sure that the team's resources are used to best advantage.
- **Shaper.** An organizer role. The incumbent sets objectives and priorities and generally ensures that the team's effort is focused and directed.
- **Monitor evaluator.** An analytic role. The incumbent analyzes problems and evaluates solutions to ensure a balanced approach to decision making.
- **Teamworker.** The incumbent is the glue that keeps the team working harmoniously and in a coordinated fashion. He or she supports team members in areas of weakness and generally fosters team morale and spirit.
- **Implementer.** The role that makes things happen. The incumbent takes concepts and turns them into practical procedures and takes plans and carries them out.

Completer/finisher. The person in this role pays attention to the details. The incumbent makes sure that all work is complete as required in the plan.

Specialist. Teams need subject matter experts. These roles are filled with people who bring a special and scarce skill to the team. They are single-purposed in that they contribute their expertise, and that's all. Rarely would you expect them to fill any other roles on the team.

Belbin's research was limited to senior management teams, but it applies equally well to project teams.

Belbin Associates has developed a software package called INTER-PLACE that assesses role preferences for individuals and characterizes the team with respect to its balance across those role preferences. INTER-PLACE uses a computer-based survey to measure an individual's attraction to each of the 9 team roles. There are 7 questions, each of which has 8 responses. The individual is asked to distribute 10 points, in any way he or she chooses, across the 8 responses. The point value given to each response to each question is categorized into one of the 9 team roles and the team role total calculated. The resulting scores for an individual are calibrated to normed percentiles and presented as shown in Figure 3.1.

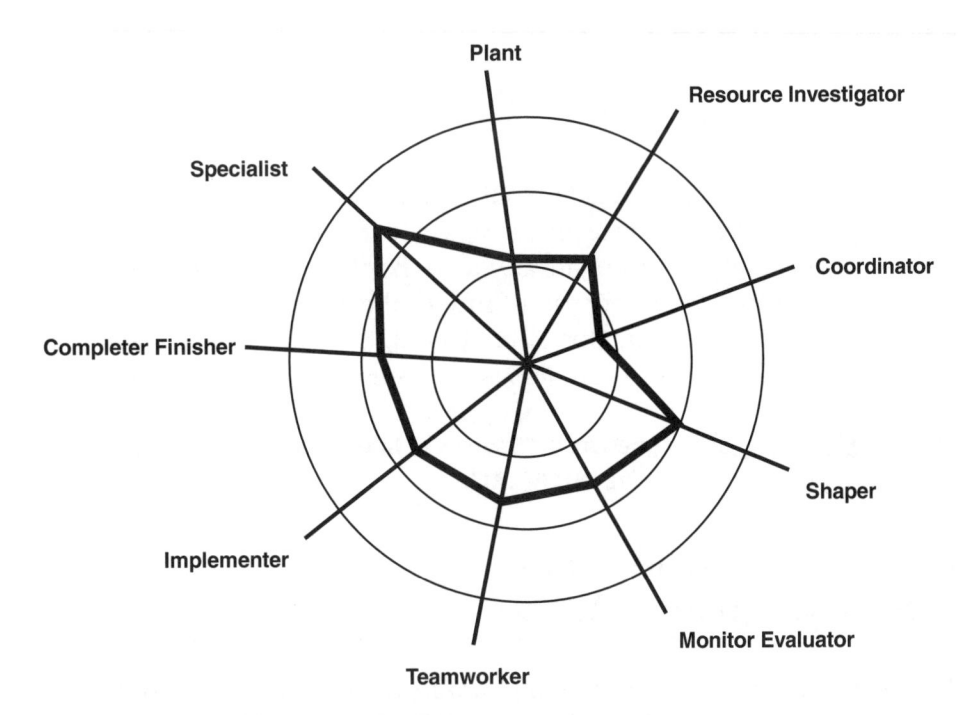

Figure 3.1 Individual team role profile.

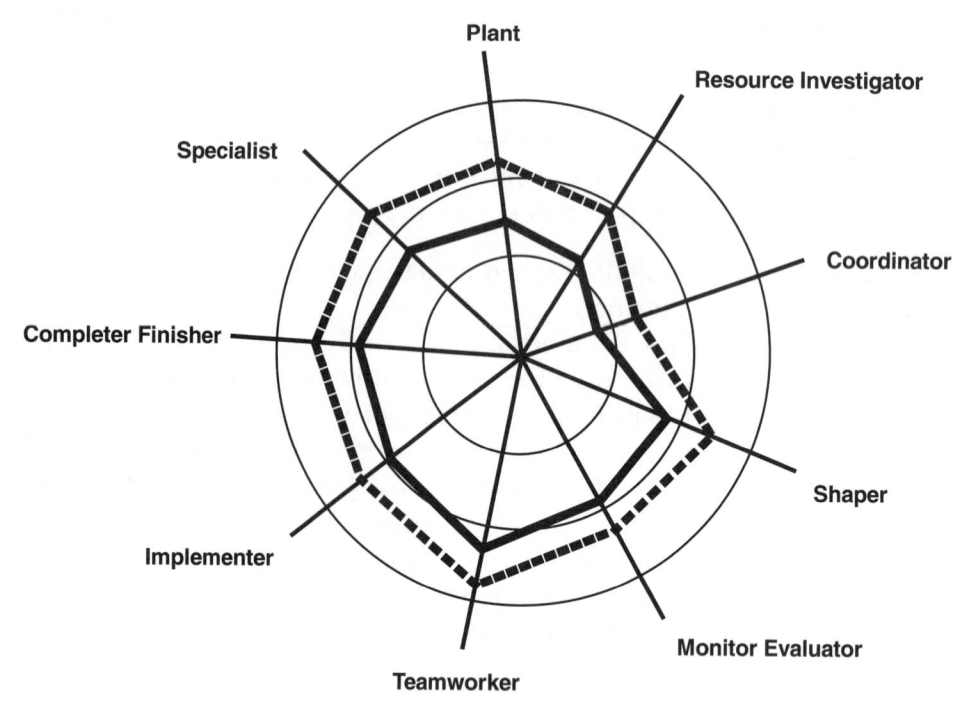

Figure 3.2 Team role profile.

The individual shown in this figure has the greatest affinity to X and the least affinity to Y.

The data can also be aggregated to the team level, as shown in Figure 3.2. The solid line represents the team average on each team role, and the dotted line represents that maximum affinity to each role by a team member. As a team, this team has the strongest affinity to the Teamworker role and the least affinity to the Coordinator role. Overall, the team is reasonably well balanced. Its only obvious weakness is the absence of strong leadership.

FURTHER READING Appendix B, "Sources of Information," contains more details on acquiring and using INTERPLACE.

Margerison and McCann Team Management Wheel

The next significant contribution in team formation came in 1990 with the publication of Charles Margerison and Dick McCann's book, *Team Man-*

agement: Practical New Approaches (Management Books 2000 Ltd.). In that book, Margerison and McCann report the results of research conducted primarily in Australia over an eight-year period. Their work involved collecting data from more than 100,000 managers working in the United Kingdom, United States, Australia, Southeast Asia, and Europe.

In their quest to discover why some teams succeeded while others didn't, Margerison and McCann interviewed team managers and asked what recurring problems they saw. Among the many comments they received were comments such as these:

- Weak on implementation
- Not coordinated
- Don't handle change very well
- Don't understand one another
- Poor communications

Their conclusion was that the teams involved were not balanced. To determine whether a team was balanced would require a definition of the key work functions of every team. These work functions would be robust —that is, they would be independent of the specific technical functions that the team was involved in doing.

As a result of their extensive research, Margerison and McCann defined nine key work functions that broadly describe the work that every team must support. These nine work functions are as follows:

Advising. Gathering, organizing, and presenting information and data to the team.

Innovating. Creating ideas and discovering new ways of doing things.

Promoting. Selling new ideas and obtaining the resources to get the job done.

Developing. Getting the product or service developed so that it can succeed in the market.

Organizing. Getting an infrastructure and a plan in place to deliver the product or service.

Producing. All aspects of the production function.

Inspecting. Ensuring that the resulting product or service meets customer expectations for quality, safety, and security.

Maintaining. Ensuring that the infrastructure works as expected and the necessary support services are operating.

Linking. Coordinating all other work activities to ensure an effective team.

Magerison and McCann determined that a team must cover each of these nine functions in order to be balanced. They had very little to say on how these roles should be distributed across the team or even what team size would be needed to cover all nine roles. They did, however, suggest that a team member could very likely exercise more than one team role.

Magerison and McCann further defined the work functions in terms of nine *roles* in which that work takes place. These nine roles are as follows:

Creator-innovators. The people in this role are idea generators. They like to introduce new ways of doing things, which at times can be rather upsetting, especially in more stable environments. They are focused on change, and they need to be closely managed. They do, however, need to be encouraged to express their thoughts because every team needs their input.

Explorer-promoters. The people in this role gather information from outside the organization, present new ideas, and sell them effectively to the organization. They build a network of outside contacts, which may be helpful to the organization at a later date. They tend to be proactive and bore easily when not involved in something new and exciting.

Assessor-developers. The people in this role can take new ideas and test them against actual needs to determine their business feasibility. They are a good bridge between ideas and their practical implementation.

Thruster-organizers. The people in this role get things done. They are good at establishing the infrastructure of procedures, processes, and the organization to turn ideas into reality. They are good planners and are results oriented as well.

Concluder-producers. The people in this role thrive on standards and procedures. They get satisfaction out of successfully repeating a process to produce a deliverable. They operate on high standards of quality and prefer a stable environment in which to do their work. Change is not a favorite of theirs.

Controller-inspectors. The people in this role are the detailed people. They are careful to ensure that their work is complete and accurate to the last digit. They abhor errors of any kind and will go out of their way to avoid them. Where details and accuracy are at a premium, these are good team players to have.

Upholder-maintainers. The people in this role like to make sure that everything is progressing, as it should. They follow the process to the letter and will strongly defend it. They are good support people, but they tend not to be the front-line leaders. Their word is golden, and you can count on them to deliver according to established procedures. There are no surprises where they are concerned.

Reporter-advisors. The people in this role are very deliberate. They diligently gather facts and figures and analyze them until they are sure of the results. They are driven to present a complete picture of a situation before drawing any conclusions.

Linkers. The people in this role are the coordinators. They ensure that cooperation and communication exist between all members so that the team can progress according to plan.

Margerison and McCann established Team Management Systems and developed a portfolio of indices to measure work preferences, leadership skills, and decision-making styles. The flagship product is the *Team Management Index* (TMI), which is a 60-item assessment that attempts to understand how an individual approaches work. Work preferences are explored in terms of how an individual relates to others, how an individual gathers and uses information, how decisions are made, and how individuals organize themselves.

FURTHER READING For more information on TMI and other tools and related services available from Team Management Systems, see Appendix B.

As you might have observed, there is a great deal of commonality between this team-role model and the one developed by Belbin. It is interesting that even though the two models were developed independently of each another, they bear such remarkable similarity. With few exceptions the mapping is one-to-one, as shown in Figure 3.3. Because of this similarity, the researcher would probably draw some conclusions regarding the face validity of the two models. In other words, these models appear to be measuring exactly what they claim to be measuring.

DISC System

The third model is the *DISC System*. Developed by the Institute for Motivational Learning, in the United States the DISC System is the best known and most widely used of the three models.

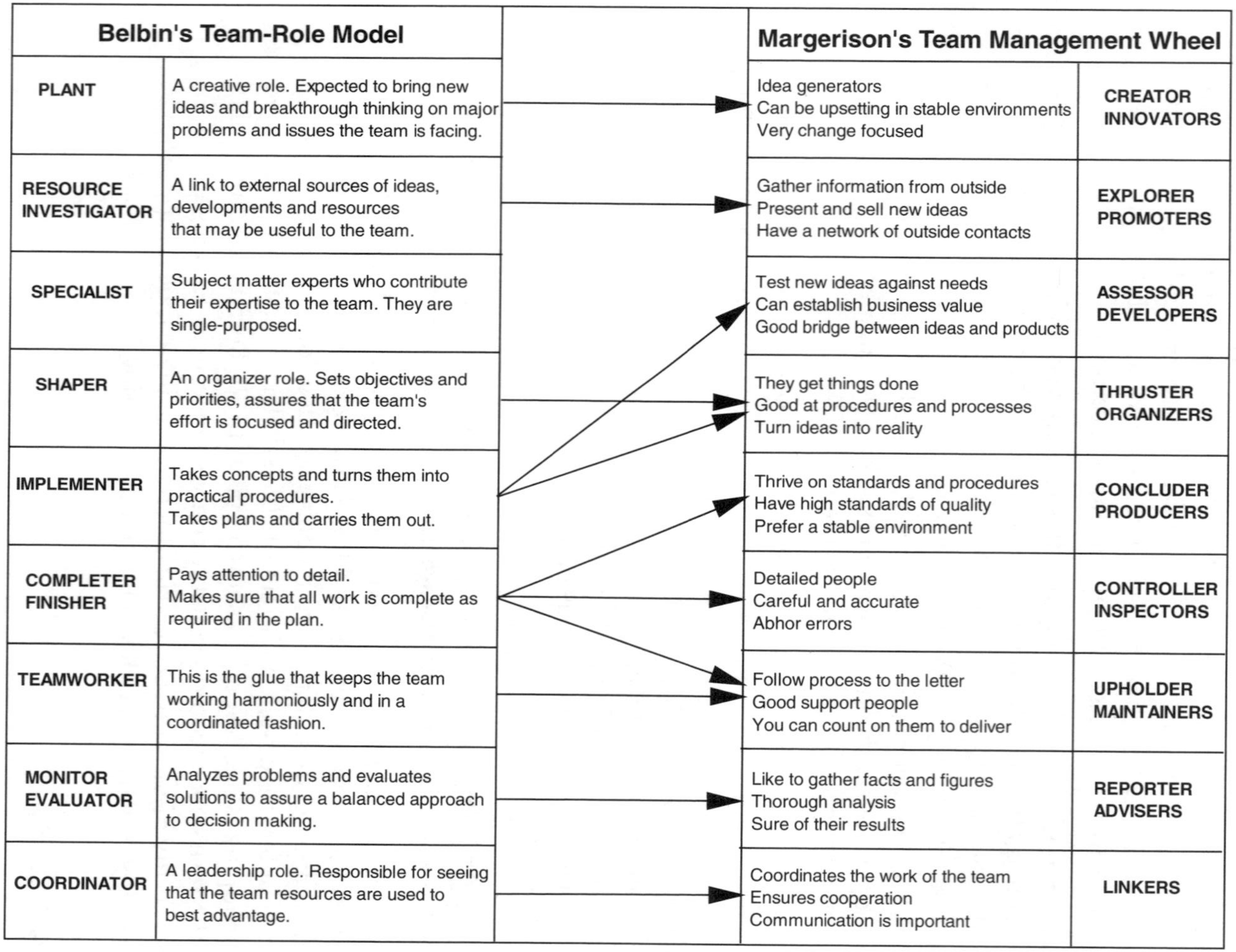

Belbin's Team-Role Model		Margerison's Team Management Wheel	
PLANT	A creative role. Expected to bring new ideas and breakthrough thinking on major problems and issues the team is facing.	Idea generators Can be upsetting in stable environments Very change focused	CREATOR INNOVATORS
RESOURCE INVESTIGATOR	A link to external sources of ideas, developments and resources that may be useful to the team.	Gather information from outside Present and sell new ideas Have a network of outside contacts	EXPLORER PROMOTERS
SPECIALIST	Subject matter experts who contribute their expertise to the team. They are single-purposed.	Test new ideas against needs Can establish business value Good bridge between ideas and products	ASSESSOR DEVELOPERS
SHAPER	An organizer role. Sets objectives and priorities, assures that the team's effort is focused and directed.	They get things done Good at procedures and processes Turn ideas into reality	THRUSTER ORGANIZERS
IMPLEMENTER	Takes concepts and turns them into practical procedures. Takes plans and carries them out.	Thrive on standards and procedures Have high standards of quality Prefer a stable environment	CONCLUDER PRODUCERS
COMPLETER FINISHER	Pays attention to detail. Makes sure that all work is complete as required in the plan.	Detailed people Careful and accurate Abhor errors	CONTROLLER INSPECTORS
TEAMWORKER	This is the glue that keeps the team working harmoniously and in a coordinated fashion.	Follow process to the letter Good support people You can count on them to deliver	UPHOLDER MAINTAINERS
MONITOR EVALUATOR	Analyzes problems and evaluates solutions to assure a balanced approach to decision making.	Like to gather facts and figures Thorough analysis Sure of their results	REPORTER ADVISERS
COORDINATOR	A leadership role. Responsible for seeing that the team resources are used to best advantage.	Coordinates the work of the team Ensures cooperation Communication is important	LINKERS

Figure 3.3 A comparison of the Belbin and Margerison Team-Role Models.

The DISC System is based on the theory that a balanced team must include four personality styles, which form the acronym for its name: Drive, Influencing, Steadiness, and Compliance. Research has shown that these four personality styles are present to some extent in every person. Some people will exhibit more or less of a style than others, but everyone has some measure of each style.

- **Drive.** The D-personality style is characteristic of individuals that have a high energy level. These individuals are direct and decisive and are results oriented, risk takers, and problem solvers. They tend to be self-starters and often take on too much at one time. They thrive on the non-routine and like challenges. If you say to a D-personality "I don't think you can do that," step aside and watch—he or she will rise to the challenge. It's an ego thing with D-personalities. They like to be in charge, thrive on task variety, and are always looking for assignments that offer them professional development opportunities.

- **Influencing.** Individuals who fall under the I-personality style are people people. They have a very positive outlook, have a sense of humor, are optimistic and emotional, are often motivators of others, and are good negotiators. They like attention and acceptance. They are not detail oriented and prefer a work environment free from rules and regulations. As a result, they are not results oriented and can often stray from the task.

- **Steadiness.** You can go to the bank on what the S-personality people say they will do. They are excellent team players, reliable and dependable. They have strong interpersonal skills and resolve conflicts well. They like a stable and predictable work environment and are not in favor of change, although they will adapt given enough time. With them you don't have to worry about any surprises.

- **Compliance.** Much like the S-personality style, the C-personality is dependable but from a different perspective. C-personalities are systematic and careful as a result of their analytic and fact-finding leanings. You can count on them for quality decisions and high standards in everything they do. They want all the facts and don't like uncertainty or out-of-control situations. Tell them exactly what you want, and they are ready to act without any further meddling from their manager.

FURTHER READING Refer to Appendix B for information about how to acquire the DISC System.

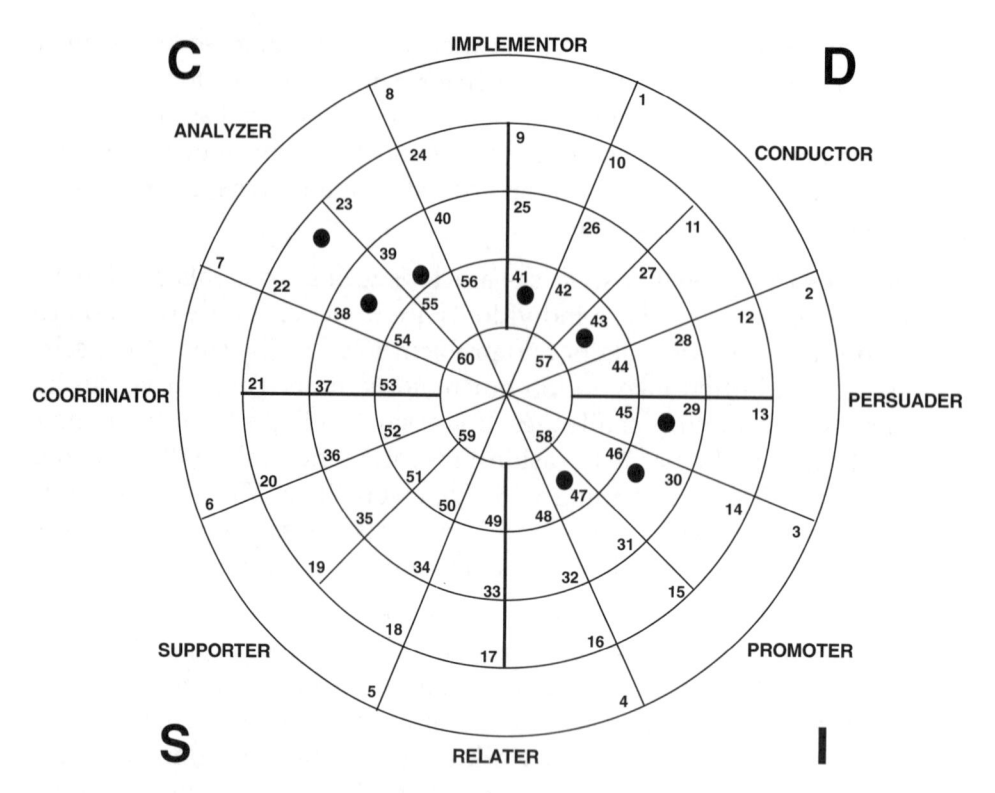

Figure 3.4 Team DISC profile.

Adapted from www.ttidisc.com/wheel: TTI's Success Insights Wheel™.

The DISC system collects data on a number of survey items and translates the data into a graphical representation of the individual and the team, as shown in Figure 3.4. The data forms a hypothetical team. The plot for the example team in this figure shows an imbalance on the team. There is no representation from the Coordinator, Supporter, and Relater types. This indicates a team that functions more like a group of individuals than it does a team.

Shortcomings

So far, so good, but as I began to think about putting these roles and functions into the project team environment, I felt that something was missing. It seemed to me that the nature of the project would have some relationship to whether the team was really balanced. Perhaps an example will help illustrate my point.

Looking ahead briefly to Chapter 10, "Establishing the Profile of the Project," we compare a design project to a development project to an implementation project with specific reference to creative team members. For the project to be successful we argue that the design project needed a significant dose of creativity but that the development project required less and the implementation project even less. In fact, creativity on an implementation project could easily increase the risk of project failure compared to implementation teams that had little creative preferences among its team members. While every team member is sure to have some creative leanings, it seems obvious to me that the creative role takes on more or less importance as the characteristics of the project change. In other words, to build an effective team the characteristics of the project should have been factored into each of the role models described in this chapter. The issue is not whether the role belongs on the team. It does, as all three models have concluded. The real question is to what extent should the role be a dominant influencer on the team. We will have much more to say about that in Chapter 4, "Project/Team Alignment Model," and in Chapter 10 as well.

Team size should also be considered in forming the effective project team. While none of the three models offers much discussion on team size, it is an important factor. As team size increases, teams tend to lose the characteristics of a team (shared leadership, mutual accountability, collective deliverables, proactive involvement in meetings, direct performance measures) and take on the characteristics of a group (strong leader, individual accountability, individual deliverables, reactive involvement in meetings, indirect performance measures). In *The Wisdom of Teams* by Katzenbach and Smith (Harvard Business School Press, 1993), a team is defined as "a small number of people with complementary skills who are equally committed to a common purpose, goals, and working approach for which they hold themselves mutually accountable." So how small is small? Figure 3.5 offers some guidelines.

Most researchers would agree that teams of 8 to 10 members are most effective. Teams of 15 to 20 members can also be effective, but the tendency is for them to break apart into subteams. Teams of 50 members are probably not teams at all but groups. We just call them teams because it feels good to be an advocate for teams. How many organizations do you know that follow this silly labeling practice? Probably a lot!

So, what is a project manager to do when the people who will work on the project number, say, 100? My advice would be to consider the project to be a program made up of several interdependent projects with each one having a team size nearer the 8 to 10 number. The trade-off is that this

Team effectiveness

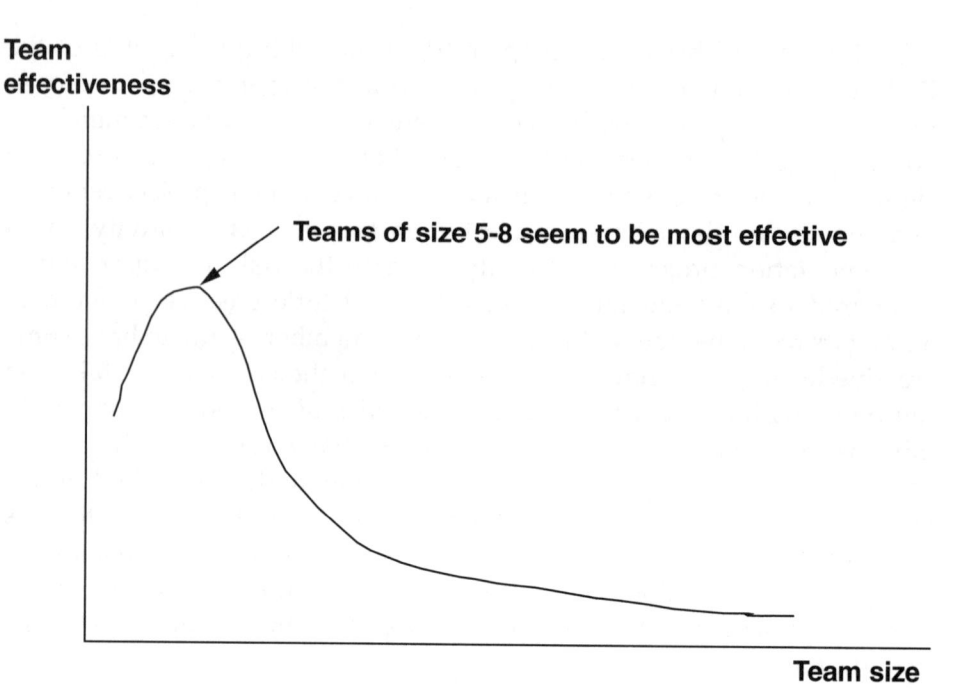

Teams of size 5-8 seem to be most effective

Team size

Figure 3.5 Team size versus team effectiveness.

program structure will require a more demanding communications program and an additional management layer to coordinate schedules and deliverables between the projects. On balance, I believe that to be a good trade-off.

Putting It All Together

The three models discussed in this chapter are well known worldwide and are the most practical models that I know of. They are accessible and affordable. Appendix B has all the details you will need to investigate them further and acquire them for your use.

Despite their validity and reliability, all three models have the same limitation. The characteristics of the project are not considered a factor in the definition of balance on the team. I believe that that is a fatal flaw for the project manager. Chapter 4 introduces a new approach that I designed as an add-on to these three models. The TeamArchitect approach is a way to rectify this flaw.

CHAPTER 4

Project/Team Alignment Model

When I first started to examine team effectiveness, something seemed to be missing from the models put forth by Belbin and Margerison. I had always thought that the characteristics of the project would somehow determine the characteristics the team should possess if it wanted to increase its chances of success. All three models, as you saw in Chapter 3, "Team Models," did not take the project into account.

As a simple example, let's consider Harry, a database administrator (DBA), Harry is an excellent implementer and is able to use his database skills quite effectively, even when he works with less technically oriented people. He has consistently demonstrated good people skills. Because he was available and there was an opening for a DBA on the design team of a new project, he was assigned. Even though his DBA skills would be needed in both types of projects, there is no reason to believe that his success in an implementation project would in any way ensure his success in a design project. In other words, the Belbin and Margerison definition of team roles were the necessary conditions for team success, but they were by no means sufficient. Somehow, the characteristics of the project had to be factored into the equation for forming an effective project team.

And so we have seen how two parts of the project environment (project and team) are linked to one another. The third part, project management methodology, is also linked to the project, and that is how we get the system that I discuss in this chapter. These observations led me to the Project/Team Alignment model.

This model combines the project, project team, and project management process as dynamic parts of a system—a system that can be defined at the outset of the project and, as project work commences and the project changes, will adjust and change as well. In this model, the initial definition of the project team is based on the nature, scope, and characteristics of the project. The three entities are always maintained in alignment or balance with respect to one another. As any one of the characteristics of the project changes, the project team and project process will have to change to preserve that balance.

This chapter takes a look at the four premises and the P^4 System that form the basis of the Project/Team Alignment Model. It then takes a look at how the project and the team are integrated together to create the model for an effective and balanced team.

The Basis of the Model

There are four premises that underlie the Alignment Model. The first is a restatement of the Belbin and Margerison team role model. It represents the necessary conditions for team success. The next three premises are project-driven and represent the necessary and sufficient conditions for team success. By necessary and sufficient I mean that all of the premises are needed for team success and none of the premises are superfluous. The four premises map to four parts of a dynamic system that, when aligned, create the balanced project team.

> **Premise #1: There are specific role preferences that must be present on every successful project team, which are independent of the profile of the project.** This premise is in line with the team models constructed by Belbin and Margerison. There are certain fundamental roles (necessary but not sufficient conditions) that every successful project team must practice, regardless of the type of project on which they are working. Recall from Chapter 3 that both Belbin and Margerison identified 9 roles. There is quite a bit of overlap, as you saw in Figure 3.3. At least 1 team member must be inclined to each role. Team members may prefer more than 1 role, and there may be more than 1

team member per role. Team size may be larger or smaller than 9 members. Smaller is better. When team size reaches 15, teams tend to become dysfunctional. When team size pushes up against 25, the team begins to take on the characteristics of a group, and members tend to form smaller work groups, which become teams unto themselves. In the worst case, the team completely degenerates and becomes nothing more than a herd of cats. And you can't herd cats very well!

Premise #2: The characteristics of the project determine the type of project management process that will be employed. One size does not fit all. The type of project to be undertaken should be used to determine which features or variations of the project methodology to use. For example, a very small, familiar, and simple project should not require the extensive risk management effort of a large, complex, and bleeding-edge technology project. To ignore these differences and require the same methodology for each is simply a waste of resources and time. I recall several clients whose project management process was less effective than expected because they insisted on a one-size-fits-all approach. My advice is to require the minimum that the project manager and other managers will need and let the project manager decide if there is personal value in using more comprehensive variations of the project management process. It is beyond the scope of this book to discuss these project classification rules and the subsequent choice of project management process. For a detailed discussion, refer to *Effective Project Management, Second Edition* by Wysocki et al. (Wiley, 2000).

Premise #3: The characteristics of the project determine the profile of the successful project team. There certainly are some necessary roles and hence behavioral characteristics that every team must have in order to perform, as defined by Belbin and Margerison. But there are also other behavioral characteristics dictated by the project that a specific team must possess in order to be balanced with respect to the characteristics of their project. For example, let's consider two projects. Project Alpha involves solving a very difficult process improvement problem. It is expected that a significant reengineering effort will be required. Project Beta, on the other hand, is a project to install the company's customer technical support system, which has been customized to meet the specific needs of your largest customer. How would these two project teams differ? Project Alpha clearly requires a team composed of analytical, conceptual, and creative problem solvers. To put this type of team to work on Project Beta would be to risk disaster. They would be looking for problems that didn't exist rather than focusing on the established process of systems installation. They would be looking for opportunities to be innovative when the project simply does not require that type of approach. Neither the Belbin nor the Margerison models account for this variation between projects.

Premise #4: The profile of the successful project team does not remain constant over the life of the project. If you agree with the third premise, this statement follows naturally. The project takes on different characteristics as it progresses through its life cycle. As you move from phase to phase in a project, the characteristics of the project will change. For example, a software applications development project might follow a linear systems development life cycle defined by the six phases: define, design, build, test, train, and implement. I think you would all agree that the profile of the team needed in the first phase is certainly different from the profile of the team needed in the design phase and so on. Don't limit your thinking to just technical skills—those are obviously different—but consider personal and interpersonal skills as well. How about the team member's ability to interact with the customer? What about conflict management, decision making, and problem solving? Certainly these will differ by phase. How about thinking styles? Would you not agree that the need for a particular analytical or creative skill would vary depending on the phase?

Now we know that the profile of the ideal team does not remain constant over the life of the project. That's fine, but we seldom have the luxury of changing the composition of the team whenever the project scope changes or if progress into other phases of the project indicates that the profile of the project team should change. What can we do under these conditions? The answer is actually very simple, but the result may be less than ideal. I am assuming that team membership does not change. What you see is what you get. But what can change is who does what or who is trained to do what.

This is the rationale behind Premise #4. Instead of changing team members, change the task assignments to reposition team members to take advantage of their strengths and minimize their weaknesses. For example, the creative problem solvers on the team will lead the team's efforts in the design phase, the process and procedures team members will lead the team's efforts during the installation phase, and the people-oriented team members will lead the team's efforts during the implementation and training phases. Consider what would happen if you assigned creative people to the implementation phase. Being creative, these team members are adverse to routine and defined process. They like challenge. They live outside the box and can be expected to be looking for better ways to do things. They will be inventing problems just so they will have something to solve. This is not what you want on your implementation team.

P⁴ System

The four premises identify four interacting parts, which when combined make up the P⁴ System:

- Project scope
- Project profile
- Profile of the team
- Project management process

This system is shown in Figure 4.1.

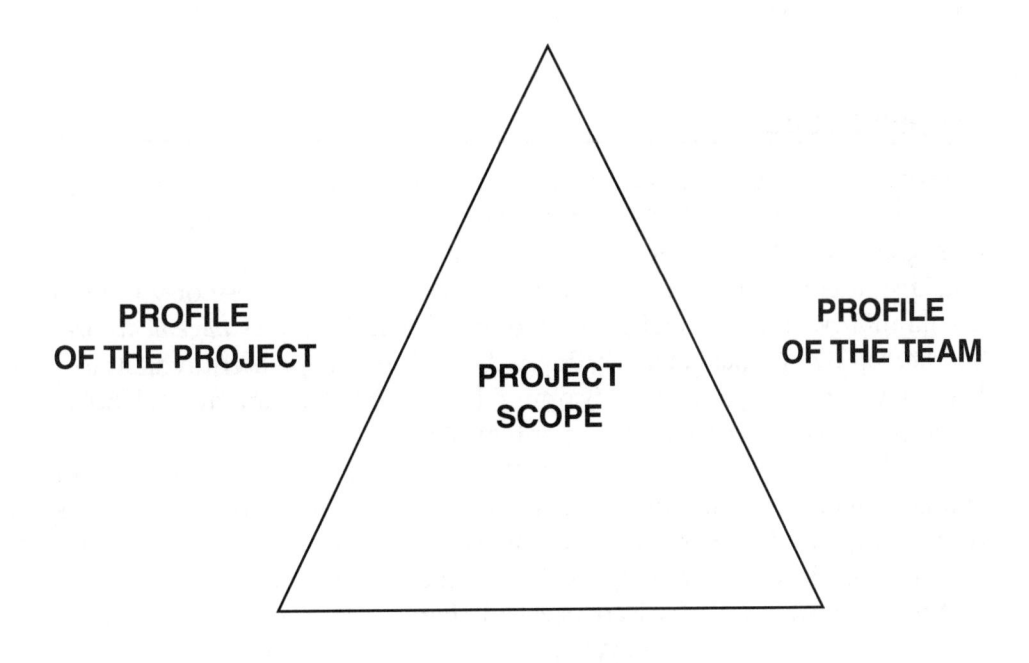

Figure 4.1 The P⁴ System.

All four parts are functionally dependent on one another, and when properly aligned, this system is in balance. If any part should change, the system will be out of balance, and one or more other parts must then change in order to restore balance to the system. For example, a change in the business environment (i.e., a new competitor enters the market; a competitor introduces an enhanced version of a competing product; a new technology that will significantly affect development time is introduced) might necessitate a change in the project scope or the team profile or even the project management process. Any one of these changes will ripple through the system and result in changes to other parts of the system in an effort to restore itself to a balanced state. If a competitor's action necessitates a change in project scope, the profile of the project and the profile of the project team will have to change to restore balance to the system. In extreme cases it might even affect the project management process. If a new technology is introduced, the profile of the project team will have to change to assimilate the new technology. Similarly, the project management process will have to adjust to correct whatever imbalance the new technology causes.

Project Scope

The scope of the project is derived from the discussions and agreements between the requestor and the provider. As a result of that interaction a common understanding of what is to be done is agreed to by both parties and documented in what is called the *project scope*. For those of you who are familiar with the model presented in *Effective Project Management, Second Edition* by Wysocki et al. (Wiley, 2000), project scope is equivalent to a Project Overview Statement, Scoping Document, Document of Understanding, Project Initiation Document, or Statement of Work.

Project scope is not a constant in this model. It changes as a result of changing market conditions or changing technology or through the process of learning and discovery as project work commences. Those of you who are involved in Web applications development will certainly attest to the fact that the processes of discovery and change are constant through the life of these types of projects. Whatever the impetus for that change, it will definitely affect the profile of the project, may affect the profile of the successful team, and in rare circumstances (massive change to the project scope, for example) will affect the project management process that is being followed.

Project Profile

The project profile is derived from the project scope. This is a fully automated process, which is done under the control of TeamArchitect. TeamArchitect is a Web-based decision support system; it was briefly introduced in the "Introduction." TeamArchitect accepts, as input, a narrative statement of the project scope and produces, as output, the project profile. The technique is very powerful and robust. No specific format of the project scoping document is required. Good results have been obtained with documents having as few as 300 words. That is roughly equivalent to one typed page of information.

FOR YOUR REFERENCE Refer to Appendix C, "How to Get TeamArchitect Tools," for more information about TeamArchitect.

As the project moves through its phases (design, build, test, implement, for example) it is often useful to profile each phase independently. The resulting phase profiles will be different from one another and will often contain additional information about improving team effectiveness that cannot be extracted from the overall project profile.

Profile of the Team

The profile of the project team is derived from assessments of each team member. In many organizations a database housing all previously collected assessments will be available to construct the team profile. These assessments may include skill and competency profiles, thinking styles, decision-making styles, problem-solving styles, and conflict management styles.

Project Management Process

I strongly advocate an adaptive approach when choosing or adapting the project management process that will be used on a specific project. Projects vary in terms of risk, business value, duration, total cost, technology, and organizational impact. In some cases, the project will be very simple and repetitive and will require the use of only a minimal part of the project management process. Projects that are very complex and carry high risk will require the use of the entire project management process. The bottom line is that the project manager must see value in the chosen methodology, or it will not be used as intended. Those organizations that have insisted on a "one size fits all" mentality for their project management process have typically been disappointed with the continuing high rate of project failure. In other words, the project management process must be tailored so that it is appropriate for the project, and it must be chosen because it has value to the project manager and team; that is, all parts are in balance with one another.

FURTHER READING For a more complete discussion of my adaptive approach to project management consult *Effective Project Management, Second Edition* by Wysocki et al. (Wiley, 2000).

Project Management Life Cycle

Regardless of the specifics of your project management process, it will always conform to the standard project management life cycle. Let's put that life cycle in place now because we will refer to it later in the chapter.

There are several variations as to how the project management life cycle can be described. I prefer the five-phase model shown in Figure 4.2 and described in the paragraphs that follow. This model is the same as the model presented in *Effective Project Management, Second Edition* (Wysocki et al., Wiley, 2000). The Project/Team Alignment Model is based on this five-phase project management life cycle.

Initiating Phase

One of the first tasks for project managers is to define the work that needs to be done in their area of responsibility. Exactly the same task applies to people management. Unlike project management, though, the initiating phase is very informal in people management.

There is a parallel in project management. For the project manager, defining the tasks to do is a preliminary and important phase of the project

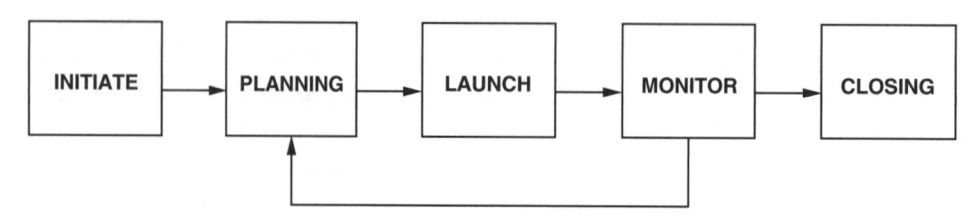

Figure 4.2 The project management life cycle model.

life cycle. In this phase, the requester (also known as the customer) and the project manager come to an agreement about several important aspects of the project. Regardless of the format used, every good initiating phase answers five basic questions:

- What is the problem or opportunity to be addressed?
- What is the goal of the project?
- What objectives must be met to accomplish the goal?
- How will we determine if the project has been successful?
- Are there any assumptions, risks, or obstacles that may affect project success?

The initiating phase sets the scope of the project. It forms the basis for deciding if a particular function or feature is within the scope of the project. It also produces the project scope document that is used to create the project profile.

Even the best of intentions to define project scope will fall short of the mark. The scope of the project can change for a variety of reasons—sometimes far more frequently than the project manager would prefer. Scope creep can be the bane of the project manager if it is not dealt with effectively. Scope creep can occur for a variety of reasons—from something the client forgot to include in the business requirements document, to a change in business priorities that must be reflected in the project, to the availability of a new technology, to a learning process inherent in the project work itself.

The project manager must respond to scope creep by documenting the alternative courses of action and their respective consequences on the project plan. The alternative courses of action will affect the project team. For example, a significant scope change will change the profile of the project and hence the profile of the project team. Remember that we are trying to maintain balance between the project, the project team, and the project management process. Any change to one of the parts will require a compensating change in one or more of the other components in order to preserve balance.

Planning Phase

How often have you heard it said that planning is a waste of time? No sooner is the plan completed than someone comes along to change it. These same nay-sayers would also argue that the plan, once completed, is disregarded and merely put on the shelf so that the team can get down to doing some real work. In people management, the planning activity involves deciding on the types of people resources that will be needed to discharge the responsibilities of the department. That means identifying the types of skills needed and the number of people possessing those skills.

The project plan is indispensable. Not only is it a roadmap to how the work will be performed, but it is also a tool for decision making. The plan suggests alternative approaches, schedules, and resource requirements from which the project manager can select the best alternative.

A project plan is *dynamic*. We expect it to change. A complete plan will clearly state the tasks that need to be done, why they are necessary, who will do what, when it will be completed, what resources will be needed, and what criteria must be met in order for the project to be declared complete and successful.

There are three benefits to developing a project plan:

Planning reduces uncertainty. Even though we would never expect the project work to occur exactly as planned, planning the work allows us to consider the likely outcomes and to put the necessary corrective measures in place.

Planning increases understanding. The mere act of planning gives us a better understanding of the goals and objectives of the project. Even if we were to discard the plan, we would still benefit from having done the exercise.

Planning improves efficiency. Once we have defined the project plan and the necessary resources to carry out the plan, we can schedule the work to take advantage of resource availability. We also can schedule work in parallel; that is, we can do tasks concurrently, rather than in series. By doing tasks concurrently we can shorten the total duration of the project. We can maximize our use of resources and complete the project work in less time than by taking other approaches.

Just as Alice needed to know where in Wonderland she was going, so does the project manager. Not knowing the parameters of a project prevents measurement of progress and results in never knowing when the project is complete. The plan also provides a basis for measuring work performed against work planned.

Planning affects the profile of the effective project team in formation, deployment, and development decisions. In formation decisions the project plan will identify specific combinations of skills that are needed, which will help with team selection. Equally as important, the plan will assist the project manager in deployment decisions. For example, when a client requests a scope change that will be difficult for the team to accommodate, the project manager will want to assign team members with good negotiation skills to resolve the change request with the client. Finally, once the project is underway and changes occur, the revised project plan may identify additional skills beyond those already possessed on the team. To accommodate these additional skills the project manager may have to provide development opportunities to prepare the team for their new responsibilities.

Launching Phase

Launching the project plan is equivalent to authorizing your staff to perform the tasks that define their respective jobs. Each staff member knows what is expected of him or her, how to accomplish the work, and when to have it completed.

Launching the project plan involves five steps. In addition to organizing the people who will work on the project, a project manager also needs to do the following:

1. Identify the specific resources (people, facilities, materials, and money) that will be required to accomplish the work defined in the plan.
2. Establish team operating rules.
3. Schedule activities with specific start and end dates.
4. Assign workers to activities.
5. Launch the plan.

Launching has a minimal impact on the profile of the project team, but it does use the team profile in a number of ways. For example, the team will have to decide very early on how it will make decisions and resolve conflicts. In Chapter 7, "Problem-Solving and Decision-Making Styles," and Chapter 8, "Conflict Management Styles and Strategies," we will learn how to profile the team with respect to its conflict management and decision-making abilities. This will identify strengths and weaknesses on the team, which need to be discussed by the team. In other words, as part of the launch phase we create an awareness of the team's strengths and weaknesses so that the project manager can plan how to deal effectively with situations that arise.

Monitoring Phase

As part of the planning process, an initial schedule is created. The schedule lists the following:

- What must be accomplished in the project
- When each task must be accomplished
- Who is responsible for completing each task
- What deliverables are expected as a result of completing the project

No matter how attentive the team is when creating the plan, the project work will not go according to plan. Schedules slip—this is the reality of project management. The project manager must have a system in place that constantly monitors the project's progress, or lack thereof, and adjusts the plan as required. The monitoring system summarizes the completed work measured against the plan and also looks ahead to forewarn of potential problems.

Monitoring and team deployment/development are closely related. Events will occur (i.e., schedule slippages, the loss of a team member, a significant change request by the customer, an unexpected shift in the market, etc.), and the project team will have to respond with the appropriate corrective measures. Assignments may have to be adjusted. Additional training may be required. Here is where the profile of the project team will be an invaluable aid to decision making for the project manager.

Closing Phase

Closing a project is a formal means of signaling the completion of the project work and the delivery of the results to the customer. In managing people, the equivalent action is to signal the end of a task with some sign of completion and assign the individual to another task.

The closing phase evaluates what occurred during the project and provides historical information for use in planning and executing later projects. This historical information is best kept in a document called a *project notebook*. To be useful, the notebook should be in an electronic form so that it is easy to retrieve and summarize project information for use in projects currently being planned. Every good closing provides answers to the following questions:

- Do the project deliverables meet the expectations of the requester?
- Do the project deliverables meet the expectations of the project manager?
- Did the project team complete the project according to plan?
- What information was collected that will help with later projects?

- How well did the project management methodology work, and how well did the project team follow it?
- What lessons have we learned from this project?

The closing phase is very important to project management, but unfortunately it is the part that is most often neglected or omitted by management. Rather than spending time in the closing phase of this project, the project manager is under pressure to get started on the next project. Often the next project is already behind schedule, and work hasn't yet begun. It is easy for management to skip the closing phase because it is perceived as an overhead expense, is easily overlooked, and delays getting the next project underway.

Team Life Cycle

Just as a project has a life cycle, so also does a team. A team life cycle consists of four interdependent parts: assessment, formation, development, and deployment. These parts are not to be confused with the forming, storming, norming, performing stages through which a team evolves. The stages refer to an evolution of a specific group of people into a high-performance team. The life cycle that we are talking about here focuses on who should be on the team, why they should be on the team, and how they will contribute to the team. Once these three questions are answered, the stages model will explain the further evolution of the team.

Let us be clear up front that this is a new way of thinking about the team. Until now, team membership was largely focused on what the individual brings to the project. And most of those considerations were based entirely on technical skills. The approach that I have taken here is to consider the team as the focus, and membership on the team is based on how the individual contributes to the alignment of the team to the project. By focusing on the individual, we can form a team of very skilled and experienced individuals but end up with a team that is seriously misaligned to the project. By focusing on the team's alignment to the project, we can form a team of varied skills and experiences and end up with a team that is closely aligned to the project. The difference is subtle but significant. I have developed a new way of thinking about the life cycle of a project team. This approach is original with me, and so any shortcomings or flaws are mine to assume and defend. I am continuing to improve the model through ongoing research efforts and through feedback from the early adopters.

Before we put these two life cycles together we need a little more detail on how the four parts of the team life cycle operate and interact with one another. That is the topic of the next section.

Creating an Effective Project Team

There are four stages to the creation of an effective project team:

Assessment stage. Understanding the profile of the team.

Formation stage. Putting a team together.

Development stage. Trying to do the best we can with the skills and competencies we are fortunate to have on our team.

Deployment stage. Deploying and redeploying the team members to the work of the project as the project moves through its stages.

Every project manager should go through these four stages regardless of the constraints the organization places on team formation. For some project managers, the stages will be supported by the organization. For others, forming an effective team will be a constant struggle. Let's take a look inside each stage.

Assessment Stage

The assessment stage is a data collection stage. A number of assessment tools, which are discussed in great detail in Chapters 6 through 9, will be used. Each one is designed to profile a potential team member. This data may have been collected at some earlier time and made available to any project manager at the time he or she is putting a team together. Alternatively, the data might be collected at the time a proposed team is identified. That means that the assessment stage and the formation stage would occur in parallel.

Individual assessment is the first step in this stage and involves collecting data about individuals in the resource pool who are available for project assignments. Assessment includes measuring thinking styles, learning styles, conflict management strategies, skill assessment, and competency assessment.

At the individual level, assessment can precede or follow team formation. If it precedes the formation stage, it will usually be the result of an enterprise effort to assess all potential project team members on a number of instruments. If it follows the formation stage, it will usually be the result of the project team being formed based on availability or because of limited staff resources. At the team level, assessment usually follows the team formation stage.

Team assessment is the second step in the assessment stage. In this step you will already have assembled the group that will become the project team.

In most organizations the project team is formed based solely on availability and technical skills. The members may have had little opportunity to work together as a team on previous projects. In other words, they are a herd of cats. If you have ever tried to herd cats, you know what I am talking about. It is very difficult. Each has a mind of its own. They do things in their own way and at their own pace. They are not accountable to anyone else on the team. They resist being organized. Fortunately, my analogy is only a temporary one because I am going to show you how to turn this herd of cats into an effective project team.

In order to do that, you need to summarize the individual assessment data at the team level and assess the results. The objective will be a development and deployment strategy for each team member so that he or she can be used to the best advantage. Openness is going to be critical. The results of the team assessment must be shared and discussed candidly in the initial team meetings. Team members must be comfortable in their honesty and directness in dealing with one another. To expect to have a true team environment in the absence of this is unrealistic.

Formation Stage

The formation stage is the stage in which team members are selected. There is a continuum of possibilities for this stage that stretches from fixed to variable. At the fixed end of the continuum, the members of the team have been determined previously and are assigned to the team. Circumstances, availability, size of the resource pool, timing, and other variables may have dictated team membership and left little or no room for adjustment. At the other end of the continuum, team membership is totally variable. The project manager is free to recruit and hire each team member. The organization is supportive of this approach and provides an infrastructure within which this process takes place.

All possibilities in between these two extremes are possible. I have clients at both ends of the continuum and in between as well. Unfortunately, most of them are near the end of the continuum, where team members are given to the project manager and he or she has to make the best of it.

Development Stage

However you arrived at the development stage, it is now time to take a look at the development needs of your team. If you handpicked the team, there should be very little that you have to do to develop their skills. Your efforts will be centered around assigning specific tasks to team members based on skills and preferences.

On the other hand, if you inherited all or most of your team members, you have a much different problem. You will have to assess the strengths and weaknesses of each team member with respect to the needs of the project and make the best assignment you can. In some cases, those assignments may be risk avoidance strategies, rather than positive choices. Face it, you are going to have to do the best you can with what you've got. To the extent that you will have opportunities to train your team on the job or off-site, you will have to plan for who gets trained, in what, and when. At the same time you have project work to do, and the schedule is probably aggressive.

Deployment Stage

At the deployment stage, the team has been formed and all meaningful development has been planned or completed. It is now up to the project manager to determine specific assignments.

To the extent possible the project manager will try to avoid assignments that expose known team weaknesses. The project manager will try to put the team's best foot forward. Our friend Harry the database administrator is a good example. He does well in implementation assignments but not in design assignments. His involvement in the design phase of a project should be minimized. That doesn't mean he won't be doing design work. It just means he will not take the lead in such activities. He might play the role of consultant to the team member who does take the lead in the design phase. It is your job as project manager to evaluate the individual assessments and deploy your team members appropriately. By doing so, you will have formed an effective team. Failing to do so will result in project failure.

The Project/Team Alignment Model

The Project/Team Alignment Model takes the project management life cycle and the team life cycle and combines them together into six phases. This section gives an overview of each of the phases. The details of each phase are discussed in Chapters 10 through 13. As we discuss each of the six phases you will see how the four stages of team formation are threaded throughout the model.

Phase I: Establish the profile of the project. Phase I is to establish the project profile. In this phase the project scope document is analyzed and a profile of the project produced. That profile describes the underlying characteristics of the project, which will eventually be related to the characteristics of the project team. The details of how this is done are described in Chapter 9, "Project Management Skills and Competencies," and Chapter 10, "Establishing the Profile of the Project." A project team will be effective only if it has been formed with consideration given to the type of project the team will be tasked to perform.

Phase II: Establish the profile of the ideal project team. The profile of the ideal team will be derived from the profile of the project. In a certain sense the creation of the ideal team is equivalent to the design of the system. The successful completion of the project is the function that the system is expected to perform, and the ideal team is the system that can perform that function. Think of the project profile as the average profile of the project team. That is, we will use a tool called the Herrmann Brain Dominance Instrument (HBDI) to collect data on each individual that will make up the ideal project team, compute the average score of the team on each of the four quadrants, and plot the profile. The resulting graph is the same as the project profile. While this ideal team can be defined in these terms as well as in terms of specific skills and proficiency levels that are required, resource constraints are such that it is very unlikely that such a team can ever be formed. It does, however, give us a goal to focus on as we try to build the best team possible from the resources available to the project. Phase II is discussed in detail in Chapter 11, "Establishing the Profile of the Project Team."

Phase III: Form the actual project team. There are two situations to consider when forming the actual project team. The first, and least likely to occur, is that we will actually have the luxury of choosing the members of the project team. I call a team that has been formed in this manner an "actual team."

The second, and most frequently encountered, is the situation where team membership is a given. In many cases, we will not have the luxury of choosing who will be on our team. That is most obvious in cases where we have scarce people resources. For example, we have only one fiber optics expert (or equivalently, there is only one available), and we need one on our team. It makes little difference as to the degree of fit of our fiber optics expert to the ideal team profile. That person will be on the team. I call a team that has been formed by circumstance rather than by choice an "accidental team." We may be able to change one or perhaps two of the accidental team members, but for the most part we are stuck with whatever we get. Phase III is discussed in detail in Chapter 11.

Phase IV: Assess the gap between the project and the actual project team. Using the project profile as a template of the ideal team, we can compare the profile of an actual team to the ideal team. By making changes to the actual team membership we can converge the actual team profile toward the ideal team profile. This process of changing actual team members will continue until the actual team profile is as close as possible to the ideal team profile, and hence no additional improvements in the actual team are possible. The actual team becomes the system that will perform the function of successfully completing the project. Further improvements in the actual team will come from development and deployment strategies based on assessments of the actual team strengths and weaknesses with respect to each phase of the project.

When team membership is fixed, we have the accidental team situation. In this case, we begin by comparing the accidental team profile to the ideal team profile, but now we are looking for development strategies or risk mitigation strategies rather than the altering of team membership. Phase IV is discussed in detail in Chapter 12, "Assessing Team Alignment and Balance."

Phase V: Plan and implement a strategy to manage the gap. There are two strategies to manage the gap: development and deployment. Development will occur first at the team level and then at the individual level. The focus of our development strategies will be on the team's decision-making styles, problem-solving styles, conflict management styles, skills, and competencies. At the team level the strategy is one of temporarily augmenting team membership to correct the alignment gaps. In large organizations there may be several options available; in smaller organizations the choices may be very limited. In any case, we will exhaust all possibilities for augmenting membership and then proceed to development strategies at the individual team member level.

Once we have implemented as many team-level development strategies as possible, we turn to development strategies at the individual level. Here the focus is on individual training programs to further ameliorate any remaining alignment gaps. Depending on the duration of the project some of these strategies may not be sufficiently completed in time to be useful on the project. We will simply do the best we can and leave it to our deployment strategies to correct the remaining alignment gaps as much as possible.

Once all development strategies have been implemented we will look to deployment as a further means of correcting any significant alignment problems. Regardless of the extent to which we have been successful in our development strategies there will still be alignment gaps at the team level. Phase V is discussed in detail in Chapter 13, "Developing and Deploying the Project Team."

Phase VI: Maintain team-to-project alignment over the life of the project.
Once team membership has been established and a development and deployment strategy put in place, project work can commence. The beginning of Phase VI of the project team life cycle is concurrent with the beginning of the project management life cycle. As changes occur during the life of the project and as the project progresses through its five stages, the project needs will change, and so will the project profile at that point in time. The new project profile will drive corresponding changes to the ideal team profile and hence to the actual team profile best suited to the now-changed project. In terms of the project team life cycle, this creates a feedback loop from Phase VI to Phase IV. In this case, Phase IV will reassess the gap, which is now different from the gap assessed earlier. Then, moving into Phase V the strategy will be revised accordingly, and Phase VI will continue until the next project change occurs and the cycle repeats itself once more.

Phase VI highlights the fact that project teams are dynamic systems. As the project moves through the five phases the needs of the project will change. In order to keep the team aligned to the project the team profile and/or the deployment of the team members may need to change as well. Phase VI is discussed in detail in Chapter 13.

The Project/Team Alignment Model is shown in Figure 4.3. The right side of the figure displays the five phases of the project management life cycle. The left side of the figure displays the six phases of the team life cycle. The four stages of effective project team development are easily discerned within the six phases of the team life cycle. The letters A through L signify state transitions from phase to phase within and between the two life cycles. Also note that there are five state transitions between the two life cycles. These are labeled A, D, F, I, and L.

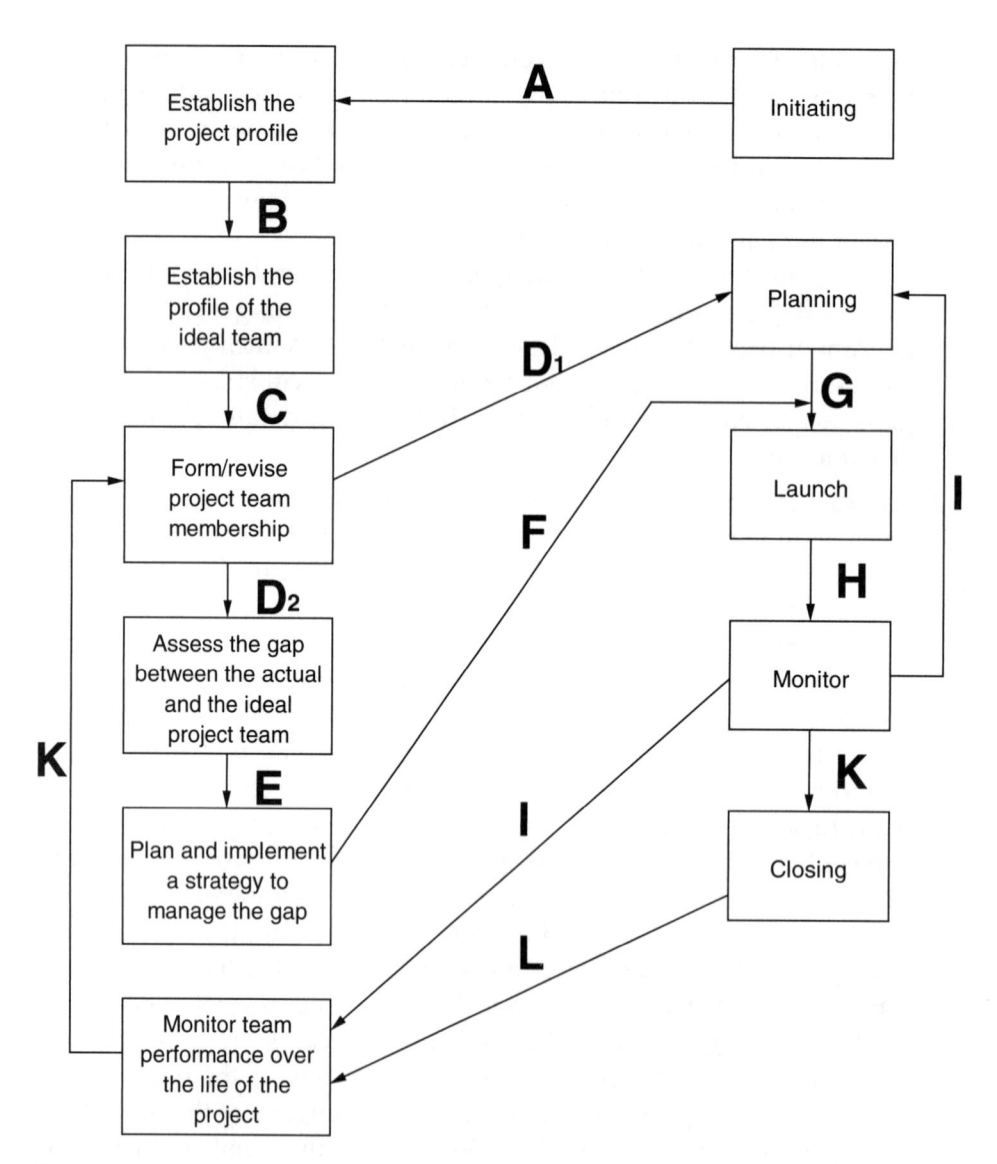

Figure 4.3 The Project/Team Alignment Model.

The two processes are tightly coupled and dependent on one another. Let's examine the Project/Team Alignment Model a little more closely. The deliverable from the initiating phase is a scope document. It is a narrative description of the project. The scope document is input (A) to the process that will develop the project profile. The project profile is input (B) to the process that establishes the profile of the ideal project team. This profile is simply an expanded view of the project profile but with a focus on the project team. Using that ideal profile (C) the actual project team can be formed. At this point two parallel transitions take place. The team moves to (D), the planning phase, and an assessment of the gap between the actual and the ideal team is undertaken (D). That assessment results in a strategic plan to manage the gap (E). The strategic plan includes development and deployment alternatives as well. That plan and the project plan are input to the launch phase (F and G).

Early reports from colleagues who have reviewed the model and its implications are very encouraging. Incorporating the project profile in the decision process for team formation is seen as a significant step forward in improving overall project team effectiveness. The Project/Team Alignment Model is certainly one component. In the remaining chapters of this book we will explore this model in considerable depth.

Putting It All Together

This chapter marks a departure from conventional thought on team formation. We have seen how the selection of team members is based not only on the generic team roles talked about in the pioneering works of Belbin and Margerison but also on the characteristics of the project itself. This opens up all sorts of possibilities for how we can form project teams and also how project changes will influence further team development and deployment. This chapter ends Part One of the book. In Part Two, we will introduce and examine the assessment tools that will be used for team formation decisions. To fully understand the power and insight that these tools give us we will introduce a case study that applies these tools. That is the topic of the next chapter.

PART Two

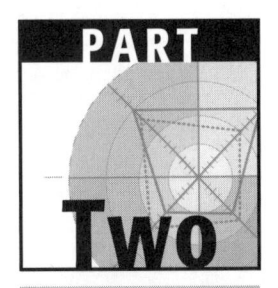

Assessment

CHAPTER 5

The Case Study

I have long felt that the best way to learn how to do something is to actually have a chance to do it as part of the learning experience. I use that approach extensively in *Effective Project Management, Second Edition* (Wysocki et al., Wiley, 2000), and have received excellent feedback from my readers. Not to be outdone by that effort, I have included one of my favorite cases to illustrate the concepts and principles underlying *Effective Project Teams*. It is a hypothetical case. None of the characters are real. I have tuned the case and the data to allow me to effectively illustrate the points without burdening you with a ton of data.

The case involves O'Neill & Preigh and a project to build a new type of organ. O'Neill and Preigh is a hypothetical organization, the Gold Medallion Organ Project is a hypothetical project, and the professional staff from which the project team is assembled are fictitious as well. (I do have to admit that some of them look an awful lot like people I have worked with in the past, but I suspect that that is mere coincidence.) As you become familiar with the staff you will undoubtedly see similarities to people who are part of your work world. Perhaps I will give you some ideas in this book as to how you might work more effectively with them or use them more productively on your project teams! O'Neill & Preigh was originally introduced in the first edition of *Effective Project Management*, and it has gone through a lot of changes since then. Its situation is updated in this book.

The O'Neill and Preigh Business Situation

O'Neill & Preigh is an 800-year-old manufacturer of church equipment. Originally established in a small village on the outskirts of Rome, it now operates out of its corporate offices in Lancaster, Pennsylvania. It clearly is recognized as the market leader in both stock and custom-built furnishings and equipment for churches of all denominations. Its quality and craftsmanship are undisputed as the best in the industry. Its sells its products in international markets through its own sales staff as well as through a network of manufacturer's representatives and distributors in major cities around the world.

All is not good, however. For the past six quarters business has dropped off dramatically. It is generally agreed that the company's problems are both internal and external.

Internally the company has always operated rather loosely. Operating budgets are held at the officer level so that department managers have not been involved in operational-level details. Its long history as an organization is to focus on the highly skilled craft of building custom furnishings for which it is very proud and for which it is world class. One could say that it is more an organization of artisans than an organization of business managers.

Externally the market is changing and the company is concerned. Its president, Del E. Lama, has just concluded the quarterly "State of the Business" meeting of the senior officers at which he reported that part of the problem is certainly the result of the aggressive pricing strategies of a Southeastern Asian conglomerate that recently introduced its product to the American market. While the Asians do not compete on quality, it seems that the American market is more price-sensitive than in the past. Del exhorted his management team to take a good hard look at the business. "Leave no stone unturned" were his exact words. He went on to talk about a likely reengineering effort. (He attended the Chamber of Commerce breakfast that week at which the speaker was a reengineering consultant from a large Philadelphia firm.) There would also be a good hard look at the information systems that support the business. Here his concern was that the few computer applications it has were developed in the company's decentralized, laissez-faire style. Maybe it was time to look at information as a competitive weapon and see what might be done to increase its impact on the future. Del has also heard much about information technology and automated manufacturing so that he wonders whether the company, in its zeal for craftsmanship, has overlooked opportunities to remain competitive without sacrificing quality. To spearhead this computerization effort he hired his grandson, Sal Vation, to join the firm as Director of Information Resources. Sal had just graduated from a prominent New England business school with an MBA in Information Systems.

Needless to say, the management team was taken aback. They certainly used computers, but only as a backroom tool. Computers ran the accounting functions, and that was just fine. Del was talking about a whole new way of doing business. Many would find that uncomfortable.

In the few years since Del issued that quarterly "State of the Business" report a number of things have happened. The company did implement a cost-containment program. All department heads are now responsible for their own operating budgets. As a result, a number of productivity improvements have been made, and costs have been significantly reduced. That allowed for some minor price reductions that have positively affected sales. Market share is holding steady but has not returned to its former levels. With the implementation of departmental budgets the computer has become a significant tool for the department heads. The company has overcome its resistance to computers and feels more comfortable working with them. That bodes well for the Gold Medallion Organ project because department heads are now more willing to accept technology in their venerable product line.

The Gold Medallion Organ Project

Below is a profile of the Gold Medallion Organ project. Rather than constantly having to repeat the name "Gold Medallion Organ project," from this point forward I will shorten it to the "Gold Project."

Hal E. Lewya is the Vice President of Manufacturing for O&P. He has been with the company for nearly 30 years, having been aggressively recruited away from a leading manufacturer of church musical instruments. Hal has always been the champion for new and innovative instrumentation. In fact, a few years ago he presented an idea for a new line of church organs that utilized the latest computer technologies. He believed strongly in using current technology and had devised an idea for replacing the usual pulls and stops with a touch screen. The performer could easily and more quickly reconfigure the organ with a few finger moves, rather than the physical process heretofore required. Hal had shared his idea with a few musicians, and they gave it their approval. The old guard, however, did not receive his idea very well. They saw it as a compromise of the traditions for which O&P had been known. Somehow computers and craftsmanship didn't mix very well in their minds. Del's proclamation changed the game, however, and Hal was preparing to resurrect his idea once more. Surely they would buy it this time.

Before going forward with his proposal, he decided to take some time to polish it up a bit. After all, there had been a lot of technology breakthroughs since he first put his ideas on paper almost two years ago. He began by listing the features and functions he saw in his new organ:

- All stops and pulls would be replaced with a color touch screen menu.
- The touch screen would have to be physically integrated in the design of the organ. It would have to be as inconspicuous as possible.
- The screen would use a graphic interface. There would be no text to read.
- Once the performer had set the configuration, the screen would display a description of the configuration that had been input. This was a final check that the correct data had been entered.
- The organ should be online to the O&P offices for remote diagnostics and tuning.

Hal knew that his proposal would not be received enthusiastically. O&P was a company of craftsmen, not of technologists. And that meant that this project was going to be a big challenge.

One thing in his favor, however, was that the Del E. Lama was open to new ideas. The fact that the company was in trouble may be just the thing that he could draw on to sell his idea. His initial proposal would have to be very carefully crafted and worded.

The Gold Medallion Organ Project Team

What follows is a profile of each of the professional staff from which the actual team members will be chosen to work on the Gold Medallion Organ project. Rather than constantly having to repeat the name "Gold Medallion Organ Project Team," from this point forward I will shorten it to the "Gold Team."

The candidate pool consists of 16 professionals from which an 8-person team will be chosen. There are 7 roles on the team: a project manager, a manufacturing engineer, a project administrative assistant, a manager of applications development, two programmers, a systems analyst, and a mechanical engineer. They are introduced here according to the project role they are qualified to fill.

Project Manager

There are two choices for project manager.

> **Hal E. Lewya.** Hal, the VP of Manufacturing, reports directly to Del. He has been with O&P for 30 years. He is a true craftsman who has been quite successful with O&P. Despite the fact that he has a high regard for the craft he is open to new and creative ideas to improve the business as long as quality is not sacrificed.
>
> **Pearl E. Gates.** Pearl, the VP of Product Development, reports directly to Del. She has been with O&P for only two years. In that time, however, she has established a reputation for sticking to process and has always shown a high regard for her fellow workers.

Project Administrator

There are two choices for the project administrator. Both candidates report to Pearl E. Gates in their regular job duties.

> **Olive Branch.** Olive has been a project administrator for nearly 20 years. They make a dynamite team. She doesn't make waves and avoids confrontation whenever possible. She would rather spend her time finding common grounds on which agreements can be reached than using the power of her position to dictate.
>
> **Dick Tator.** Dick has also been a successful project administrator for several years but has a style quite different from Olive's. He is a stickler for detail and insists on rigidly following process and procedure. At times he seems to act with complete disregard for people but has never failed to meet his responsibilities. His projects always seem to finish on time even though he doesn't cultivate many friends along the way.

Manager of Applications Development

There are two choices for the manager of applications development.

> **Sal Vation.** Sal is the grandson of the president, Del E. Lama. He just received his MBA with a specialization in Information Systems from a

prominent New England business school. His grandfather hired him into the position of Director of Information Resources and charged him to bring O&P into the computer age although he is not sure exactly what that will mean to the company. He is surely taking some risk given the culture of the company.

Anita Kaskett. Shortly after joining O&P Sal hired Anita into her present position. She is a veteran and has had a successful career in applications development in the manufacturing industry. She brings the much-needed industry experience that Sal lacks, and he knows it.

Programmer

There are four choices for the two programmer positions on the project team. All four candidates report to Anita Kaskett in their regular job duties.

Terri Tory. Terri is definitely not a team player. She is a very skilled senior programmer but works effectively only if she is responsible for an activity from start to finish. She makes it very clear that she doesn't want to be assigned to complete work begun by others. Her greatest strength is that she can be counted on to deliver as promised.

Mack N. Tawsch. Mack is a very outgoing and creative programmer. His style always seems casual, but he is able to produce clean and crisp code with seemingly little effort. One can usually count on him for finding a unique and intuitive approach to most any problem.

Sy Yonara. Sy is quite different from Mack. His style is very analytical and organized. He doesn't spend too much time socializing with his fellow workers, and he can be counted on to meet expectations. There are no surprises when it comes to his work.

Mike Rowtoys. Mike is unique among IS professionals. While he is a junior programmer, he is unequalled in his ability to solve very complex systems design problems. He is also unequalled in his ability to deliver complex solutions that no one can understand. He seems to delight in other people's confusion. Mike is very much a loner. He doesn't like to work with people, and they share a similar feeling for him. If it weren't for his exceptional analytical and programming skills he would be long gone. He is rumored to have said "This would be a great place to work if it weren't for all the people." I suspect it has been blown out of proportion through numerous repetitions, but it does tell you in no uncertain terms what Mike is like.

Systems Analyst

There are two choices for systems analyst. Both candidates report to Anita Kaskett in their regular job duties.

Barry deBones. Barry is the only senior systems analyst at O&P. Many have commented on his ability to see to the heart of the problem, offer a number of alternative solutions, and work with users through implementation. He is an effective negotiator. His only shortcoming is his intolerance of incompetent or poorly committed professionals. He makes no bones about letting them know his opinions, not so much through words as through actions.

Doug deGrave. Doug is very people-oriented and likes to engage others in brainstorming and other creative pursuits. He is effective as an analyst as long as he is aligned with the things that interest him.

Manufacturing Engineer

There are two choices for the manufacturing engineer. Both candidates report to Hal E. Lewya.

Justin Case. Justin is widely recognized as the best manufacturing engineer at O&P. He is a recent hire and despite his youth is the only senior manufacturing engineer at O&P. He has demonstrated the sound judgment and decision-making characteristics of an executive, and some day he will be a strong contender for a position as VP of Manufacturing at some company.

Justin Tyme. Justin Tyme was hired at the same time as Justin Case. He bears many of the same characteristics as his counterpart but has not progressed at as fast a pace. He has a bright future at O&P.

Mechanical Engineer

There are two choices for mechanical engineer.

Mel Otious. Mel is just a simple but hard-working mechanical and industrial engineer. He has been with the company only a few years and was hired by Hal to improve manufacturing processes. Mel has made it very clear that he would like to work on this project and has shown great enthusiasm for it. Give him a well-defined task and you can count on him to deliver. His skill set includes the ability to integrate computer technology with other processes. To the technically challenged employees he seems to perform miracles with the computer. He is personable and well liked. He is a good learner and has demonstrated a definite potential for growth.

Lou Neetoon. Lou is a mechanical engineer and has also been with the company only a few years. Her style is refreshing and inventive and characterized by delivering beyond expectations. She can usually be counted on to come up with a different approach than many might have expected. She is good at what she does but often needs to be reminded of the scope of her assignments. Her coworkers have commented that she looks and acts like an inventor.

Organization of the Gold Team

While the members of the Gold Team are yet to be chosen, the organizational structure has been determined in order to assist in staffing the team. Hal E. Lewya is responsible for staffing the team from the available candidates. Notice that Hal himself is a possible choice for project manager. Figure 5.1 shows the team structure. It is shown hierarchically, but that does not imply that the team will be run as a hierarchical structure. That will be a decision that the project manager and team will make.

Putting It All Together

And so this is the cast of characters from which the Gold Team will be chosen. Throughout the rest of this book, I will call on them to provide additional data both as individuals and as a team. This will mostly be for illustration purposes and to show you the true power in the TeamArchitect approach to assessing, forming, developing, and deploying effective project teams!

For your entertainment and edification I have assembled five different project teams: Team Alpha, Team Beta, Team Gamma, Team Delta, and, of course, Team Epsilon. These teams are very different from one another, having been formed using different criteria. I'll leave it to you to determine what that criteria might have been. In any case, these five teams give us a rich environment in which to learn about team effectiveness.

Much of our analysis will utilize graphics created specifically to present the data in a format that meets our interpretive needs. To the extent that I can, these graphics are intuitive. You look at them, and you immediately

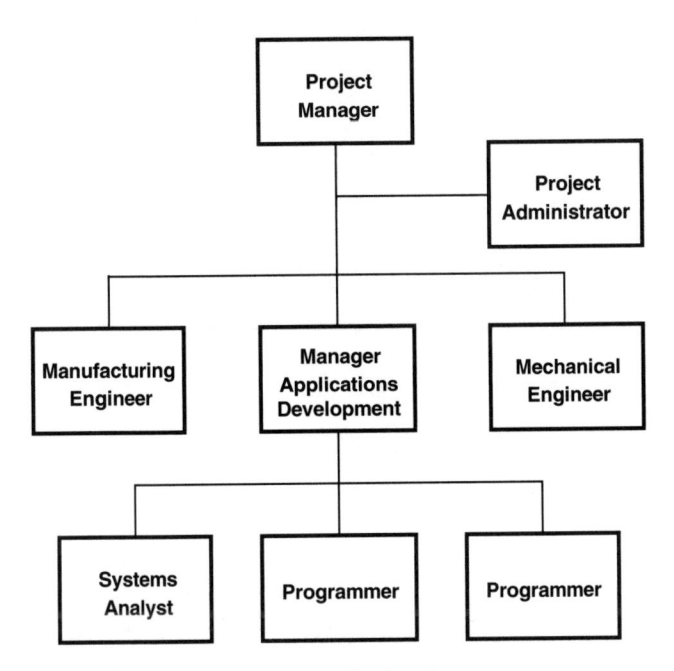

Figure 5.1 Gold Team organizational structure.

understand the message they are conveying. Others, generated by TeamArchitect, will be screen shots and will be stored on the CD-ROM for your retrieval and further analysis. And for those who are really inquisitive, you may link to the Web site (www.teamarchitect.com) where you may conduct independent analyses on your own. In other words, I have created as comprehensive a learning and practicing environment as I can. After this experience you may decide that you would like to use these tools on your own projects and project teams. Appendix C tells you how to do that.

Beginning with Chapter 6, "Thinking Styles," and continuing through to Chapter 9, "Project Management Skills and Competencies," we will learn about the tools that will be used to assess each potential team member. Chapter 6 introduces the Herrmann Brain Dominance Instrument, the major tool used in TeamArchitect, because it will be used to assess not only each team member but the project as well.

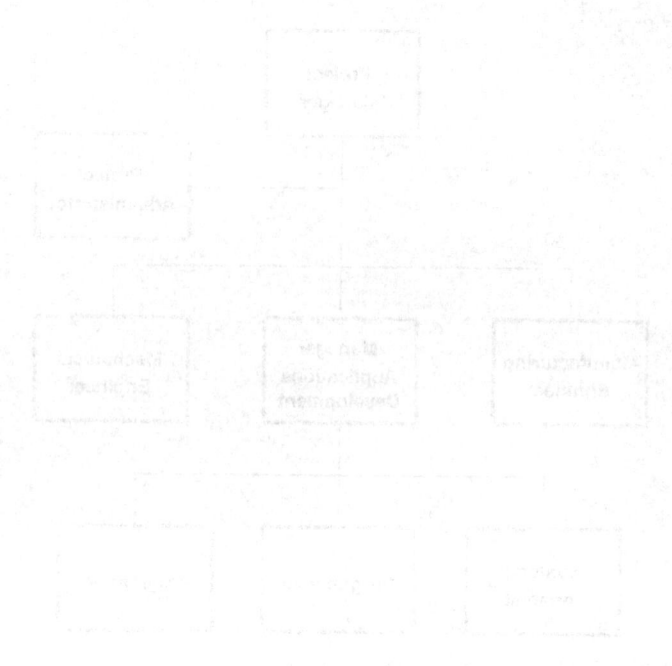

CHAPTER 6

Thinking Styles

How people think is somehow related to what they prefer to do, and the things that they prefer to do are things that they probably do well. It would seem then that if we can align people with the things they like to do, we would probably get better performance and high motivation as well, which will, in some way, positively affect team effectiveness. How many of you are in work situations where you have to masquerade as someone you are not in order to perform up to expectations? Probably quite a few. After a while that masked behavior gets to be old hat and you revert to your normal preferences. You just aren't happy, and it shows!

There are several tools that measure thinking styles. Most people have heard of the *Myers-Briggs Temperament Indicator* (MBTI). It is a powerful assessment tool, but it requires a trained consultant to help interpret the results. *The Learning Styles Inventory* (LSI) can also be used to assess how a person thinks. I will use it but for a different reason. Instead of the MBTI, I prefer to use the *Herrmann Brain Dominance Instrument* (HBDI) because it has additional benefits that we will be able to further apply to the project itself as we look for ways to improve team effectiveness later in the book.

88 Building Effective Project Teams

> **FOR YOUR REFERENCE** For those who would like more information on how to acquire the HBDI, information is provided in Appendix B, "Sources of Information," and Appendix C, "How to Get TeamArchitect Tools."

Herrmann Brain Dominance Instrument

The Herrmann Brain Dominance Instrument (HBDI) is a very powerful tool because it can be used to describe a project, to describe an individual team member, and to describe the entire team. I know of no other tool that has this breadth of application to project management. Ned Herrmann developed the HBDI in the 1970s during his tenure as Manager of Management Education at General Electric. He established a series of 120 questions, the answers to which could map a person's thinking styles into the four-sided graphic shown in Figure 6.1.

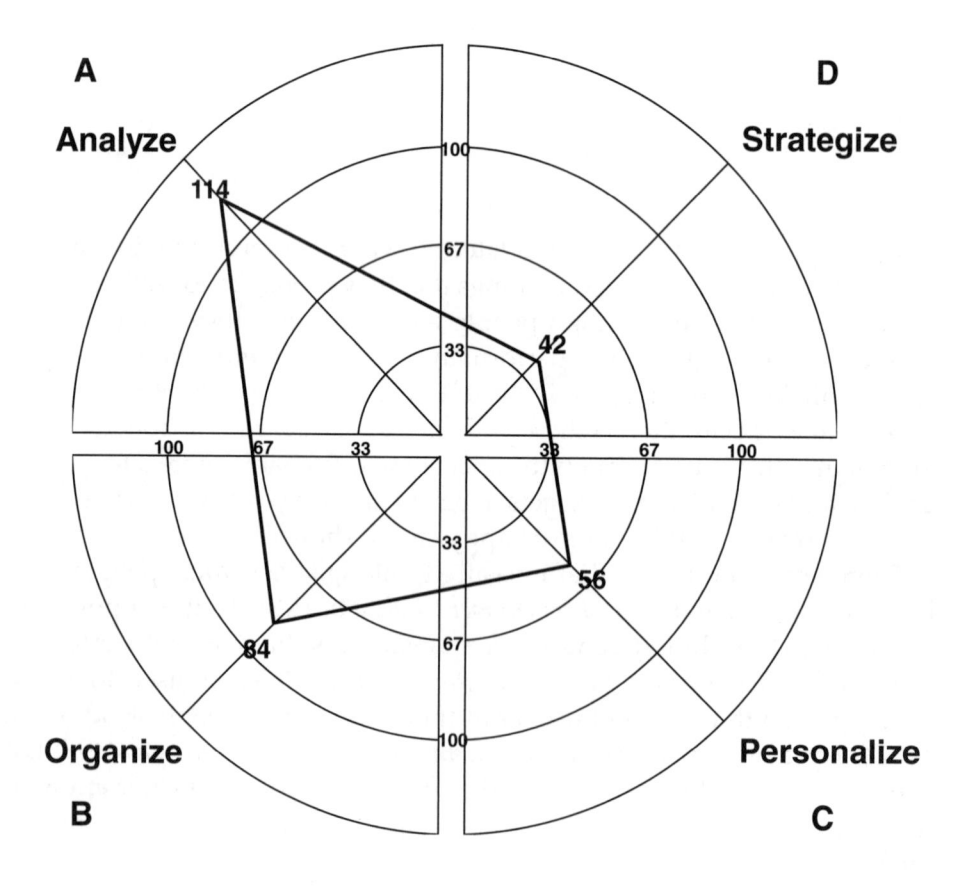

Figure 6.1 A typical HBDI profile.

Thinking Styles

When Ned Herrmann became interested in the subject of thinking, brain researchers were suggesting that people are either right-brained or left-brained in their preference. Those who prefer left-brained thinking would deal with logic, analysis, order, and so on, while the right-brained individuals would be more conceptual and less orderly in their thinking. As he studied the literature and tried to understand people in his training programs, he decided something was missing.

He eventually postulated that thinking was influenced by another dimension of the brain, which he surmised were the cerebral and limbic components of the brain. By adding these dimensions, he could map thinking styles using the four-quadrant metaphor shown in Figure 6.1. The A- and B-Quadrants represent left-brain thinking styles. The C- and D-Quadrants represent right-brain thinking styles. The A- and D-Quadrants represent cerebral thinking styles. The B- and C-Quadrants represent limbic thinking styles. Every individual is a composite of all four thinking styles.

Ned had postulated that thinking styles are a function of brain physiology and that different parts of the brain relate to different thinking styles. Whether thinking preferences are actually determined by brain physiology remains open to question, but after nearly 30 years of research, I believe that the folks at Herrmann International have demonstrated the face validity of the four different thinking preferences. At this time, more than a million individuals have taken the HBDI, and over 300,000 profiles are stored in the Herrmann computer, representing almost every imaginable job discipline and many different nationalities. Let's take a look at a typical profile in order to get a basic understanding of the profile and an understanding of the terminology that is used.

Figure 6.1 is a typical profile of an individual. It is generated from answers to a 120-question survey. It is important to note that there are no right or wrong answers. All the instrument measures are preferences. The answers are processed through a proprietary algorithm, and scores are generated for each of the four quadrants. As part of the algorithm the scores are normalized and currently range as follows:

A-Quadrant: 11–149

B-Quadrant: 15–153

C-Quadrant: 11–149

D-Quadrant: 9–189

For the purposes of interpretation the four-quadrant map is divided into sectors (the solid concentric circles) at scores of 33, 67, 100, and 133. The profile shown has quadrant scores of 114, 84, 56, and 42. There is also a shorthand scoring template that translates scores as follows:

- 1 represents scores above 67
- 2 represents scores between 34 and 66
- 3 represents scores less than 33

For the given example, the profile would simply be referred to as a 1122 profile. In this codification scheme a 1 designates a preferred thinking style, a 2 designates an available thinking preference, and a 3 often designates a style that the individual prefers to avoid. Using this coding scheme, there are 81 distinct thinking style profiles.

Individuals will display preferences for one or more quadrants. They can be single-dominant, double-dominant, triple-dominant, and quadruple-dominant. The pattern displayed in the example is double-dominant in quadrants A and B. That means that this individual prefers to use the thinking styles associated with those two quadrants. On the other hand, an individual with a quadrant score below 67 does not have a preference for that thinking style. There are two cases to consider. If the quadrant score is between 34 and 66, the individual has that thinking style available and will use it on occasion. The other case is where the quadrant score is 33 or below, in which case the individual actually avoids using that thinking style.

Now let's take a closer look at each of the four quadrants.

The A-Quadrant

The thinking associated with the A-Quadrant can be described as logical, analytical, technical, mathematical, and problem solving. People with a strong preference to think in these ways are also attracted to professions that require such thinking. Examples of such careers include technical, legal, and financial areas, including accounting and tax law, engineering, mathematics, and some middle management positions.

A project manager with a single-dominant profile in the A-Quadrant could be expected to be very logical, to be interested in technical issues affecting the project, to be inclined to analyze status reports carefully, and to be keen on problem solving. If he or she has very little preference for thinking in the other quadrants (particularly the C-Quadrant) this person may be seen as cold, uncaring, and interested only in the problems presented by the project.

The B-Quadrant

The B-Quadrant has some similarity to the A-Quadrant in that both are left-brain thinking preferences, but there are significant differences as well. Words that describe the B-Quadrant are organizational, administrative, conservative, controlled, and planning. This is the preferred thinking of many managers, administrators, planners, bookkeepers, foremen, and manufacturers. Individuals who have single-dominant profiles in the B-Quadrant could be expected to be concerned with the detailed plans of a project and with keeping everything organized and controlled. Note that individuals with financial interests who are dominant in the A-Quadrant will probably be financial managers, whereas those with dominant B-Quadrant profiles may be drawn to cost accounting.

If you want someone to pay attention to detail, to dot all the letter i's and cross all the letter t's, then you want someone who has a strong preference for this quadrant. If that person has a single dominant profile, however, he or she may see the trees and be unaware of the forest.

The C-Quadrant

People with single-dominant profiles in the A- or B-Quadrants probably see individuals with strong C-Quadrant preferences as being very "touchy-feely." Words that describe this quadrant are interpersonal, emotional, musical, spiritual, and talker. Individuals with single-dominant C profiles would be very "feeling" and people-oriented. Such individuals are often nurses, social workers, musicians, teachers, counselors, or ministers.

A project manager with a single-dominant C profile would naturally be concerned with the interpersonal aspects of the project, perhaps to the detriment of getting the work done. Such an individual would be drawn to the coordination of project activities with people both inside and outside the team and would be a relationship builder. For highly political projects, this would be a good bias to have, as long as other members of the team are attending to the work itself.

The D-Quadrant

Words that describe this quadrant are artistic, holistic, imaginative, synthesizer, and conceptualizer. Individuals who have single-dominant D-Quadrant profiles are often drawn to careers that involve entrepreneurial effort, facilitation, advising or consulting, being sales leaders, and artists. These are the "idea" people in a team, and they enjoy synthesizing ideas from several sources to create something new from that combination.

This is the natural domain of people who are thought of as being creative. You may conclude that if you are primarily a "left-brain" thinker, having strong preferences for A- or B-Quadrant thinking, and low preference for thinking in the D-Quadrant, then you are out of luck. Not so. It turns out that it is easier for left-brain thinkers to learn to do conceptual or creative thinking than it is for conceptual thinkers to do analytical or detail thinking.

Project managers who have single-dominant D-Quadrant profiles could be expected to be very "big picture" in their thinking. They may run the risk of seeing the forest without realizing that it consists of a bunch of trees. They are generally good at thinking strategically, so in planning a project; the D-Quadrant thinker will develop a game plan but will need help from B-Quadrant thinkers to turn it into something practical.

Double, Triple, and Quadruple Profiles

As you can imagine, you have a wide variety of profiles (81 to be exact). I have discussed single-dominant profiles and what they may mean for project managers. They represent about 5 percent of the population. But suppose that you have strength in two quadrants (58 percent of the population). Or three (34 percent of the population). Or all four (3 percent of the population). How would team members or project managers with these profiles operate? Let's look at a few of the more frequently occurring multiple dominant profiles.

There is an interesting finding about how we behave in terms of our least-preferred thinking styles. Jim Lewis, a project management trainer and consultant colleague of mine, has a very strong D-Quadrant preference, with B-Quadrant being his least preferred. This means that he loves developing concepts and dislikes doing detail work. If he must do detail work in order to see one of his ideas see the light of day, then he is very motivated to do so. What this means, then, is that you can be motivated to deal with the "touchy-feely" stuff if it means achieving success in terms of your other thinking preferences.

I, on the other hand, have very strong A- and D-Quadrant preferences with the B- and C-Quadrants being least preferred. I hold a Ph.D. in mathematical statistics and have always viewed myself as a problem solver. My B- and D-Quadrant scores need some further clarification. I like process but only from the design aspect, not from the execution aspect. While I eagerly approach the design of processes, the last thing I want to do is manage the processes. In my mind that is maintenance work, and I don't like maintenance work! My weak C-Quadrant score may be testimony to the fact that I am, shall we say, musically challenged—a fact to which my wife will testify. My weak C-Quadrant score does not reflect a disinterest in people. I enjoy and I think I excel in my people management skills with particular interest in helping people improve professionally. The bottom line is that we all have different thinking style preferences, and it is those differences that will make our project teams strong.

A- and B-dominant Profiles

An A- and B-dominant profile is the profile of the left-brain thinker. There is an internal coherence between the A- and B-Quadrants. That is, they tend to reinforce each another. For example, the analytical and logical processes of the A-Quadrant support the structural and procedural characteristics of the B-Quadrant. This is a very common profile, especially among males. People with this profile are logical, analytical, technically oriented, and good problem solvers. They are also good planners, organizers, and implementers. They do not shy away from administrative details.

A- and D-dominant Profiles

The A- and D-dominant profile is the profile of the cerebral thinker. The great minds and great inventors of our time exhibit these two thinking styles. People with this profile have all of the thinking preferences of the A-Quadrant plus a preference for the conceptual, creative, and integrative styles. They like to invent things and new ways of doing things and are quite happy to be individual contributors.

C- and D-dominant Profiles

The C- and D-dominant profile is the profile of the right-brain thinker. People with this profile are creative and inventive because of their D-Quadrant preferences but are also people people. They are intuitive, holistic, and interpersonal. Entrepreneurs, teachers, salespersons, and trainers often exhibit this thinking style pattern.

B- and D-dominant Profiles

So far we have talked about double-dominant thinking styles where the two thinking styles were compatible with each another. They were both right-brain, or left-brain, or cerebral, or limbic. Interesting cases arise when the two dominant thinking styles are fundamentally different from one another, either B and D or A and C. An example is shown in Figure 6.2.

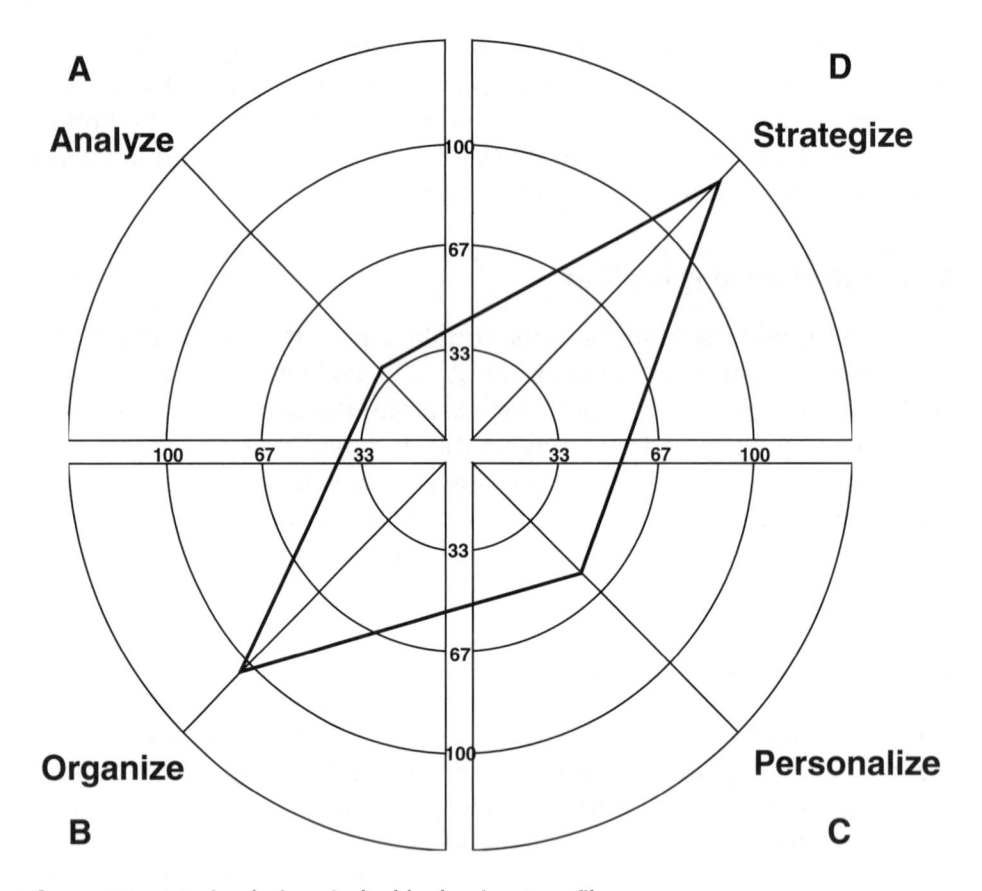

Figure 6.2 Interior designer's double-dominant profile.

This individual has a double-dominant profile, but interestingly, it is across the diagonal between quadrants B and D. The person was an interior designer, and she was asked, "Do you sometimes talk yourself out of some good ideas?" She admitted that she did. The reason was that she would conceive the idea using her D-Quadrant thinking, and then when she tried to work out the details of how to execute the idea, she would begin to find problems and throw it out.

On the positive side, though, she did have the desire to make her designs a reality, something that a person with a single-dominant D-Quadrant profile may not otherwise do. The single dominant person may conceive all kinds of good ideas but not have much interest in implementing them.

Think of this person in a project manager's role. We would guess that she would be good at seeing the "big picture" of the project and at developing project strategy, but she would also be interested in doing detailed implementation planning as well. In other words, she could see both the forest and the trees.

B- and C-dominant Profiles

This is the profile of the limbic thinker. Because of his or her dominant B-Quadrant score this person has a strong preference for conservative thinking and the need for structure and detailed procedures for all that he or she does. The dominant C-Quadrant score indicates a strong preference for interpersonal relations and concern for how the individual will react to situations. These people are results oriented, and they respond well to deadlines and enjoy working with others.

A-, B-, and C-Dominant Profiles

Simply put, this is a left-brain individual with the added concern for the individual. He or she makes a good team player and enjoys analyzing data, building things, and seeing things work. Technical managers will often display this thinking style profile.

A-, B-, C-, and D-dominant Profiles

Only about 3 percent of the population exhibits a preference for all four quadrants. People with this profile are well balanced and can understand the thinking modes of all types of people. They are good facilitators and can deal effectively with every situation. They are adaptable and make good leaders because of their whole-brain approach and even-handed ways. The successful CEO will often display a four-quadrant thinking preference.

Project Manager Profiles

What would you guess the profiles of the most competent project managers would look like? Actually, there isn't a best. Or to put it another way, a person can be an effective project manager regardless of the shape of his or her HBDI profile. The Herrmann International database bears this out. The point here is not to confuse thinking styles with skills. Every person utilizes all four thinking styles at various times. He or she just happens to prefer one style over another. Being an effective project manager will call on all four thinking styles. The project manager must recognize this and know when each style is required.

Test-Retest Reliability

Research on the test-retest reliability is underway, and at this point there is not a lot of scientifically supporting evidence. There is anecdotal data on people who have repeated the instrument. The instrument gives highly repeatable results. It would seem to me that radical changes in a person's professional, family, and faith life could alter the results. I have had occasion to take the survey twice. The first time was in February 1998, and the second was in October 2000. Figure 6.3 is the result.

The A- and B-Quadrant scores do not reflect any real change other than the reliability of the instrument and perhaps some other random perturbations caused by my changing work situation as described in the text that follows. The C- and D-Quadrant scores were different, however. The first thing I noticed was a shift away from left-brain toward right-brain think-

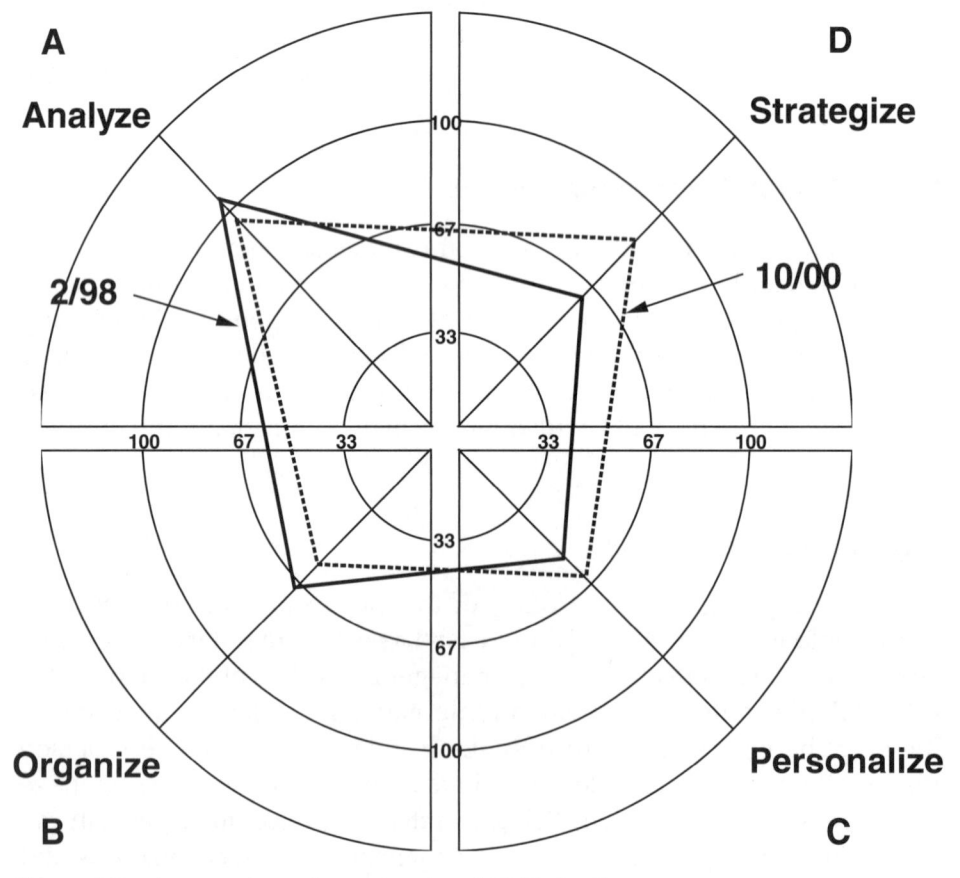

Figure 6.3 A comparison of two completed HBDIs by the same person.

ing styles. It was moderate for the C-Quadrant (51 to 63) and more dramatic for the D-Quadrant (62 to 87).

I talked to Ann Herrmann, CEO of Herrmann International, about those differences. She asked me a number of questions to determine if I had had any lifestyle changes between the two dates. In November of 1998 I had just completed a consulting engagement that had occupied me full time since September of 1994. That engagement was not a happy time in my professional life. The person to whom I was accountable was a terrible manager and even worse decision maker. He finally destroyed the business and was terminated. My behavior through that engagement was masked, that is, I had to act quite differently than I preferred. Ann Herrmann saw that reflected in my HBDI profile. My work situation changed radically starting in November of 1998 and continues to this day. I was able to be my real self, and it was reflected in the retake of the HBDI in October of 2000. Although my own personal experience is not scientifically valid proof of the reliability of the HBDI, I'm not concerned about the test-retest variability.

Candidate Pool Members' HBDI Data

To better understand and become more familiar with interpreting HBDI profiles, let's examine the profiles of five of the candidate pool members. They were chosen because they represent differing thinking styles. These individuals are not real, but they are typical of the types of people that I have had as team members over the years. Their HBDI profiles were chosen to demonstrate a variety of thinking styles that you can encounter and to give us a rich source of data on which to be able to demonstrate the power of this assessment tool.

Hal E. Lewya HBDI profile. Hal is one of the two possible choices for project manager for the Gold Project. His quadrant scores are 98, 54, 63, and 87 and are shown in Figure 6.4. Using the scale discussed previously, Hal's thinking style pattern is 1221. The A-D double-dominant profile denotes a cerebral thinker. Note also that Hal's scores on the B- and C-Quadrants are high in the range of the two profile scores. In other words, Hal is nearly balanced across all four quadrants, which is a great asset to have in a project manager. Having that balance means that Hal is comfortable with all four thinking styles.

Pearl E. Gates HBDI profile. Pearl is the other choice for project manager. Her HBDI kite is shown in Figure 6.5. First, note that she has very

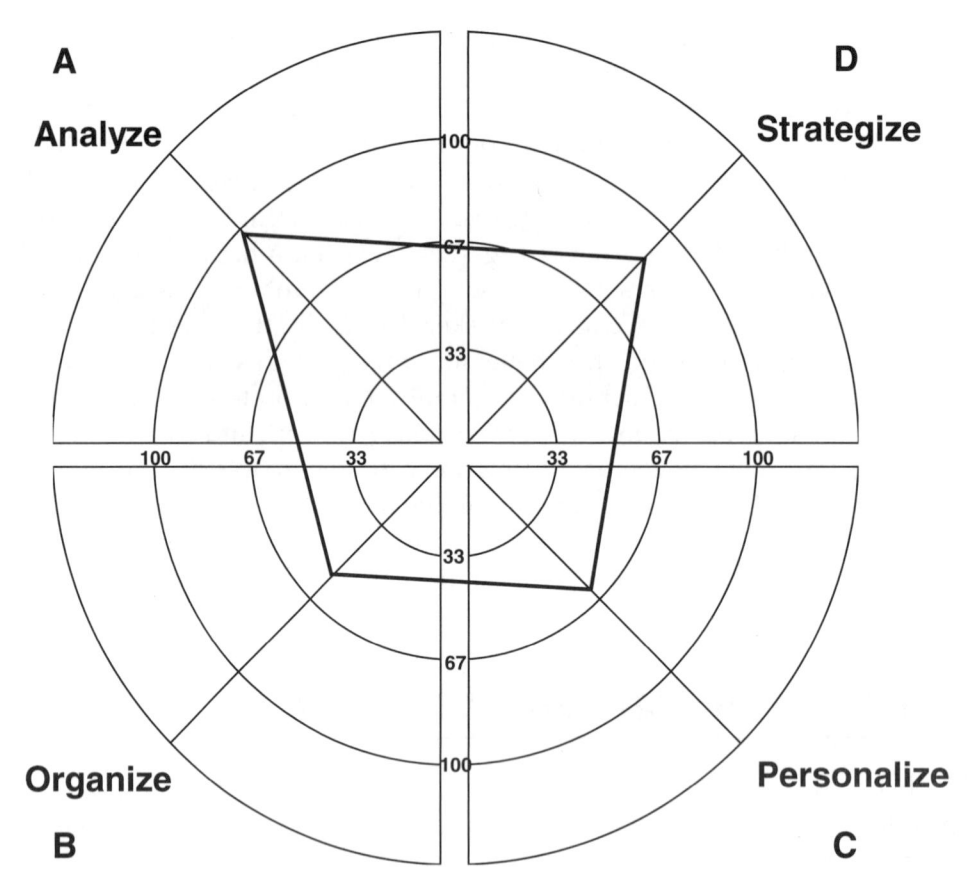

Figure 6.4 Hal's HBDI profile.

different thinking style preferences from Hal. Pearl's thinking style pattern is 2113—the exact opposite of Hal. Pearl is strong in the limbic quadrants (B and C). Because the B-Quadrant is a primary for her, she displays a strong sense of order, and she is a follower of established process. Her C-Quadrant primary indicates that she is sensitive to people and how they might react to order and compliance to processes that she practices. Her D-Quadrant score is very low, which indicates that she avoids strategic and creative thinking styles. In other words, don't expect her to initiate new ideas. Her strong B-Quadrant score tells you that she sticks to established procedure.

Olive Branch HBDI profile. Olive is one of the two choices for project administrative assistant, and her quadrant-scores are 60, 107, 67, and 36, as shown in Figure 6.6. Her thinking profile is 2122—a single-dom-

A
Analyze

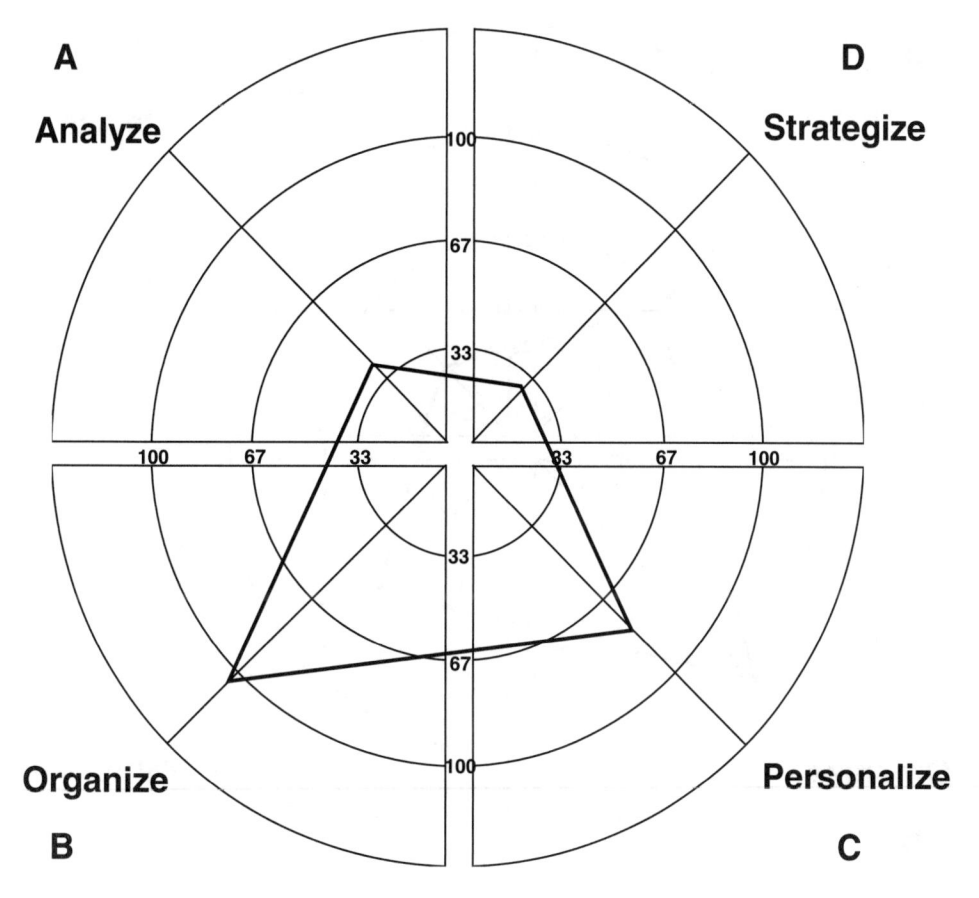

D
Strategize

Organize
B

Personalize
C

Figure 6.5 Pearl's HBDI profile.

inant B. Olive has some affinity for analysis and problem solving. Within the scope of her responsibility there will be some evidence of this, but this is not a strong area for her, as is indicated by her A-Quadrant score. She does bring exceptional organizational and administrative preferences to the team, as indicated by her very high B-Quadrant score. The team can depend on her for the myriad of details that they may not be very interested in doing. She can be expected to keep them in sync with the project plan. Olive tries to get along with people but will maintain her position if at all possible. She is not a negotiator and would rather avoid confrontation than take it on. Little in the way of creative input should be expected from her. In team situations this may become an obstacle because she will always be pointing to established procedures to dampen any creative energies that come from the team.

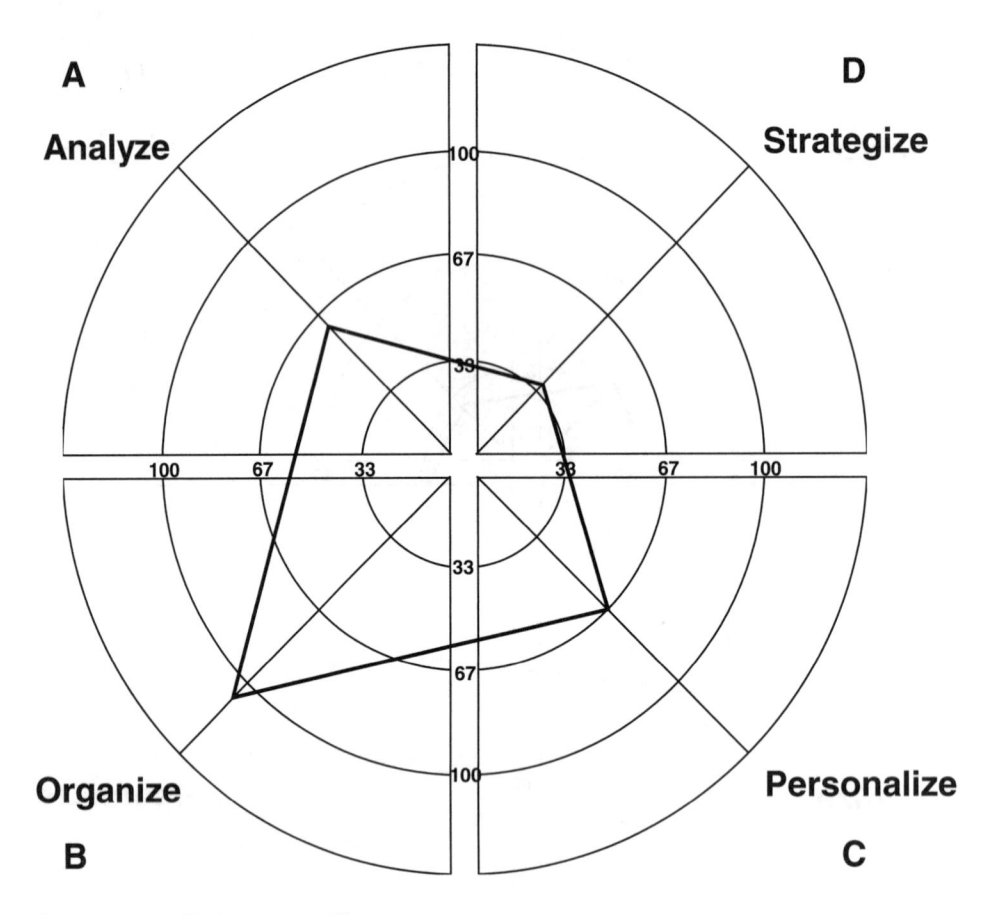

Figure 6.6 Olive's HBDI profile.

Dick Tator HBDI profile. Dick is the other choice for project administrative assistant. His HBDI profile is shown in Figure 6.7. Note that his thinking style pattern is 1133. Note the stark differences between his profile and that of Olive. Dick is AB-dominant—and like Hal he is a very strong left-brain individual. Note that his B-Quadrant score is very high. This means that Dick has high expectations and places a lot of value on order and procedure. He is unlikely to deviate from that model if at all possible. He will be deadline driven and results oriented. If Dick says he will do something by a certain date, you can go to the bank with that. His C- and D-Quadrants are so weak (3, 3 respectively) that he actually avoids those thinking styles. This means that he may, in fact, appear robotic and quite insensitive in the way he comports himself and relates to others. His weak D-Quadrant score

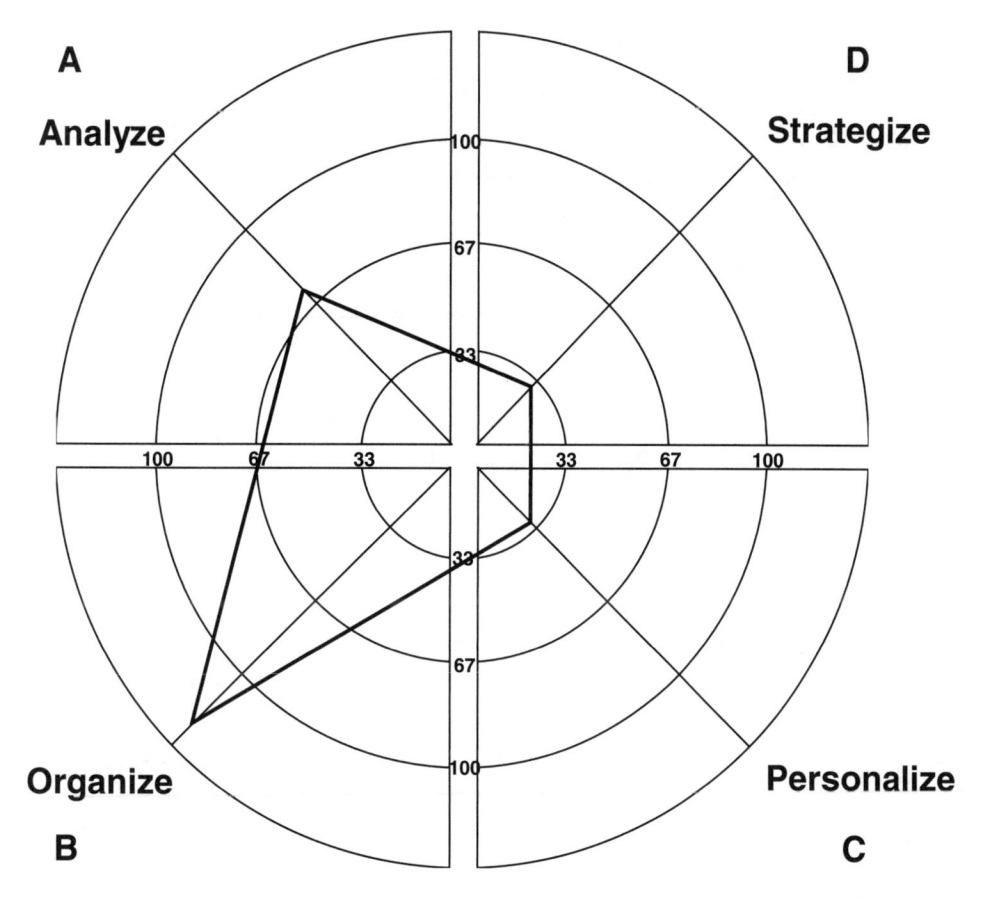

Figure 6.7 Dick's HBDI profile.

means that you can't look to him for any creative ideas and new ways of thinking. He is fixed on current process and procedure.

Mike Rowtoys HBDI profile. Mike is one of the four candidate programmers, two of which will be chosen for the Gold Team. His quadrant scores, shown in Figure 6.8, are 118, 33, 34, and 128. His thinking style pattern is therefore 1321. Actually, he is very close to being a 1331. Mike is very dominant in the two cerebral quadrants (A and D), and we have already commented on that profile. His very weak B- and C-Quadrant scores indicate that he will avoid process and procedure and look for different ways to do things with little concern for how others might react to his style. As it turns out, Mike is the most analytical and strategic member of the team. No challenge will be too great for him. This can be both an asset and a hindrance to the team if not

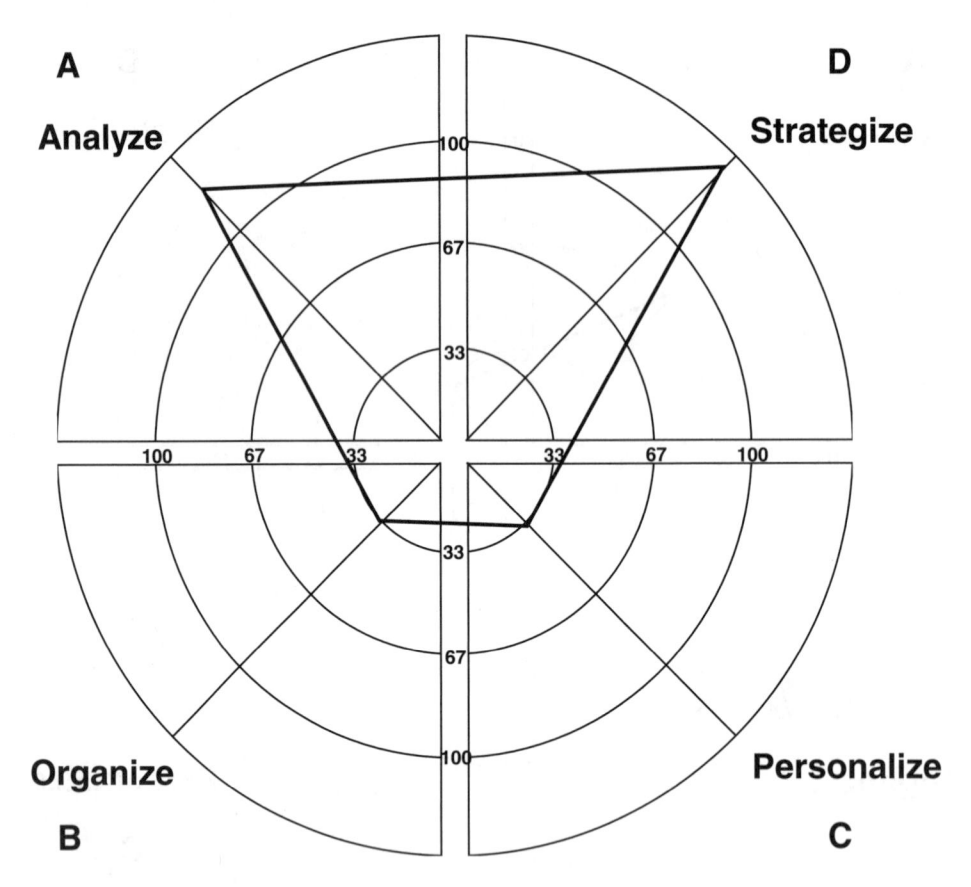

Figure 6.8 Mike's HBDI profile.

managed properly. Procedure and process are not in Mike's mindset, and he avoids them whenever he can. He can be a significant management challenge for the project manager. Mike is not a people person. He will be very valuable when the team is confronted with a particularly difficult system and process integration problem, but his focus will not be on how people will react to his proposals. Mike is the most creative person on the team. He is a rugged individualist, and that creativity will need to be focused and channeled to be effective. The project manager will need to stay on top of what Mike is doing and ensure that it is within the scope of the project.

Putting It All Together

Now, based on the kite that is generated from a person's answering the 120 questions of the HBDI, we know how to interpret a person's thinking styles. You should have guessed that the team, in order to be a balanced team, will have to display a diversity of thinking styles. Table 6.1 shows the thinking style profiles for all 16 members of the candidate pool. It gives you some indication of the challenges you will face as you try to build a team that is balanced with respect to its HBDI profile. We will return to that analysis in Chapter 11, "Establishing the Profile of the Project Team," Chapter 12, "Assessing Team Alignment and Balance," and Chapter 13, "Developing and Deploying the Project Team." You should also have guessed that, when team membership is a given, you can analyze the team's profile to determine where the imbalances lie. Later in the book we will discuss strategies for dealing with those imbalances. In the next chapter we will look at a tool that can be used to profile a person's problem-solving and decision-making styles.

Table 6.1 HBDI Profiles of the Candidate Pool

CANDIDATE	HBDI PROFILE
Hal E. Lewya	1221
Pearl E. Gates	2113
Olive Branch	2122
Dick Tator	1133
Sal Vation	1122
Anita Kaskett	1113
Terri Tory	1221
Mack N. Tawsch	2111
Sy Yonara	1122
Mike Rowtoys	1321
Barry deBones	1122
Doug deGrave	2211
Justin Case	1121
Justin Tyme	1121
Mel Otious	1122
Lou Neetoon	1221

CHAPTER 7

Problem-Solving and Decision-Making Styles

I have practiced project management for over 35 years, and I have yet to be involved with a project that went according to plan. That is not intended to be a reflection on any lack of planning skills on my part but rather on the fact that something unexpected always happens. The unexpected sent me and my team back to the drawing board, scratching our heads and looking for a way out of the dilemma.

All project managers need to be able to assess every situation that arises and find an acceptable resolution. That will call on their team to define the problem, gather the data, formulate alternative courses of action, evaluate and rank alternatives, pick the best alternative, sell stakeholders on the decision, implement the solution, and follow up to make sure the solution worked. This applies equally well to problem solving and decision making.

The tool that I have found most useful in assessing the team's capacity to resolve these situations is the *Learning Styles Inventory* (LSI), which was developed by David Kolb in 1981 and is marketed through the Hay McBer Training Resources Group. I have used the LSI for several years in a variety of project management consulting situations and always found it to be a valuable asset. The LSI and its application to problem solving and decision making are the focus of this chapter. Once we have a good understanding of the LSI we will take a closer look at problem solving and decision making to see exactly how to apply the LSI to team effectiveness.

How We Learn

The American education system tends to create in students a bias to be solution-minded. A great deal of problem solving is done throughout a child's school years, but most of it deals with structured problems that are called *closed-ended*. These are problems that have a single answer. Examples include math or physics problems at the end of a chapter in their textbook. They all know that the key to solving the problem is somewhere in the chapter material. All they have to do is find it and apply it. They will get it right or wrong—there is no other possible outcome. Their thinking is limited to the inside of the box as defined by the pages of their book.

Entirely different categories of problems exist and are called *open-ended*, in which there are several acceptable solutions, some of which are better than others. Examples include how to design something or how to develop a strategy for a project. Many of these problems have a number of effective solutions; other problems are extremely complex, and finding even one solution that works is very challenging.

If you think about the types of problems you encounter on a day-to-day basis, you'll find that most of them are open-ended. Our schooling has created in us a bias for single-answered solutions, and this sometimes paralyzes us when we deal with open-ended situations. A lot of our instincts for creativity have been suppressed by the way we have been taught to solve problems. We might even be tempted to come up with the "quick fix" that does little more than temporarily eliminate one or more of the symptoms of the problem, but that does not really address the problem itself. Somehow I can't help but think that our school system has done us an injustice by driving a lot of creativity out of the problem-solving process, but that is a topic far outside the scope of this book.

I have found that projects typically fail at the very beginning because people on the team do not correctly define the problem to be solved by the project. We consider this skill vital to your success as a project manager and recommend that you set for yourself a goal to develop these skills.

FURTHER READING If you want an overview of how to solve both closed-ended and open-ended problems, you may want to consult *The Project Manager's Desk Reference, Second Edition* by Lewis (McGraw-Hill, 2000).

If you are a strong process-oriented person, you may not be a good creative person. In this area it is especially important to draw on the resources of your project team members. Think outside the box. Don't be shackled by conventional thinking and practice. If you are ever going to be different, this is the time.

In Chapter 6, "Thinking Styles," we discussed the fact that some individuals are naturally creative thinkers and some are more analytical or detailed thinkers. It turns out that it is easier to help analytical thinkers learn to do creative thinking than the reverse. In fact, there are numerous books on this subject, and listing them all would be impossible.

FURTHER READING A few that I have found particularly useful are *Thinkertoys* by Michalko (Ten Speed Press, 1991), *Serious Creativity* by de Bono (HarperCollins, 1992) and *A Whack on the Side of the Head* by von Oech (Warner Books, 1983).

All of this leads to the facts that people learn in different ways and that learning is the basis of problem solving and decision making. We need a way to assess learning styles so that we can balance the team with respect to its problem-solving and decision-making capabilities. A tool I have used for several years in my consulting practice is the Learning Styles Inventory, which is the topic of the next section.

Learning Styles Inventory

The LSI consists of 12 questions that are designed to help you evaluate the way in which you learn. While you may already know that you prefer to experiment with something new rather than to have someone lecture you on its use, the LSI will help you understand exactly how you learn and what you can do to improve your learning abilities. Each question asks you to rank your preferences for four different choices in several different learning situations. For example, one of the questions asks the following:

I learn best when: _____ I rely on my feelings

_____ I rely on my observations

_____ I rely on my ideas

_____ I can try things out for myself

You rank the four choices from the one that is most like you (rank 4) to the one that is least like you (rank 1). The inventory is self-administered and self-scored. Following an algorithm that is explained in the inventory the rankings are tabulated and presented in four learning preferences as follows:

Abstract conceptualization. This style of learning is best thought of as learning by thinking. The individual analyzes ideas and data and draws conclusions based on his or her intellectual understanding of the situation.

Active experimentation. This style of learning is best thought of as learning by doing. The individual simply goes ahead and does things. These individuals are risk takers, results oriented, and influencers of others through their taking action.

Concrete experience. This style of learning is best thought of as learning by experience. The individual draws conclusions from the experiences he or she has had with these situations. These individuals typically do this in a collegial environment by relating to the feelings and practices of others.

Reflective observation. This style of learning is best thought of as learning by watching. The individual observes others practicing the situation and draws out meaning after careful reflection.

A simple example will help clarify these four dimensions. Let's assume you want to learn to swim. If you say "I'd like to read about the principles of buoyancy in a liquid medium," that is abstract conceptualization. If you say "I'd like to get in the pool, but I want someone next to me in the event I start to sink," that is active experimentation. If you say "Throw me in the pool, and I will figure it out on the way down," that is concrete experience. And finally, if you say "Can't I just watch for a while and see how it is done," that is reflective observation. All four are valid modes of learning, and all four are used to some extent by every one of us. We just happen to prefer one over the other in certain situations.

Each of the 12 questions has four responses, and each response maps to one of these four dimensions. The scoring key that accompanies the LSI shows you how to map your rankings on each answer to each of the four dimensions. In effect, you are adding up the rankings for all of the responses that map to a specific dimension. The resulting scores are mapped to the diagram shown in the figures that follow. The higher the sum of the rankings on a dimension, the more that dimension is your preferred learning style; that is reflected by an extended portion of the "kite" in that dimension. The kite conveys a lot of information about the individual. The larger the penetration of the kite into a particular quadrant, the more the individual prefers that style. This will become clearer as we examine some of the more typical learning styles in Figures 7.1 through 7.4. The learning styles diagram resembles the HBDI template, but it is not related to the HBDI in any way.

Individual Learning Style Types

The four learning preferences (abstract conceptualization, active experimentation, concrete experience, and reflective observation) map into four learning style types as follows:

Assimilating. A combination of reflective observation and abstract conceptualization.

Diverging. A combination of concrete experience and reflective observation.

Accommodating. A combination of active experimentation and concrete experience.

Converging. A combination of abstract conceptualization and active experimentation.

Let's take a closer look at each of these learning styles and then relate them to the problem-solving and decision-making models introduced in the text that follows.

The assimilating learning style is characterized by high scores in the reflective observation and abstract conceptualization learning preferences. Figure 7.1 shows two examples of typical results from individuals who strongly favor abstract conceptualization and active experimentation over concrete experience and reflective observation. These individuals prefer the *assimilating style*. Assimilators are people who excel at collecting and representing data in crisp and logical form. They are focused on ideas and concepts rather than people. These individuals like to put data and information together into models that explain the situation from a larger perspective. As a result, they are more interested in something making sense logically than they are in any practical value. They are not results-oriented people. These types of individuals are generally found in the more technical or specialist careers, such as project managers.

The diverging style is characterized by high scores in the concrete experience and reflective observation learning preferences. Figure 7.2 shows two examples of typical results from individuals who favor concrete experience and reflective observation. These individuals prefer the *diverging style*. Individuals who are characterized by these kites like to look at alternatives

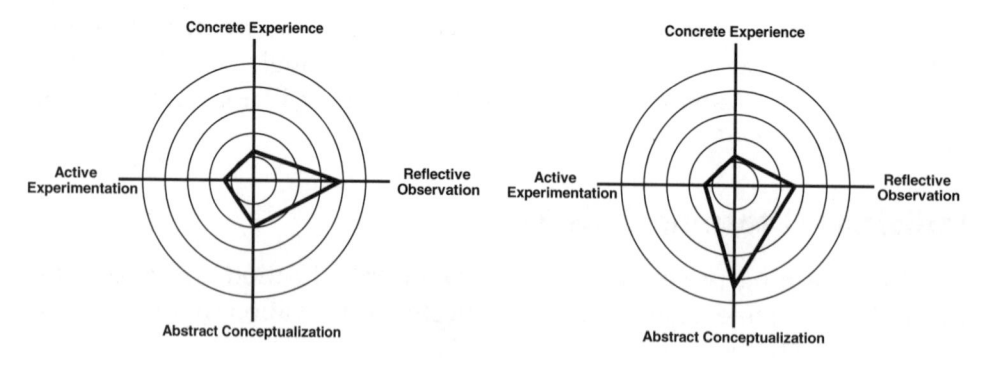

Figure 7.1 Examples of the assimilating learning style.

and view the situation from a variety of perspectives. They would rather observe than take action. Divergers like brainstorming and generally have a broad range of interests and like to gather information. On a project team these people will often suggest outside-the-box thinking and offer suggestions for other approaches than those that may have already been identified.

The accommodating style is characterized by high scores in the active experimentation and concrete experience learning preferences. Figure 7.3 shows two examples of typical results from individuals who favor active experimentation and concrete experience. These individuals prefer the *accommodating style*. Individuals who are characterized by this kite are results oriented and want to put things into practice. They are adaptive and can easily change with the circumstances. Accommodators are people persons. They are strong at implementation and hands-on activities and

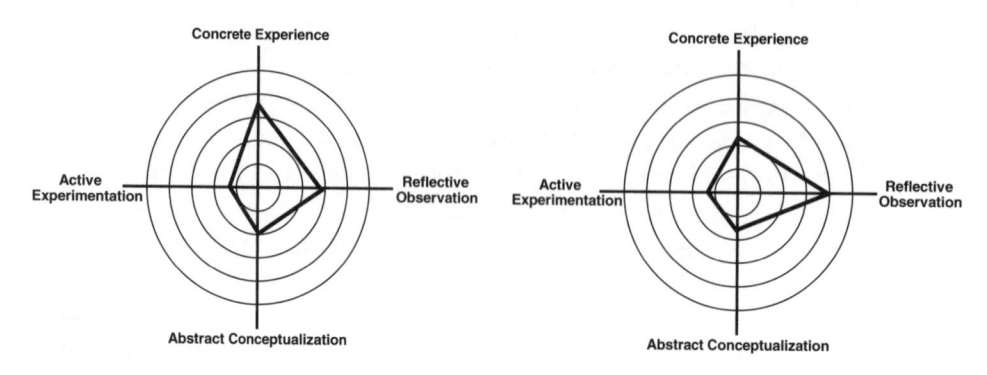

Figure 7.2 Examples of the diverging learning style.

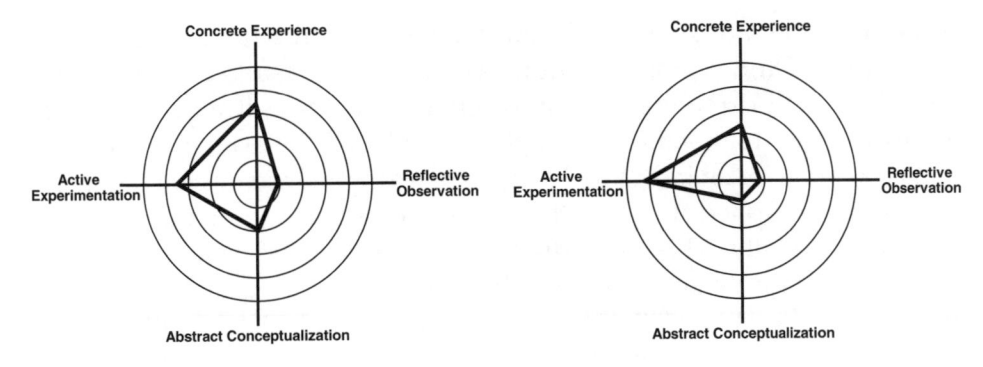

Figure 7.3 Examples of the accommodating learning style.

are good team players. They tend to be action oriented and more spontaneous than logical. As problem solvers they rely on people for input rather than on any technical analysis. On the project team you can count on these people to help foster a strong sense of teamwork, and they will often be found facilitating the working together of team members. They will often be the peacekeepers as well.

The converging learning style is characterized by high scores in the abstract conceptualization and active experimentation learning preferences. Figure 7.4 shows two examples of individuals who favor abstract conceptualization and active experimentation. These individuals prefer the *converging style*. Individuals who are characterized by this kite like to assemble information in order to solve problems. They like to converge to the correct solution. Convergers are the solution finders but not the solution implementors. Their strength lies in their ability to take concepts, models, and ideas and turn them into practical use. They are not particularly people oriented and would rather work with technical tasks and

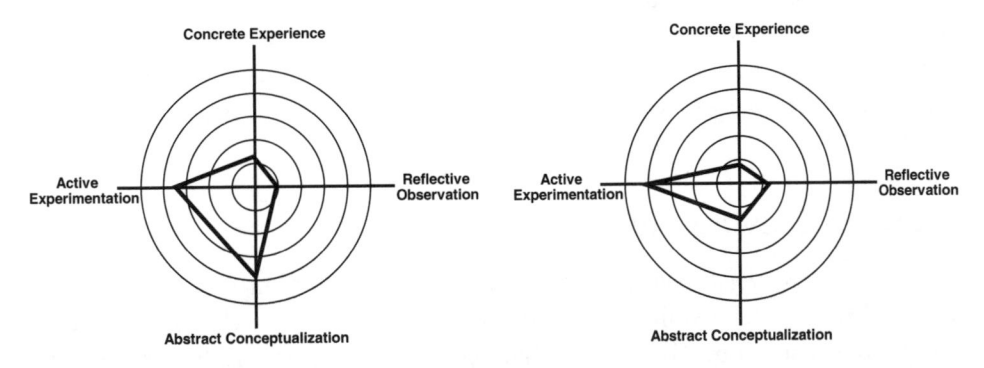

Figure 7.4 Examples of the converging learning style.

problems. They are good at picking the best option among a number of alternatives. On the project team these will be the results-oriented members. They will drive the team into action by helping it focus on which approach to a situation is best and then mobilizing the team into action.

It is possible for an individual's LSI to reveal similar scores in each quadrant. When graphed, the kite that these scores form penetrates all four quadrants equally. This individual is considered balanced, and the kite indicates that the person is comfortable with and practices all four learning preferences. Because of this balance and ability to relate to all learning preferences, he or she will be a stabilizing force on the project team and will function very well in a coordinating role across the team.

Once you determine the preferred learning styles of your team, you are better prepared to choose among alternative assignments. The data will tell you where the individual's strengths and weaknesses lie. A particularly weak quadrant score suggests an area of improvement for the individual. It would be unusual for an individual to be strong in all four quadrants. Use the scores to play to the individual's strengths and take corrective steps to mitigate the weaknesses in the future.

FOR YOUR REFERENCE For those of you who would like more information about how to acquire the LSI refer to Appendix B, "Sources of Information," and Appendix C, "How to Get TeamArchitect Tools."

LSI and the Problem-Solving Process

Creativity and problem solving go hand in hand. A good problem solver will think outside the box. He or she will conceive of approaches that may have been overlooked. The ability to think outside the box and suggest other approaches is the territory of the creative person. As we will discuss next, each of the learning styles relates to a different part of the problem-solving model. That means that the team must have all learning styles represented in order to solve problems effectively. In this section, we will see how the LSI relates to the problem-solving process.

Problem-Solving Model

In his work *Creative Problem Solving and Opportunity Finding* (Boyd and Fraser Publishing, 1995), J. Daniel Couger points out that there are dozens of models for problem solving. The model that seems most appropriate for business problem solving is one put forward by Couger and shown in Figure 7.5.

Stimulus ➡		Required Learning Styles
Step One	Delineate opportunity and define problem.	Assimilator
Step Two	Compile relevant information.	Assimilator
Step Three	Generate ideas.	Diverger
Step Four	Evaluate and prioritize ideas.	Converger
Step Five	Develop implementation plan.	Accommodator
		➡ Action

Figure 7.5 Couger's creative problem-solving model.

Couger's process begins with an outside stimulus—an event has occurred that creates an out-of-control situation that must be rectified. That launches a series of actions that clarify the situation, identifies and assembles relevant data, gets a number of ideas and approaches on the table, analyzes the ideas, selects the one that would appear most promising as the way to rectify the situation and return it to nominal, and finally puts an action plan in place and executes it (the exit point of the model is the action itself). We will see how all of the learning styles are needed to complete each step in the model. Couger identifies five steps to the problem-solving process.

Step 1: Delineate the opportunity and define the problem. This is a scoping step in which the team members attempt to establish a formulation and definition of the problem and the desired results that a solution to the problem will provide. It helps the team develop the boundaries of the problem—that is, what is in scope and what is out of scope. This step is best performed by team members who have a preference for the assimilator style. These individuals will look at the problem independently of any focus on people and try to present the problem at the conceptual level and put it into a logical framework. Their penchant for collecting and concisely reporting data is an early activity in this model.

Step 2: Compile the relevant information. With a definition of the problem in hand the team can now identify and specify the data elements that will be needed in order to further understand the problem and provide a foundation on which possible solutions can be formulated. Again, the assimilator is well suited to this activity.

Step 3: Generate ideas. This step typically begins with a brainstorming session. The team needs to identify as many solutions as possible. This is the time to think outside the box and look for creative and innovative ways to approach a solution. Ideas will spawn new ideas until the team has exhausted its creative energies. The diverger is well suited to the activities that take place in this step. The job of this individual is to look at the problem from a number of perspectives. Like the assimilator, the diverger also has an interest in data and information with the purpose of generating ideas, but he or she is not interested in generating solutions.

Step 4: Evaluate and prioritize ideas. In this step the list of possible solutions needs to be winnowed down to the one or two solutions that will actually be planned. Criteria for selecting the best solution ideas need to be developed (that's a job for the converger), metrics for assessing advantages and disadvantages need to be developed (again, a job for the converger), and the metrics will be used to prioritize the solutions. This is a straightforward exercise that anyone on the team can perform. This individual has the ability to take a variety of ideas and turn them into solutions. His or her work is not finished, however, until he or she has established criteria for evaluating those solutions and making their recommendations for action.

Step 5: Develop the implementation plan. The solution has been identified, and it's now time to build a plan to implement the solution. This is a whole team exercise that will draw on the team's collective wisdom for planning and implementation. When it is results that you want, call on the accommodator. His or her contribution will be to put a plan in place for delivering the recommended solution and making it happen. The accommodator is a good person to lead this planning and implementation exercise.

Couger then identifies 22 techniques that are useful in one or more of the five phases of the model. One of those techniques is brainstorming. From the previous discussion we can see that it is used in Step 3, generating ideas. Another technique is the Crawford Blue Slip, which can be used in opportunity delineation, problem definition (Step 1), and Step 3 (generating ideas). The Crawford Blue Slip technique can be used to collect a large number of ideas in a short time. The technique works as follows. Everyone gets a stack of blue slips of paper. The facilitator presents the situation in the form of a "how to" statement such as "How can we reduce the order-entry-to-order-fulfillment time? The group is given five minutes to write as many answers as possible—one to a slip. The slips are collected, sorted, and grouped by similarity of ideas. A complete discussion of Couger's 22 techniques is beyond the scope of this book, but you can consult Couger's work for the details. Most of his book is devoted to a discussion of these techniques.

Problem Solving and the LSI

Each of the steps in Couger's problem-solving model directly relates to one of the four learning styles that are identified in the LSI. Figure 7.5 indicates which learning styles relate to which steps of the problem-solving process. Note that all four learning styles have a role to play in the problem-solving process. If the team is lacking in any learning style, it will compromise the team's ability to effectively complete the step that requires that learning style.

For example, if the project team did not have a single diverger, let's see what impact that would have on the team's ability to solve a typical problem. The assimilator would have helped define the problem and collect the necessary data. In the absence of the diverger the team would quickly converge on a single solution and would not take the time to identify any alternatives (remember that is the role of the diverger). If the single solution that was identified happened to be a good solution, the team would be on safe ground. If the single solution that was identified happened to be a bad solution, the team, in its rush to judgment, would use it and would not have anyone (the diverger) to help identify other solutions.

LSI and the Decision-Making Process

Just as the LSI relates to the problem-solving process, the four quadrants of the LSI also directly relate to the stages of the decision-making process. While it is true that decision making and problem solving are closely related, it is instructive for us to see just how the LSI relates to decision making as well. Problem solving cannot happen without some decisions having been made. In that sense, decision making can be thought of as a subset of problem solving. But decision making can also occur outside of the problem-solving context. For example, the project is behind schedule, and the design phase is not yet complete. We could start some preliminary programming, but at the risk that when the design is complete we may have to rework some of the earlier programming. Do we begin programming to make up lost time and take the risk, or do we wait for design to be finished before we begin programming? This is clearly a decision-making situation, not a problem situation.

In this section we will establish the decision-making process and show how the four quadrants of the LSI relate to it.

Decision Styles

The particular situation that a project team finds itself in can be used to decide which of three decision styles (command style, consultative style, or consensus style) should be used. Let's define each of these and see how best to use them in concert with the learning styles represented on the project team.

Command style. The person with the most in-depth knowledge of the situation makes the decision. Often this will be the project manager. This style has more to do with the quality of the decision than it does with the acceptance of the decision. In difficult or tough situations, this style may be the better approach. If this decision style is used, the person making the decision should exhibit a balanced approach to learning. Each learning style must be equally preferred. Any balance that the team possesses may be of some value to the project manager, but it is not germane to this decision style.

Consultation style. If acceptance and quality are both important, involvement of the project team in the deliberations leading up to the decision is the preferred style. The project manager still makes the decision but only after receiving input from the team. If this decision style is used, the project team must display a balanced preference for each learning style. That doesn't mean each person must be balanced; rather, it means that the team, as a whole, represents each learning style.

Consensus style. If acceptance of the decision is more important than the quality of the decision, all team members should be involved in making the decision. This approach works if every person has an opportunity to share his or her point of view and all team members understand it. Every team member must commit to supporting the final consensus decision whether he or she agrees with it.

Consensus ensures a better decision than either the command or consultative styles simply because it has the benefit of several thinking perspectives rather than one. A decision reached by consensus has more of a commitment of the project team members than does any other style. Unfortunately, a consensus decision requires far more time to reach than the other styles, and this may detract from its advantages in some situations. It is safe to say that a consensus decision is by far the better alternative in almost every circumstance. The question for the project manager is whether the project team can make a consensus decision. That question will be answered later in this chapter. This approach to decision making requires the same balance in learning style preferences as the consultative style.

The project manager needs to understand which learning styles are present on the team and then choose the decision style that is appropriate for those learning styles. The more balanced the team is with respect to learning styles, the more the project manager can rely on the consultative and consensus decision styles. If the team is quite unbalanced with respect to its learning styles, the project manager would do well to use the command style and rely on the consultative style only occasionally.

Decision Making and the LSI

Decision making is pervasive throughout the life of the project. Consider the following questions from *Managing the Project Team* by Verma (Project Management Institute, 1997) that must be answered at some point in the project life cycle:

- What has to be done and where? (scope)
- Why should it be done? (justification)
- How well must it be done? (quality)
- When is it required and in what sequence? (schedule)
- How much will it cost? (budget/cost)
- What are the uncertainties? (risk)
- Who should do the job? (human resources)
- How should people be organized into teams? (communication/interpersonal skills)
- How shall we know if we have done the job? (information dissemination/communication)

The answers to all of these questions require decisions. How will the project team make decisions? Will it be based on a vote? Will it be a team consensus decision? Will it be left up to the project manager? Just how will it operate? Deciding how to decide is only a piece of the puzzle. Another piece is whether the team can make a decision and, if not, what to do about it. Let's take a closer look at the decision-making environment that the project team faces.

In their book *Organizational Behavior in Action: Skill Building Experiences* (West Publishing Co., 1976), Morris and Sashkin propose the six-phase model for rational decision making. The six phases in Morris and Shashkin's approach are as follows:

Phase I: Situation definition. This phase is one of discovery for the team and clarifying the situation to make sure that there is a shared understanding of the decision the team faces.

Phase II: Situation decision generation. Through brainstorming the team tries to expand the decision space.

Phase III: Ideas to action. Metrics are devised to attach reward and penalty to each possible decision that might be made.

Phase IV: Decision action plan. The decision has been made, and the development of a plan to implement it is now needed.

Phase V: Decision evaluation planning. This is kind of a post-decision audit of what worked and what didn't work. Some lessons learned will be the likely deliverable as well.

Phase VI: Evaluation of outcome and process. The team needs to find out if the decision got the job done and whether another attempt at the situation is needed.

There is a lot of similarity between the use of the LSI in problem solving and in decision making. Phase I requires the services of an assimilator. As part of the process of discovery, the assimilator will collect data and information and formulate the situation and the required decision. Phase II, the search for alternative decisions, is the province of the diverger. This is a collaborative effort because it continues to involve the assimilator in a definition type of activity. With the alternatives identified the work can be turned over to the converger in Phase III. His or her job is to establish criteria for evaluating the alternatives and ranking the alternatives against the criteria. His or her work is complete when a plan for implementing the decision is in place in Phase IV. In Phase V the accommodator will take over and implement the decision. Then the team, under the direction of an accommodator, will take an honest look at how effective the decision was. Finally, an evaluation of the results in Phase VI puts the work back into the hands of the assimilator. If the expected results were not attained, another round may be required.

Table 7.1 provides a summary of the six phases and the required learning styles.

Table 7.1 The Six Phases of the Decision-Making Process

PHASE	DESCRIPTION	LEARNING STYLE
Phase I: Situation definition	Discovery phase. The team investigates, discusses, clarifies, and defines the situation. It is important for the team to understand the root causes and evidence that led to the need for a decision.	Assimilator
Phase II: Situation decision generation	Continuation of Phase I. Characterized by brainstorming and searching for new ideas and alternatives for resolving the situation, which should lead to better choices for the decision. Above all, the team needs to avoid a rush to judgment.	Diverger
Phase III: Ideas to action	Define the criteria for evaluating the alternative decisions. This involves identifying the advantages and disadvantages of each alternative. Whatever approach is used, the result should be a ranking of alternatives from most desirable to least desirable.	Converger
Phase IV: Decision action plan	Begins once the alternative is chosen. This is the planning phase for the project team. The team determines activities, resources, and timelines that are required to implement the decision. This phase requires a concerted effort to obtain buy-in from all affected parties.	Converger
Phase V: Decision evaluation planning	Learning opportunity for the project team. The team identifies what did and did not work, as well as areas in which it can improve and how to do so. The value of this discussion lies in the team's willingness to be honest and straightforward with one another.	Accommodator

(Continues)

120 Building Effective Project Teams

Table 7.1 (Continued)

PHASE	DESCRIPTION	LEARNING STYLE
Phase VI Evaluation of outcome and process	Focuses on the quality of results. The team evaluates the situation: Was the situation improved satisfactorily, or will another round be required? Was the situation defined correctly, or is revision required? Did the process work as expected, or will it need adjustment for the next attempt?	Assimilator

Candidate Pool Members' LSI Data

To better understand and become familiar with interpreting LSI profiles, let's examine the LSI profiles of four Gold Team members. These four were chosen because their profiles were quite dissimilar from one another, and interpreting them will give us some practice at learning about the LSI and what it can tell us about an individual.

Let's refer to Hal's profile (Figure 7.6) to explain in general what the figures represent. The left side is a display of an individual's learning preferences. The closed four-sided figure in the left panel is the individual's "kite." The farther the endpoints of the kite are from the center of the figure, the more that individual favors that learning style. Note that Hal's major preference is concrete experience followed by active experimentation. The data point in the panel on the right is derived from the scores on the four learning preferences. The formulae for deriving the data point are described in Chapter 11, "Establishing the Profile of the Project Team."

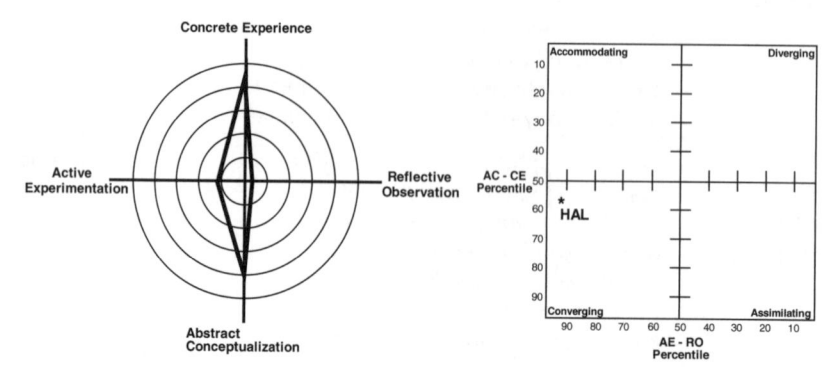

Figure 7.6 Hal E. Lewya's LSI profile.

Hal's data point falls in the converging quadrant but is not too far from the accommodating quadrant, which is what we would expect from a person who has high scores in the active experimentation and concrete experience learning preferences.

Hal E. Lewya's LSI profile. Referring again to Figure 7.6 note that because of the location of the data point, Hal is somewhat balanced between both the converging and accommodating learning styles. As a result, he is a practical person and is most comfortable working hands-on with technical tasks. Hal is a good problem solver and can switch between logical, fact-based analysis and gut feel. He often will have a strong reliance on input from others.

Pearl E. Gates's LSI profile. Pearl's scores are very high on the concrete experience and abstract conceptualization learning preferences, as shown on the left panel in Figure 7.7. This is not one of the four dominant learning styles discussed earlier. Rather, it is a combination of two very different preferences—one relying on analysis and thinking (abstract conceptualization) and the other relying on actual practice (concrete experience). Her data suggests that she is comfortable in both modes and can switch back and forth as the situation dictates. That means that she can expand current thinking and ideas into new applications and then she can put these new ideas and applications into practice. In the Gold Project she could not be expected to generate the idea for the touch screen (she is not a diverger), but she could be expected to expand on that idea and look for ways to apply it (because she is an accommodator) to the project at hand.

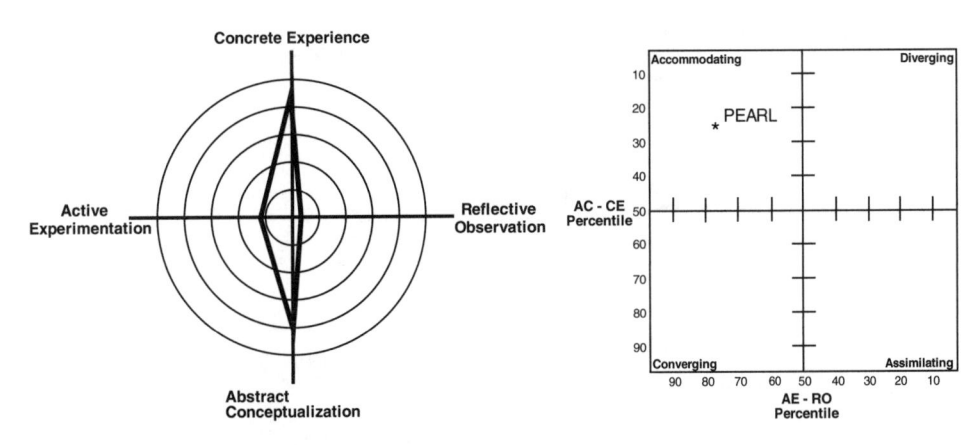

Figure 7.7 Pearl E. Gates's LSI profile.

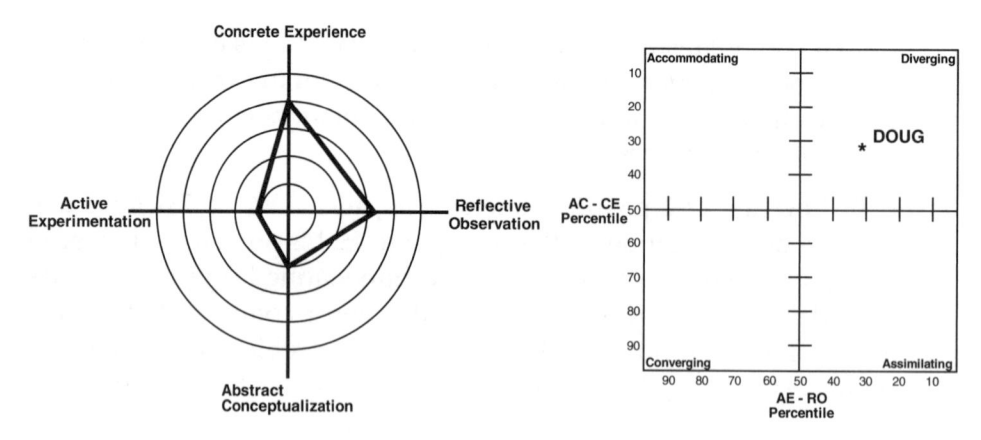

Figure 7.8 Doug deGrave's LSI profile.

Doug deGrave's LSI profile. Doug has high scores on the concrete experience and reflective observation learning preferences, as shown by the orientation of the kite on the left panel of Figure 7.8. This is characteristic of the diverger, which is reflected in the data point on the right panel. He will take different points of view as he considers issues and problems associated with the Gold Project. Doug's value to the team will be his ability to come up with alternative possibilities.

Terri Tory's LSI profile. Terri has high scores on the active experimentation and reflective observation learning preferences, as is shown in the left panel of Figure 7.9. Just as Pearl displayed a balanced use of two opposite learning preferences, so does Terri. In Terri's case she can switch between analyzing by watching and experimenting by

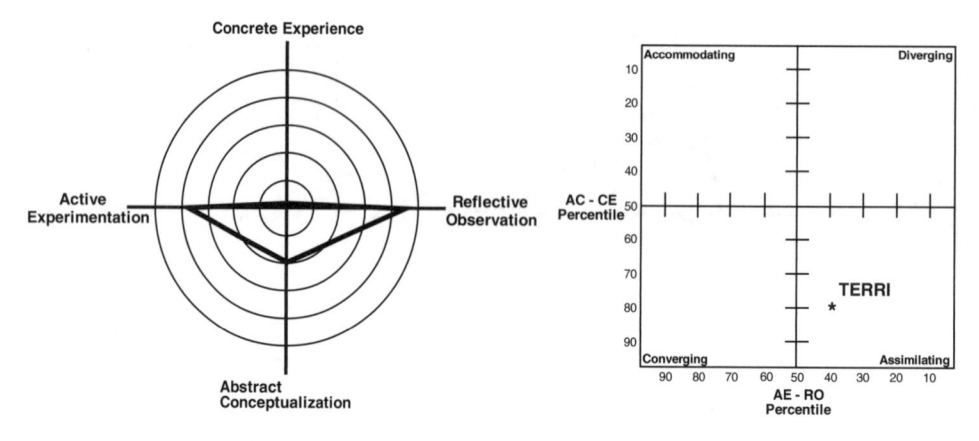

Figure 7.9 Terri Tory's LSI profile.

doing. She is comfortable in either mode. She likes to try new ideas and approaches and observe how those approaches meet the stated needs. One would expect her to apply the observed outcome back into the idea, thus modifying it and experimenting once again. This style lends itself very well to a prototyping approach to systems design and development.

Putting It All Together

We have now added another team assessment tool into our growing toolkit. The LSI data, especially the learning styles data points shown in the right panel of Figures 7.6 through 7.9, is the tool that we will use going forward to determine the team's balance with respect to its decision-making and problem-solving capabilities. Just to give you a brief look ahead, we will plot the learning styles data point for every member of the team on one graph (like the right panel on the previously cited figures). If the data points are distributed across all four quadrants, then we can say that the team is balanced with respect to decision making and problem solving. If not, we have some work to do to compensate for that lack of balance. That is the topic of Chapter 11, Chapter 12, "Assessing Team Alignment and Balance," and Chapter 13, "Developing and Deploying the Project Team." In the next chapter we will add yet another assessment tool to our toolkit—the SDI.

CHAPTER 8

Conflict Management Styles and Strategies

Every project team has to deal with conflict at all stages of the project life cycle. From planning to design to development to implementation, there are any number of conflict situations that can arise and must be dealt with effectively and decisively. Let me be clear at the outset—conflict is both good and bad.

Conflict is good because it can get other ideas on the table and can help when looking for creative solutions. It is good because in its absence the project team can easily fall into a groupthink mentality. With everyone agreeing to an issue, there is no one on the team to test the validity of the approach, to offer alternative strategies, or to challenge the team's thinking. That can only lead to trouble.

On the other hand, conflict can be bad. It is bad because it can be a roadblock to progress, a barrier to performance. When it becomes combative, the team can become dysfunctional in the face of unresolved differences. The key to a team's productive use of conflict lies in the leadership abilities of the project manager and the choice of team leadership models that are employed.

In this chapter, we'll look at the different strategies that are used to handle conflict and then talk about the Strength Deployment Inventory, a tool you can use to assist in dealing effectively with conflict.

Conflict Management

Conflict management is as important to the success of the project as any other skill—perhaps more so. This is because conflict is almost inevitable in any team situation. People have differing ideas about the importance of things and how they should be done or not done. They have conflicting personal objectives, and they have personalities that sometimes clash. A project manager must know how to effectively manage and resolve conflict.

Conflict management is important because conflict over ideas and course of action is a necessary part of the creative process, of decision making, and of problem solving. But differing positions lead to interpersonal conflict. Individuals identify with their own ideas, beliefs, and value system. If one person says, "That's a stupid idea," you can expect that the person who thought of the idea will feel personally attacked, which will lead to some type of retaliation and hence conflict between the two individuals. For this reason, members of the project team must be taught to critique ideas based on merit, saying something like, "The concern I have about this approach is that it does not address one important aspect of the problem." This evaluates the idea without attacking the intelligence of the person who offered the suggestion.

One characteristic of effective conflict management is that it draws out of the team members all of the ideas they have on how to solve a problem or make a decision without letting them get into interpersonal conflict. Still, it seems inevitable that interpersonal conflict will arise occasionally, and then the project manager must be able to channel that energy into an acceptable resolution.

Fortunately, both conflict management skills and conflict resolution skills can be acquired. Not everyone is equally good at both, any more than we are all good at any skill, but we can all develop some level of competence, if we want to do so. The key is to recognize that conflict often does not resolve itself, which is a trap into which some project managers fall. They find dealing with conflict unpleasant. They don't like emotional behavior on their teams, and they hope that the conflict will simply go away if they ignore it. This is the ostrich response. Hiding your head in the sand will not make the problem disappear, and, in fact, it usually just gets worse. Avoiding conflict is not the answer. If you give the individuals a reasonable amount of time to settle their differences and they make no headway, then you are going to have to intervene.

This is one of those areas that many project managers dislike. As we learned in Chapter 6, "Thinking Styles," individuals differ in their preferences for dealing with people problems. Many technologists and scientists have a low level of preference in this area. They may avoid the situation altogether or find it very noxious when they must intervene. If this is really a problem for you, you may want to rethink your aspirations for project management. People issues come with the turf. Remember, projects are people, not just equipment, materials, and PERT diagrams.

The best tool that I have found for assessing the conflict management styles of an individual and a team is the Strength Deployment Inventory (SDI),* from Personal Strengths Publishing, Inc. It is a 20-item survey available in both paper form and online. In this chapter, I discuss the SDI, and show how it relates to conflict management and the development of the associated strategies for dealing effectively with conflict.

FOR YOUR REFERENCE If you'd like more information about this product and how to acquire this powerful tool, refer to Appendix B, "Sources of Information," and Appendix C, "How to Get TeamArchitect Tools."

Individuals follow three basic strategies as they attempt to resolve any conflict situation that they face. These strategies are based on how they prefer to relate to people, their affinity for assertiveness and directing behavior, and their reliance on analytical approaches to situations. Every person displays some combination of all three of these behaviors, and it is in that combination that conflict management strategies unfold. Furthermore, each individual will employ these three strategies in a sequence (i.e., a series of three stages) comfortable tohim or her . Later in this chapter we will examine these stages of conflict resolution in more detail.

Conflict Management Styles

Five different strategies can be employed to deal with conflict. They are represented graphically in Figure 8.1. First, note that there are two dimensions: non-assertive to assertive and uncooperative to cooperative. All five strategies can be described in terms of these two dimensions. Let's take a closer look at each one.

---

*Strength Deployment Inventory®, SDI®, and the Interaction Triangle®, are registered trademarks of Personal Strengths Publishing. These marks are used throughout this book with permission. For ease of reading, the U.S. registration symbol is sometimes omitted. Text from the Strength Deployment Inventory is adapted for use in this book with permission.

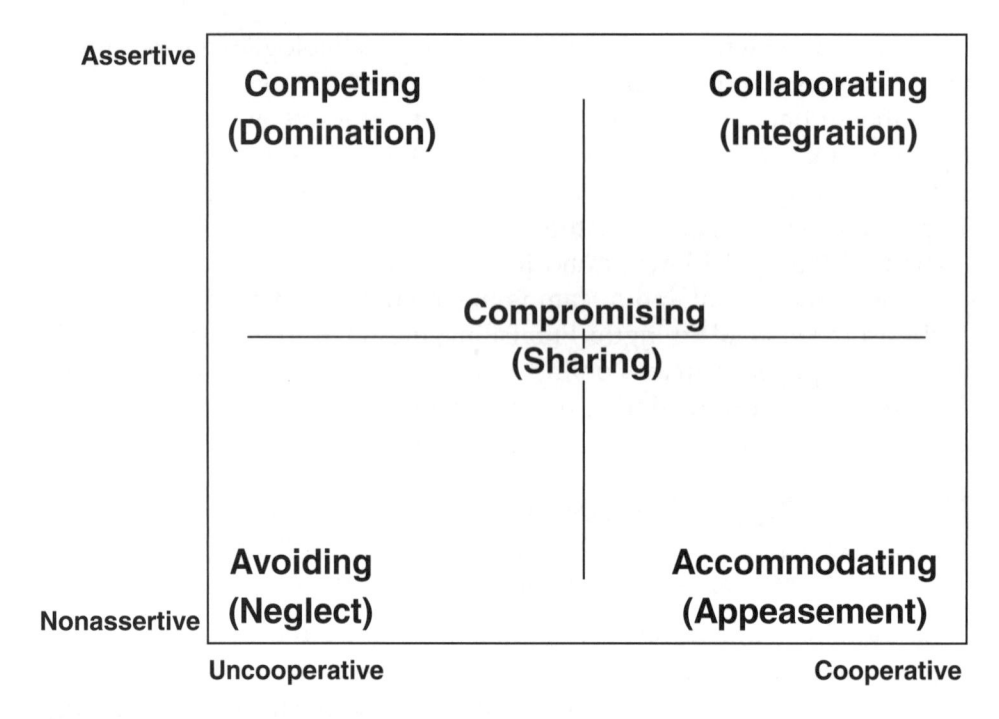

Figure 8.1 Conflict management styles.

The chart shows conflict management styles on two axes: vertical axis from Nonassertive (bottom) to Assertive (top), and horizontal axis from Uncooperative (left) to Cooperative (right). The four quadrants are: Competing (Domination) — top left; Collaborating (Integration) — top right; Avoiding (Neglect) — bottom left; Accommodating (Appeasement) — bottom right. Compromising (Sharing) is in the center.

Competing. Competing involves taking a firm stand on an issue, and it is often used to intimidate someone of lesser stature on the team. There are situations when this strategy is appropriate. For example, competing is appropriate in emergency situations when a timely response is essential and you are sure you are right.

Collaborating. A collaborative approach encourages disagreements, but they are considered opportunities and are therefore constructive. This strategy is often used to gain additional insight into an issue and to get different points of view on the table. A collaborative approach fosters ownership and can sometimes be used to overcome previous disagreements.

Accommodating. An accommodating strategy is used when you discover that you may be in error about your understanding of a situation and are willing to give in. It is a demonstration that you are a reasonable person and you know when to surrender. Often you realize that the other point of view has more merit. It is a peaceful capitulation and can build up credits for a later confrontation. Let's face it, some situations just aren't that important to you or are clearly more important to the other party. This would be a good time to implement an accommodating strategy.

Avoiding. We have already talked about this one. If there is a decision that you disagree with by accepting it without confrontation, you are avoiding it. If you withheld meaningful input, you may have caused more harm in the long run in return for a short-term peaceful resolution. If the other party is simply better equipped to deal with the situation, an avoidance strategy may be fine.

Compromising. Overall, this would seem to be the best resolution of a conflict. It represents a give-and-take resolution in which each party wins something. It is an appropriate strategy when a continued delay in resolution may simply be too costly.

Strength Deployment Inventory

Elias Porter developed the Strength Deployment Inventory (SDI), in 1971 after having spent the prior 10+ years developing it. It consists of 10 questions that ask about your behavior when everything is going well and 10 questions that ask about your behavior when everything is going wrong. Here is a question from the first 10 and one from the second 10:

I find those relationships most gratifying in which I can be . . .

_____ of support to a strong leader in whom I have faith.
_____ the one who provides the leadership others want to follow.
_____ neither a leader nor a follower but free to pursue my own independent way.

When another person insists on having his or her own way, I tend to . . .

_____ put my wishes aside for the time being and go along with that person.
_____ put up counter-arguments and try to get the person to change.
_____ respect the person's right to follow his or her interest as long as there is no interference with mine.

You answer by distributing 10 points across the three responses. The more points you allocate to a response, the more it reflects you. There are no right or wrong answers. The instrument is simply describing behavior.

One of the strengths of the SDI is that it is self-scoring and self-analyzing. You don't need a high-priced consultant to tell you what the data is saying.

The SDI booklet is self-contained. Besides the 20 questions it has all of the instructions and data templates you will need to do a complete analysis of the question responses.

Motivational Values

How people relate to others when they are free to act in a way that makes them feel good is called their *valued-relating style*. The valued-relating style forms one endpoint of the SDI. Examining how the individual relates to others when they are in a conflict situation forms the other endpoint of the SDI. The comparison between these two behaviors forms the basis of the conflict management strategy as described by the SDI graphic, discussed in the text that follows. For us this graphic will be the basis for our analysis of how the team handles conflict situations. How we handle conflict situations is the key to realizing the benefits that can accrue to the team as a result of the conflict. We will choose a strategy based on the preceding discussion and within that strategy plan how to achieve a successful conclusion.

The SDI relies on an important idea—that people choose behavior in conflict in order to defend what is important to them. So to understand and manage conflict effectively, we must first understand what is important to them. The SDI presents seven groups of Motivational Values. In order to develop a conflict management strategy for your team, you will need to be familiar with all seven. Then you will need to understand how motives change in conflict—this will be presented later in the chapter. The seven valued-relating styles are briefly described here.

Altruistic-nurturing. People with this valued-relating style are very concerned about the protection, growth, and general welfare of others.

Assertive-directing. People with this valued-relating style are focused on results and on organizing people and other resources to produce those results as efficiently and effectively as possible. These people like to win and to be seen as winners.

Analytical-automizing. People with this valued-relating style are concerned that the best approach is being used and that it has been thoroughly thought out. They tend to be individualists and self-sufficient. They do not depend on others to accomplish their results.

Flexible-cohering. This valued-relating style is a blend of the previous three valued-relating styles. People with this valued-relating style tend to take all points of view into consideration before taking action. They are good team players and, based on their values, can be effective project managers.

Assertive-nurturing. This valued-relating style is a blend of the altruistic-nurturing and assertive-directing valued-relating styles. People with this valued-relating style are concerned about the general welfare, protection, and growth of others but from a leadership and task-managed perspective.

Judicious-competing. People with this valued-relating style are a blend of the assertive-directing and analytic-autonomizing valued-relating styles. They exhibit concern for assertiveness, justice and leadership, order and fairness in competition.

Cautious-supporting. People with this valued-relating style are a blend of the altruistic-nurturing and analytic-autonomizing valued-relating styles. They are concerned with helping and supporting themselves and others become self-sufficient with regard to fairness and justice.

Project managers with different Motivational Values bring different strengths to their projects. Anyone can learn to be an effective project manager; one of the keys is recognizing your own style, how it is perceived by others, and learning to use that information to form better relationships in the project team.

The Scoring Triangle

The SDI uses an arrow plotted on the scoring triangle to represent the individual's valued-relating style and conflict management strategy. The responses to the 20 questions are self-scored, and two sets of three scores each are produced. The first set represents the situation when all things are going well and locates the base of the arrow. The second set represents the situation when things are not going well and locates the arrowhead. Figure 8.2 is an example.

The length and position of the arrow on the scoring triangle tells us everything we need to know about the individual's valued-relating style and his or her strategy for handling conflict situations. The origin of the arrow represents motives when things are going well for the person. The arrowhead represents a change in motives for the person when they feel that they are in conflict. From the arrow we can discern both the Motivational Values and the Conflict Sequence of the person to whom the arrow belongs. That is described more fully later in this chapter.

First note that the seven valued-relating styles are located at each vertex of the scoring triangle, at the midpoint along each side of the scoring triangle, and at the center of the scoring triangle. The actual scoring triangle is color coded as follows (see the CD-ROM for illustrations in color):

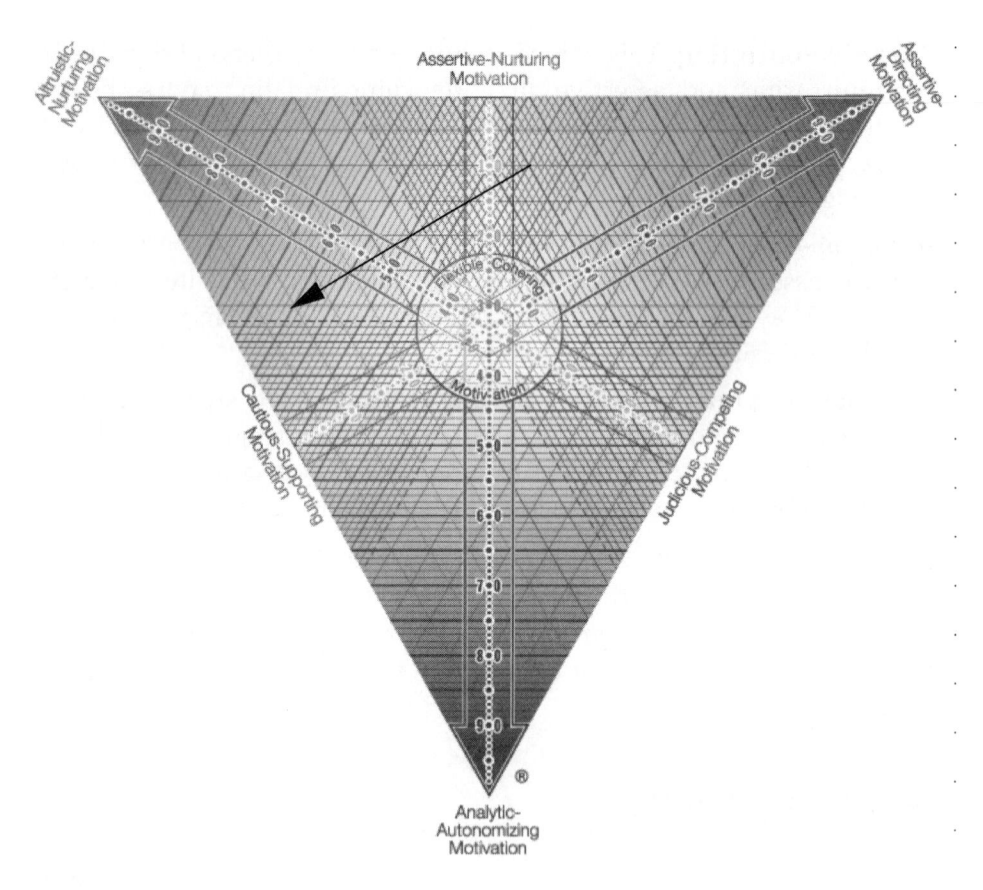

Figure 8.2 An example of an SDI plot.

- Altruistic-nurturing vertex is Blue.
- Assertive-directing vertex is Red.
- Analytic-autonomizing vertex is Green.

From now on I will refer to the vertices by their color rather than their name. Scores will always be given in the order Blue-Red-Green so that the set of scores that represents the situation when everything is going well is given by the triplet (40, 50, 10), and the set of scores that represent the situation when things are not going well is represented by the triplet (60, 10, 30). Note that the scores in each triplet add to 100. Also note that each individual is a blend of each color.

The location of the arrow with respect to the three vertices of the scoring triangle contains the interpretation of the data. This individual's valued-relating style is primarily Red and Blue with very little Green. We know this from the scores (40, 50, 10) as well as from the orientation of the base of the arrow with respect to the three vertices. The base of the arrow is closest to the Red vertex, next closest to the Blue vertex, and furthest from the Green vertex. This individual has an assertive-nurturing valued-relating style, as described previously. This individual's conflict sequence strategy is determined by the location of the arrowhead. It lies at (60, 10, 30), and therefore the conflict strategy sequence is B-G-R. When faced with conflict this individual will first attempt to retain harmony and good will by being accommodating to the needs of the other party (the Blue strategy). If that fails, he or she will try to escape from the conflict by salvaging whatever can be salvaged (the Green strategy). And finally, if that fails, he or she will simply fight for his or her rights as a last resort (the Red strategy).

Note that the sequence of the three stages of conflict resolution mentioned earlier is the same as the ordered distance of the arrowhead to the three vertices. Whichever vertex the arrowhead is closest to will describe the first-stage conflict strategy, the next closest will describe the second-stage conflict strategy, and the farthest vertex will describe the third stage conflict strategy.

Test-Retest Reliability

I have been using the SDI for several years in my consulting practice and have had the occasion to complete the SDI three times over the years (1994, 1997, and 2000). The results are shown in Figure 8.3. There has not been any noticeable change in how you would interpret the scores. The instrument itself has a test-retest reliability of plus or minus six points. In this illustration, all three of my SDI results fall within a circle with a radius of six points, thus demonstrating the instrument's reliability. All three origins and all three arrowheads are within a circle, the test re-test reliability should be considered for each part of the arrow individually.

Aside from being a very reliable measure of my valued-relating style and stages of conflict resolution, the arrows give a very interesting picture of how I deal with the project situations faced by a project manager. See the description of [BRG] later in this chapter for an interpretation of my arrows.

SDI and Conflict Management Strategies

Managing conflict involves using one of 13 possible sequences, depending on the orientation and location of your arrow on the scoring triangle. Those

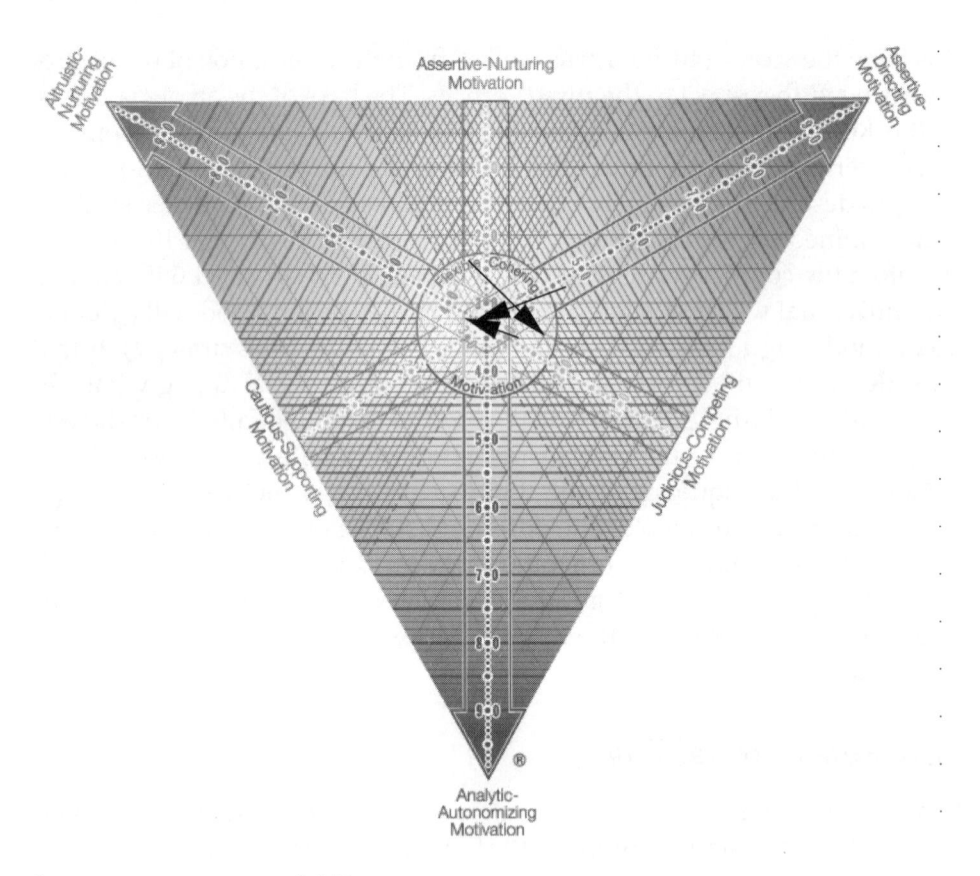

Figure 8.3 Test-retest reliability.

13 sequences are labeled in Figure 8.4. The letters indicate the sequence that an individual will follow when faced with a conflict situation The conflict sequences are denoted by the three letters, arranged in some order with brackets used in some instances.

For example, the sequence B-R-G defines the sequence of conflict strategies that this individual will use. In this case the first stage is characterized by his or her altruistic-nurturing style; the second stage by his or her assertive-directing style; and the third stage by his or her analytic-autonomizing style. I'll explain these strategies in more detail in the text that follows.

Another sequence might be B-[RG]. The brackets are used in situations where there is no measurable difference between the valued-relating styles on the vertices that are bracketed. In the example, this person's first stage is characterized by his or her altruistic-nurturing styles; the second stage will be characterized by a blending of his or her assertive-directing and

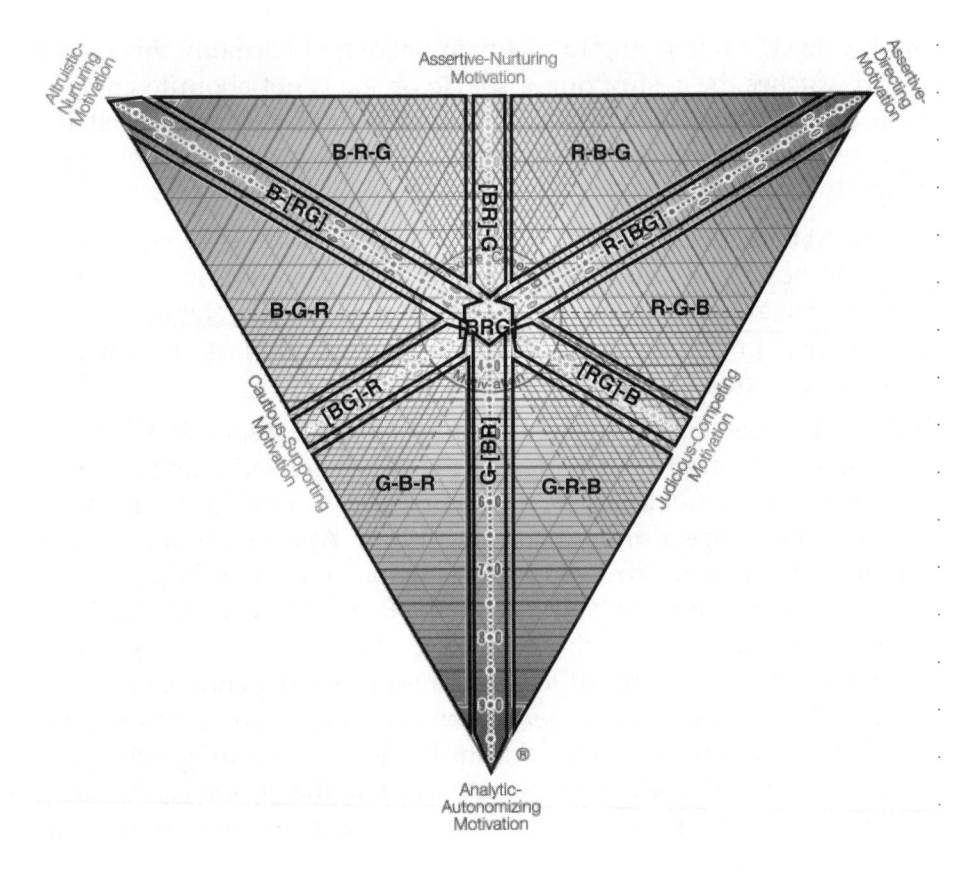

Figure 8.4 Conflict sequences.

analytic-autonomizing styles. The brackets are used whenever two vertices have numeric scores that are less than six units apart.

Let's briefly explain what each sequence entails.

B-[RG]. This person's initial strategy is to continue to seek peace and harmony by appealing to the altruistic and nurturing behaviors with which he or she is comfortable. If that fails, he or she will resort to either of two strategies. One strategy will be to appeal to the logic of the situation. That is, to attempt to resolve the conflict through pure logic and reasoning. The other strategy is to simply take an aggressive stance and not give away any ground.

B-G-R. Similar to the B-[RG] situation, this person wants to preserve harmony and good will. Unable to do that he or she will turn protective and try to retain whatever can be retained. Only as a last resort will he or she take to aggressive fighting behavior.

[BG]-R. Even while trying to maintain peace and harmony this person also watches the cost of doing so. He or she is not about to compromise beyond a point of reasonableness. If he or she cannot do that, this person will become aggressive and fight for what he or she believes is rightly his or hers.

G-B-R. At the onset of conflict these people are cautious. Being a logical person he or she will assess the facts before moving into action. If nothing of great importance is at stake, he or she will defer to the other in order to preserve peace and goodwill. Only as a last resort will he or she turn to fighting back.

[BRG]. This person is completely flexible. He or she responds differently to each situation and will weigh all the facts before adopting a conflict strategy. Because of this behavior he or she is very difficult to read and may, in fact, appear unpredictable to others. Apart from minor variations all three of my arrows lie in the region defined by [BRG].

My valued-relating styles and conflict sequence are basically equally weighted on all three vertices. That describes a person who can take any one of three different points of view depending on the situation he or she faces. This person tends to take all points of view into account before moving into action. While this due diligence is certainly a desirable style it can also appear that the person can't make a decision, that he or she is wishy-washy. I have to be very careful that I don't send that type of message.

Another interesting feature of these arrows is their length. All three arrows are short, and that means that my valued-relating styles is not markedly different from my conflict situation strategy. In other words, it is hard to tell when my behavior is that of a person in conflict or that of a person behaving the way he or she prefers to behave. I am a hard person to read because I don't display any visible signs of a behavior change, and my conflict management strategy can take any one of several directions.

With all of that said, the best project managers will have similar arrow patterns. They are balanced with respect to all three valued-relating styles, and they can work effectively with all types of people. That does not mean that someone with a different arrow configuration can't be a good project manager. He or she can. He or she just has to be aware of his or her valued-relating style and act accordingly.

G-[BR]. This person's initial position is to take a stance based on logic, order, rules, and principles. If that does not work, he or she will take one of two positions: take up the fight if the issue is important or give in if it is not important.

G-R-B. This person's first initiative is to appeal to the analytic and logical aspects of the conflict. If that fails, he or she will become assertive and only as a last resort will he or she give in.

[RG]-B. These people will analyze the situation and develop a strategy for handling the conflict. If this fails, they will give in as a last resort.

R-G-B. These people are competitors, and compete is what they do best. If that doesn't work they fall back on analysis and logic and finally will give in as a last resort.

R-[BG]. These people will immediately assert their rights and, if pressed too far, will either give in or avoid further conflict.

R-B-G. These people are assertive and will come out challenging their opponent. If that doesn't work they will try to restore harmony and peace, and only as a last resort, they will withdraw to avoid further conflict.

[BR]-G. These people will try to maintain harmony but in an assertive way. If this strategy fails, they will withdraw from the situation.

B-R-G. Peace and harmony are very important to these people, and they will do whatever they can to maintain it. If pressed further, they will stand up for their rights and withdraw only when all else fails.

Relationship between the Strategies and the SDI

While there isn't a one-to-one mapping of SDI conflict sequences to the strategies discussed previously, there are some fundamental relationships between the two. For example, the competing style is most closely associated with an R-G-B strategy. The individual competes to win his or her position, and that is what a first-stage Red strategy is all about. The collaborating style is assertive and attempts to win through logic and analysis. That is most closely associated with an [RG]-B strategy. The avoiding style is non-assertive and attempts to resolve the conflict without incident but without incurring personal cost beyond reason. That is most closely associated with a [BG]-R strategy. The accommodating style is non-assertive and cooperative, and that is most closely associated with the B-G-R strategy. Finally, the compromising style is one of fairness and equity in considering all aspects of a conflict situation. That is most closely associated with a [BRG] strategy.

Candidate Pool Members' SDI Profiles

In order to better understand and become more familiar with interpreting the SDI profiles, let's examine five Gold Team members' profiles. I chose these because they are quite different from one another and will give us some good practice in interpreting the SDI scores.

Hal E. Lewya's SDI profile. Hal, who is one choice for project manager, is described by an arrow that lies nearly inside the circle (a.k.a. hub) in the middle of the diagram. His scores are (26, 46, 28) and (35, 32, 33) for his valued-relating style and conflict sequence, respectively. Hal does not display any strong tendencies to one motivational value over another, whether in conflict or not. The short arrow is indicative of motivational values and behaviors that are very similar whether things are going well or not well. As a result, he is very difficult to read. You can't tell whether he is in a conflict mode. That can be both a strength

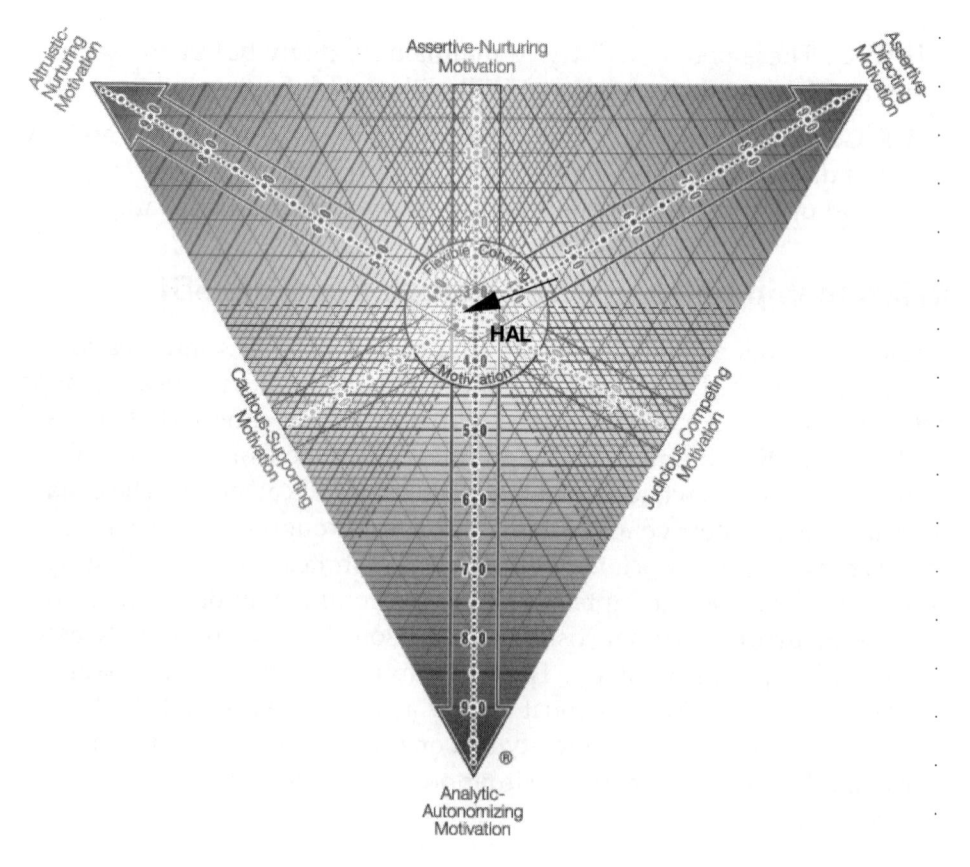

Figure 8.5 Hal E. Lewya's SDI profile.

and a weakness. It is a strength in the sense that Hal weighs input and opinions from all concerned before making any decision. It is a weakness in that because of his lack of decisiveness, he may be perceived by other project team members as a wishy-washy or unstable person.

In fact, Hal is very much influenced by the situation and may behave quite differently from one situation to the next. Hal tends to be very deliberate and not prone to knee-jerk reactions and decisions. If you have concluded that this type of pattern is typical of good project managers, you are right. That doesn't mean that your arrow has to be in the hub to be a good project manager. Regardless of how the arrow is positioned, you can be a good project manager. It is just a fact that arrows distributed in or near the hub are indicative of good project managers.

Olive Branch's SDI profile. Olive's data points are (78, 9, 13) and (43, 35, 22) when things are going well and when things are not going well, respectively. Olive, who is one choice for project administrative

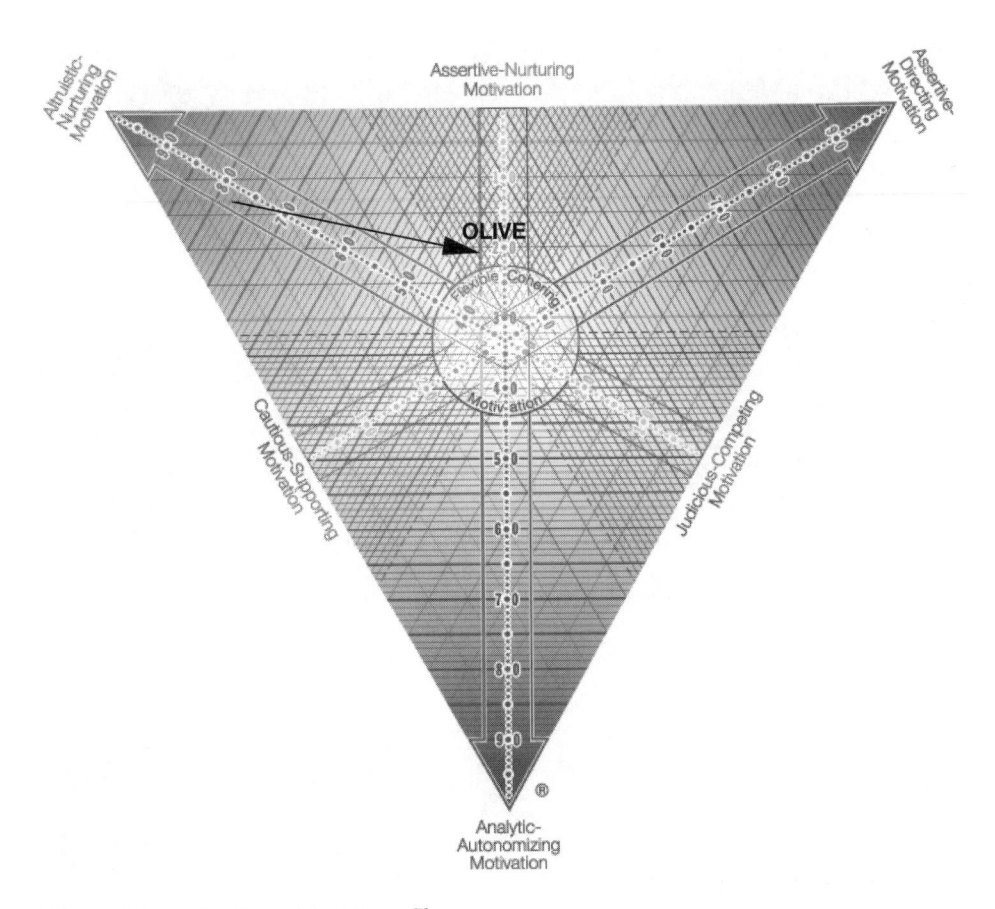

Figure 8.6 Olive Branch's SDI profile.

assistant, is quite different. Olive has very consistently shown marked concern for others, as indicated by her high Blue score. She is always very supportive and concerned about how others will react to a situation or decision and tries to placate wherever she feels the need. When placed in conflict she is still concerned about others but will resort to the leverage of her position to resolve conflicts, as indicated by her BR blend (i.e., assertive-nurturing style).

Mike Rowtoy's SDI profile. And, finally, we have Mike, one of the two programmers who might be assigned to the Gold Team. Mike's scores are (9, 67, 24) and (6, 33, 61) when things are going well and when things are not going well, respectively. He is very aggressive and results driven, as indicated by his high Red score. When placed in conflict he takes a very analytic point of view, as indicated by his high Green score. He has a solid command of performance data and bench-

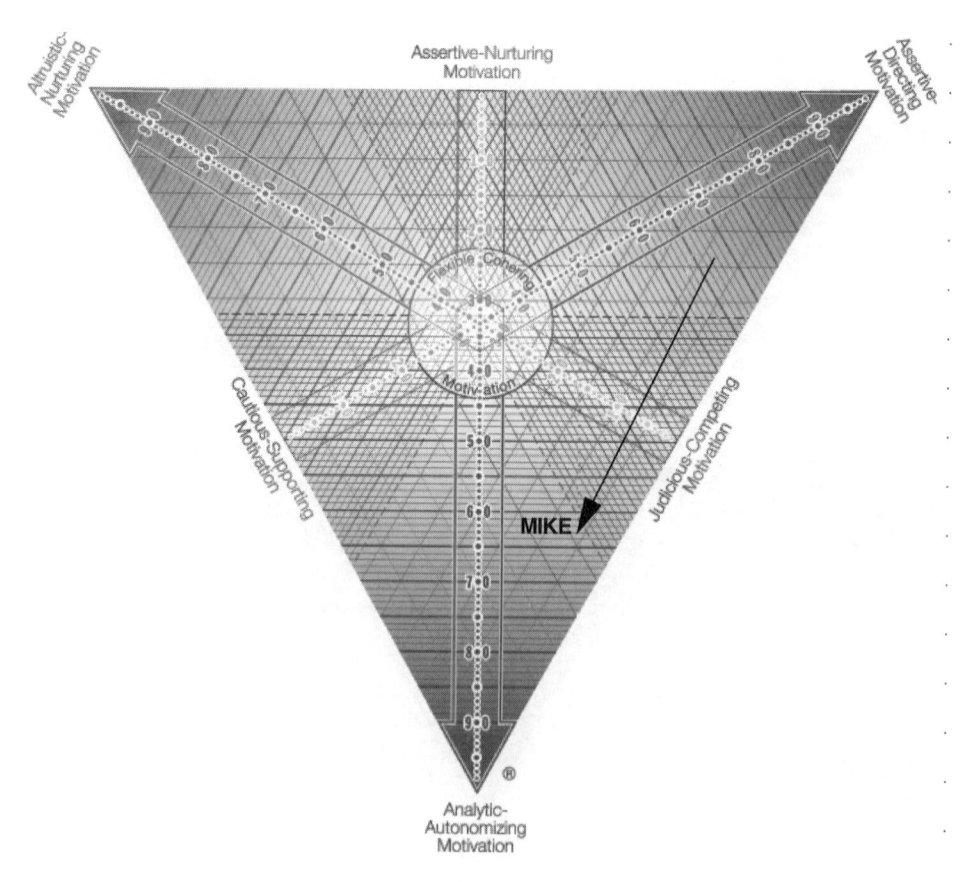

Figure 8.7 Mike Rowtoy's SDI profile.

mark studies and uses that as his first line of defense when placed in conflict situations. Mike is very weak in people skills in both normal and conflict situations, as indicated by his low Blue scores in both situations. He has very little concern for the thoughts and feelings of others. They are simply a nuisance to him.

Anita Kaskett's SDI profile. Anita, much like Hal, is another example of a person whose outward behavior in conflict situations is not very different from her valued-relating styles. Her scores are (27, 13, 60) and (27, 3, 70) when things are going well and when things are not going well, respectively. Note that her arrow is very short. This demonstrates that her outward behavior is consistent in both situations. It will be difficult to tell when she is in a conflict mode. When confronted with a conflict situation she will continue to be logical and analytic (as indicated by her high Green scores in both situations)—weighing the

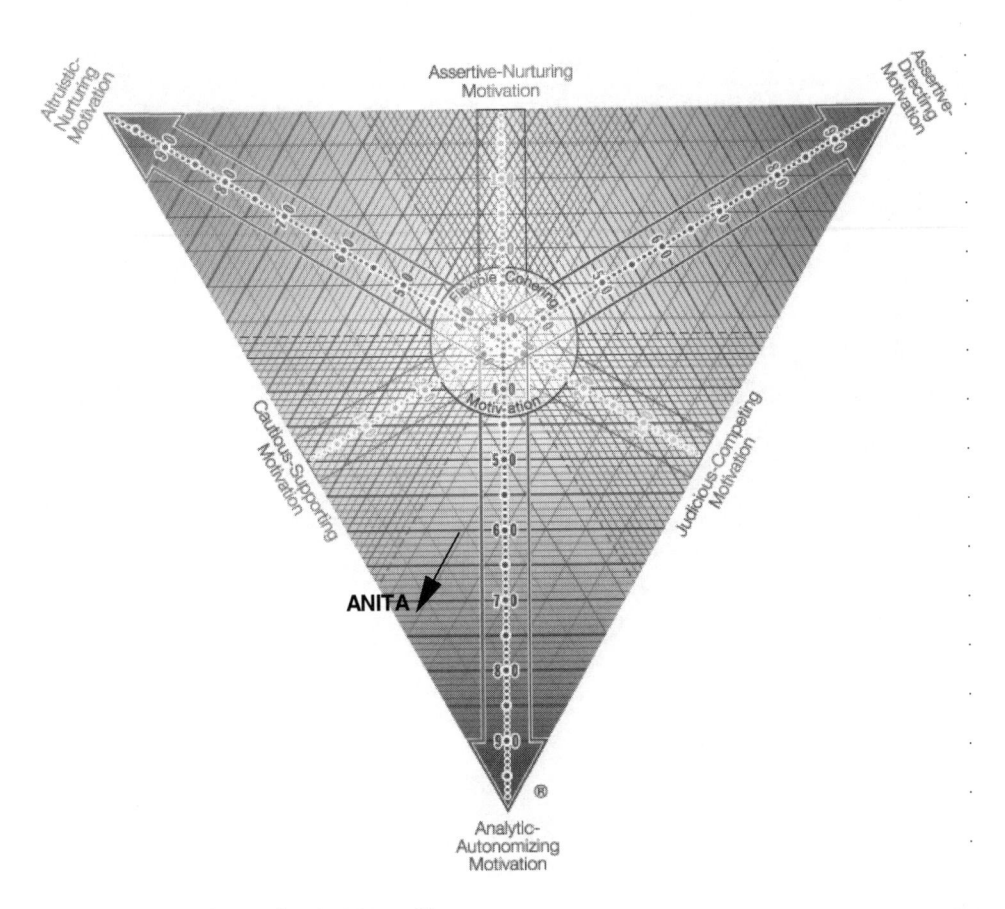

Figure 8.8 Anita Kaskett's SDI profile.

situation before she takes any action or says anything for fear that it might appear confrontational and not be relevant to the situation at all. In many cases she will settle the conflict by deferring to the other party rather than stand firm.

Sy Yonara's SDI profile. Sy, much like Olive and Mike, is another example of a person whose conflict sequence is different from his valued-relating style. His scores are (4, 31, 65) and (4, 58, 38) when things are going well and when things are not going well, respectively. Sy is an analytic person, as indicated by his high score on the analytic-autonomizing dimension. When placed in a conflict situation Sy will abandon his logical and analytic style and become competitive, as indicated by his high score on the assertive-directing dimension. He wants to win by a show of force and a take-charge attitude. He will fall back on his logical and analytic style if his challenge is not successful.

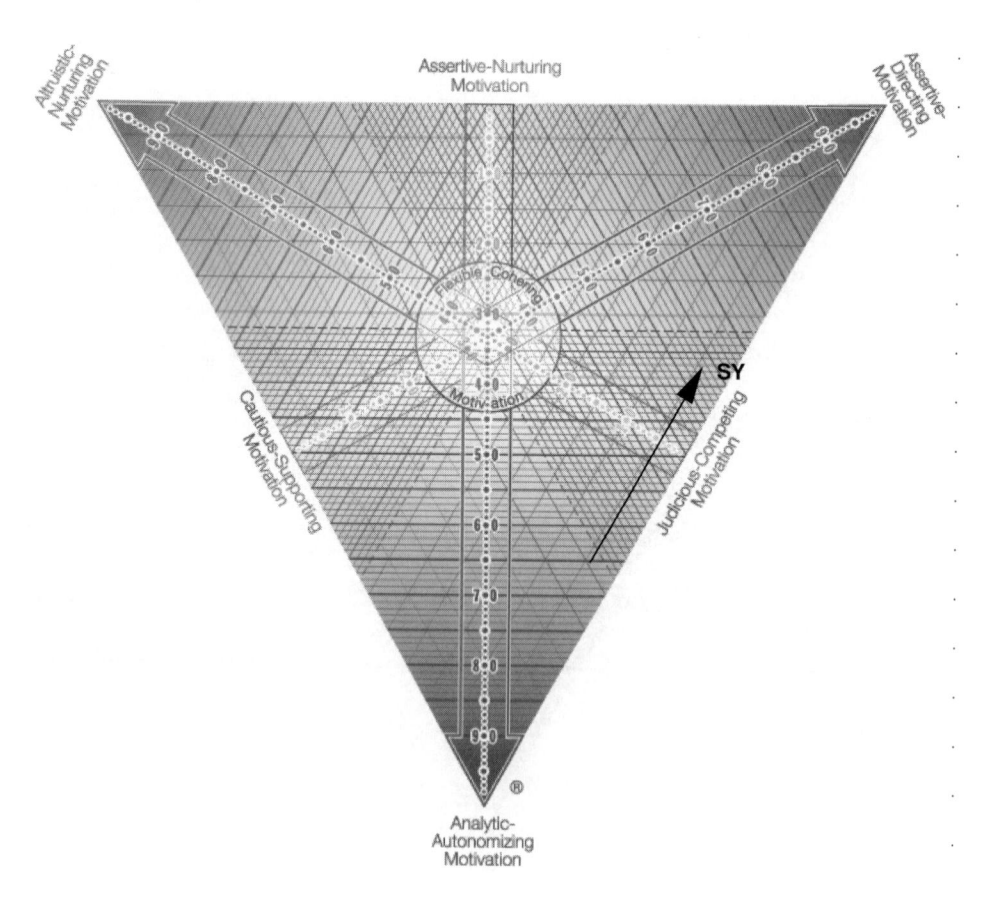

Figure 8.9 Sy Yonara's SDI profile.

He and Mike are quite similar in that they do not have a high regard for the people with whom they share the conflict, which is indicated by Sy's low score on the altruistic-nurturing dimension when things are going well as well as when he is in a conflict situation.

Putting It All Together

We have now added another assessment tool to our toolkit. Looking ahead for a moment, we will superimpose the arrows of each team member on one scoring triangle. If the team is balanced with respect to its motivational values and conflict management strategies, we should see a fairly even distribution across the triangle. This information will help us determine what types of conflict situations should be handled by which team member. If the pattern of arrows is not widely distributed across the scoring triangle we will have to put strategies in place to counter-balance that uneven distribution. That is the topic of Chapter 11, "Establishing the Profile of the Project Team," Chapter 12, "Assessing Team Alignment and Balance," and Chapter 13, "Developing and Deploying the Project Team." In the next chapter we will add the last assessment tool to our toolkit—the skill and competency data.

CHAPTER 9

Project Management Skills and Competencies

This chapter introduces two tools for measuring the skills and competencies of the project manager. Skills are the basic building blocks of competencies. They are something that we can measure directly by observing the individual at work and that the individuals can also assess by themselves. Skills can be obtained directly by training. Competencies are a bit more complex. They may consist of several skills. They are often measured indirectly.

The first tool is the *Project Manager Skill Assessment* (PMSA). PMSA consists of a set of 54 skills that are related to the practice of project management. Not all the skills are specific to the technical aspects of project management, however. The 54 skills span project management (18 skills), management (9 skills), business (14 skills), personal (6 skills), and interpersonal (7 skills) areas. All 54 can be measured and their proficiency established using *Bloom's Taxonomy*. Bloom's Taxonomy has been around for a number of years and is a well-established metric for measuring skill attainment. As presented here, skills and proficiencies are self-assessed.

A second tool is one to measure of a person's abilities in project management, called *Project Manager Competency Assessment* (PMCA). The PMCA is a 360-degree assessment where the respondents are peers, subordinates, and superiors. The respondents base their answers on observations of the individual's behavior in project management type situations. This tool helps to determine the individual's project management competencies.

> **FOR YOUR REFERENCE** For those who would like more information on how to acquire the PMSA and PMCA, refer to Appendix B, "Sources of Information," and Appendix C, "How to Get TeamArchitect Tools."

Project Manager Skill Assessment

If you think that all it takes to be a successful project manager are the block and tackle skills of project management, read on. I have some news for you. Yes, it is true that you will need skills that relate directly to scoping, project planning, execution, tracking, and status reporting, as well as closing, but you need a lot more.

Skills

In 1990, I set out to determine what it takes to be a world-class project manager. After a lot of searching and talking with project management professionals I found that the characteristics of a world-class project manager could be described by a set of 54 skills grouped into 5 general categories. There was pretty strong agreement among those with whom I had consulted that this set of 54 skills was comprehensive of the skill sets currently used by most practitioners. I felt confident that I could advocate the use of the 54 skills without any fear of having forgotten something important. Those skills, listed by general category, are as follows:

Project Management Skills

- Charter development
- Complexity assessment
- Cost estimating
- Cost managing
- Critical path management
- Detailed estimating
- Project closeout
- Project management software
- Project notebook construction/maintenance

Project organization
Project planning
Project progress assessment
Resource acquisition
Resource leveling
Resource requirements
Schedule development
Scope management
Size estimating

Management Skills

Delegation
Leadership
Managing change
Managing multiple priorities
Meeting management
Performance management
Quality management
Staff and career development
Staffing, hiring, selection

Business Skills

Budgeting
Business assessment
Business case justification
Business functions
Business process design
Company products/services
Core application systems
Customer service
Implementation
Planning: strategic/tactical

Product/vendor evaluation
Procedures and policies
Systems integration
Testing

Interpersonal Skills

Conflict management
Flexibility
Influencing
Interpersonal relations
Negotiating
Relationship management
Team management/building

Personal Skills

Creativity
Decision making/critical thinking
Presentations
Problem solving/troubleshooting
Verbal communications
Written communications

Because projects are not done independently of one or more business disciplines, the use of the 54 skills will probably be supplemented with a comparable skill assessment of such areas as information technology, accounting, finance, marketing, sales, and executive management. While these are not presented here, you can refer to Appendix B for information on how to acquire skill assessments for these business disciplines.

Measuring Skill Proficiency Levels

In order to measure an individual's mastery of each skill, you need a metric that will assess the person's proficiency in practicing the skill. The metric will have to be applied uniformly across all skills and be easy to remember and apply. Rather than create my own, I chose to use a well-established metric that is very familiar to those in the adult education and skill assessment business. I use *Bloom's Taxonomy of Educational Objectives—Cognitive Domain* to measure skill levels. Bloom's Taxonomy is a six-level taxonomy that measures cognitive abilities. It is based on observable and verifiable events as they relate to each of the skills. Listed in the text that follows is a definition of each of the six levels of Bloom's Taxonomy. For each, I present a summary of Bloom's definition and then apply it specifically to our team effectiveness application.

1.0 Knowledge (I can define it). Knowledge, as defined here, involves *the remembering or recalling* of ideas, materials, or phenomena. For measurement purposes, the recall situations involve little more than bringing to mind the appropriate material. Although some alteration of the material may be required, this is a relatively minor part of the task. If the individual can state the definition of a term or concept, he or she has a level 1 proficiency.

2.0 Comprehension (I can explain how it works). Those objectives, behaviors, or responses that represent an understanding of the literal message contained in a communication are the basis for level 2 proficiency. In reaching such understanding the individual may change the communication in his or her mind or in his or her overt responses to some parallel form more meaningful to him or her. There may also be responses that represent simple extensions beyond what is given in the communication itself. If the individual not only states the definition but also explains what it means, he or she has demonstrated level 2 proficiency.

3.0 Application (I have limited experience using it in simple situations). This skill level involves the use of abstractions in particular and concrete situations. The abstractions may be in the form of general ideas, rules, procedures, or generalized methods. The abstractions may also be technical principles, ideas, and theories that must be remembered and applied. The key here is the application for level 3 proficiency, which is the first level in Bloom's Taxonomy at which experience is a prerequisite.

A demonstration of application is that the individual will use an abstraction correctly, given an appropriate situation in which no mode of solution is specified. The ability to apply generalizations and conclusions to real-life problems and the ability to apply science principles, postulates, theorems, or other abstractions to new situations are the basis for level 3 proficiency.

4.0 Analysis (I have extensive experience using it in complex situations). This skill level involves the breakdown of a communication into its constituent elements or parts such that the relative hierarchy of ideas is made clear and/or the relations between the ideas expressed are made explicit. Such analyses are intended to clarify the communication, to indicate how the communication is organized and the way in which it manages to convey its effects, as well as its basis and arrangement. Analysis deals with both the content and form of material.

At level 4 proficiency the individual has the ability to dissect the skill and use it in more complex situations. It is distinguished from level 3 in that at level 3 the individual is merely required to repeat a series of steps without the need for any adaptation as would be the case in more complex situations.

5.0 Synthesis (I can adapt it to other uses). The putting together of elements and parts so as to form a whole distinguishes level 5 from level 4. This involves the process of working with pieces, parts, elements, and more and arranging and combining them in such a way as to constitute a pattern or structure not clearly there before. In other words, the individual has the ability to adapt the skill into areas somewhat different than those for which it was originally designed. This adaptation is clear evidence that the individual has mastered the skill to a level of broad and deep experiences.

6.0 Evaluation (I am recognized as an expert by my peers). Judgments about the value of material and methods for given purposes establish the individual as one who can choose between alternatives to pick the one best suited for the situation. Quantitative and qualitative judgments about the extent to which material and methods satisfy criteria are also part of this proficiency level. The criteria may be those determined by the individual or those that are given to him.

To make it easy to assess an individual's proficiency level I developed a set of generic statements for each proficiency level. These are shown in Table 9.1. The generic statements at a particular proficiency level are checked against the individual's knowledge and skills. If there is evidence that they have achieved all the statements at that level, then the conclusion is that they are proficient at that level. These statements are the same regardless of the skill in question. I find that that approach is much easier than having to remember skill-specific statements.

Table 9.1 Generic Knowledge, Skills, Behaviors, and Experiences for Each Proficiency Level

LEVEL	KNOWLEDGE/SKILL
Level 0	**I never heard of it** 0.
Level 1	**I can define it.** 1. Familiar with the terminology. 2. Understands the basic concepts and features.
Level 2	**I understand what it can do.** 1. Knows how it is used. 2. Can explain key issues and benefits. 3. Understands organizational relevance.
Level 3	**I have limited hands-on experience.** 1. Has a working knowledge of basic features and functions. 2. Aware of relevant standards, policies, and practices. 3. Requires assistance and supervision. 4. Can apply it in a limited (homogeneous) environment.
Level 4	**I have extensive hands-on experience.** 1. Knowledge of operational issues and considerations. 2. Understanding of benefits and drawbacks. 3. Working knowledge of interdependencies, relationships, and integration. 4. In-depth knowledge of major features, functions, and facilities. 5. Awareness of usage in other environments. 6. Can work without assistance.
Level 5	**I can adapt it to a variety of situations.** 1. Theoretical background and understanding. 2. Expertise in all major features, functions, and facilities. 3. Expertise in multiple environments (heterogeneous). 4. Knowledge of and contribution to "best practices." 5. Ability to consult with and coach others.
Level 6	**I am recognized as an expert by my peers.** 1. Extensive experience in multiple/complex environments. 2. Industry and marketplace perspective. 3. Historical and future perspective. 4. Influencing wide- or high-impact decisions and initiatives. 5. Leadership on architecture, policies, strategy, and "best practices."

What Does Your Skill Profile Tell You?

What level of project can you manage? After you have assessed your proficiency with respect to each of the 54 skills, it is time to compare your profile to that of each of the four types of project managers. By comparing your profile to each of the four types of project managers you can determine your readiness to take on the responsibility of each project manager type. Table 9.2 through Table 9.6 give the proficiency levels for project management, management, business, personal, and interpersonal areas as a function of project manager class. Recall from Chapter 2, "The Project Environment," that the four project types and their associated project manager types are defined as follows:

Simple (Type IV projects). These are the simplest projects and require an individual with the minimal set of project manager skills. This person will be at the bottom of the project manager career ladder. In some organizations he or she may be called a team leader, in which case his or her Type IV project may actually be a subproject of a much larger and more complex project.

Organizationally complex (Type III projects). Type III projects are led by a project manager or senior project manager. In addition to meeting the skill requirements of the 54 project manager skills, this individual will also have to meet additional skill and competency requirements in one or more business disciplines. The assessment of those skills and competencies is beyond the scope of this book. Consult Appendices B and C for information on how to acquire those skill and competency assessments.

Technically complex (Type II projects). Type II projects are led by a project manager or senior project manager. In addition to meeting the skill requirements of the 54 project manager skills, this individual will also have to meet additional skill and competency requirements in one or more technical disciplines. The assessment of those skills and competencies is beyond the scope of this book. Consult Appendices B and C for information on how to acquire those skill and competency assessments.

Critical mission (Type I projects). Type I projects are the most challenging projects an organization will undertake. Not only are they organizationally and technically complex, but they are also critical to the viability of the organization. A senior project manager or program manager leads these projects. In many cases, these projects are so large that they have been partitioned into several smaller projects under less demanding situations. Type I projects will generally have a program manager at the helm with several project managers accountable to the program manager.

Based on input from a number of my project management colleagues I was able to establish the baseline proficiency level for each of the 54 skills for each of the four types of projects. These are arrayed in Tables 9.2 through 9.6. In practice a number of my clients have taken these to be minimum requirements, and in selected cases they have increased the required proficiency level for several skills. As you examine the tables, note how the minimum proficiency levels in each of the skills change as you move from Type IV to Type I projects. Also note that the required proficiency level for Type II and Type III projects is the same.

There are differences in skill requirements, but they are for skills that are not part of the 54 skills defined for project managers. Those skills are specific business function skills and technical skills and should be considered in any specific application in your company. They are beyond the scope of this book. By comparing your skill profile with these profiles you can identify skill development needs as you progress through the ranks of project management.

Table 9.2 Project Management Skills of the Project Manager

PROJECT MANAGEMENT SKILL	IV	III	II	I
Charter development	3	4	4	4
Complex assessment	–	3	3	4
Cost estimating	3	4	4	5
Cost managing	3	4	4	5
Critical path management	3	4	4	4
Detailed estimating	3	4	4	5
Project closeout	3	4	4	5
Project management software expertise	4	4	4	4
Project notebook construction/maintenance	3	4	4	4
Project organization	–	3	3	5
Project planning	3	4	4	4
Project progress assessment	2	3	3	4
Resource acquisition	2	4	4	5
Resource leveling	2	4	4	5
Resource requirements	2	4	4	5
Schedule development	3	3	3	4
Scope management	3	4	4	5
Size estimating	3	4	4	5

Table 9.3 Management Skills of the Project Manager

MANAGEMENT SKILLS	IV	III	II	I
Delegation	3	4	4	5
Leadership	3	4	4	5
Managing change	3	4	4	4
Managing multiple priorities	3	4	4	5
Meeting management	3	4	4	5
Performance management	3	4	4	5
Quality management	3	4	4	4
Staff and career development	3	4	4	5
Staffing, hiring, selection	4	4	4	4

Table 9.4 Business Skills of the Project Manager

BUSINESS SKILLS	IV	III	II	I
Budgeting	3	4	4	5
Business assessment	—	4	4	5
Business case justification	3	4	4	5
Business functions	3	4	4	5
Business process design	3	4	4	5
Company products/services	3	4	4	5
Core application systems	3	4	4	4
Customer service	3	4	4	5
Implementation	4	5	5	5
Planning: strategic and tactical	3	4	4	5
Product/vendor evaluation	—	3	3	5
Standards, procedures, policies	2	3	3	4
Systems and technology integration	2	4	4	5
Testing	2	4	4	5

Table 9.5 Interpersonal Skills of the Project Manager

INTERPERSONAL SKILLS	IV	III	II	I
Conflict management	3	4	4	4
Flexibility	3	4	4	4
Influencing	–	3	3	4
Interpersonal relations	3	4	4	4
Negotiating	–	3	3	4
Relationship management	–	4	4	5
Team management/building	3	4	4	4

Table 9.6 Personal Skills of the Project Manager

PERSONAL SKILLS	IV	III	II	I
Creativity	3	4	4	5
Decision making/critical thinking	–	4	4	5
Presentations	3	4	4	5
Problem solving/troubleshooting	3	4	4	5
Verbal communications	3	4	4	4
Written communications	3	3	3	4

For a given project assignment, expect to find several areas of deficiency. These will be skills to further develop and should be part of the development and deployment strategy discussed in Part Four.

FURTHER READING For more information, you also may consult the related publication, *The World-Class Project Manager: A Professional Development Guide* by Wysocki and Lewis (Perseus Books, 2001).

Candidate Pool Members' PMSA

This skill profile is rather straightforward and needs little explanation. Because it would be repetitive to show more than one, here is the skill profile for Olive. These skills are all self-reported by Olive. The shaded columns indicate where she possesses the proficiencies needed for projects of Type IV through Type I. Note, for example, in Figure 9.1 that she has a proficiency level of 3 in complexity assessment, and that is sufficient to manage projects of Type II. On the other hand, her proficiency levels in detailed estimating, project closeout, project management software expertise, project planning, schedule development, scope management and size estimating do not even meet the minimum proficiency requirements for Type IV projects, and these are the simplest of projects. Bottom line, if Olive wants to be a project manager, she has a long way to go in skill development to qualify for the simple Type IV projects.

In some organizations skill assessments are done by the individual and by their manager, either together or independently. The two assessments are then discussed by the manager and the individual, variances are noted and resolved, and a single assessment is agreed to. This will often become the basis for career and professional development programs.

PROJECT MANAGEMENT SKILLS	SELF-ASSESSED SKILL LEVEL	PROJECT COMPLEXITY REQUIREMENT			
		IV	III	II	I
Charter Development	3	3	4	4	4
Complexity Assessment	3	-	3	3	4
Cost Estimating	3	3	4	4	5
Cost Management	3	3	4	4	5
Critical Path Management	3	3	4	4	4
Detailed Estimating	2	3	4	4	5
Project Closeout	2	3	4	4	5
Project Management Software Expertise	3	4	4	4	4
Project Notebook Construction/Maintenance	3	3	4	4	4
Project Organization	2	-	3	3	5
Project Planning	2	3	4	4	4
Project Progress Assessment	3	2	3	3	4
Resource Acquisition	2	2	4	4	5
Resource Leveling	2	2	4	4	5
Resource Requirements	2	2	4	4	5
Schedule Development	2	3	3	3	4
Scope Management	2	3	4	4	5
Size Estimating	1	3	4	4	5

Figure 9.1 Olive Branch's project management skill profile.

FURTHER READING The interested reader can consult *The World-Class Project Manager: A Professional Development Guide* by Wysocki and Lewis (Perseus Books, 2000).

Figure 9.2 reports Olive's personal and interpersonal skills. Figure 9.3 reports her business and management skills.

From Olive's skill profile, you can see that she does not possess the skills to be a project manager. Her self-reported proficiency levels fall below the minimums even for Type IV projects. Note from Figure 9.2 that Olive's personal and interpersonal skills are very strong, even for more complex projects of Type II and I. She should provide good support as a project administrator. Olive's management and business skills are strong in business functions, company products/services, core application systems, standards, procedures, policies, managing multiple priorities and quality management. In other words, she understands the company, and she seems to know her way around. She should be a good asset to the project manager in that regard.

Her real strength is in the personal and interpersonal skill areas. She works very well with people, and her skills set reflects that as well. We learned from her LSI profile in Chapter 7, "Problem-Solving and Decision-

	SELF-ASSESSED SKILL LEVEL	PROJECT COMPLEXITY REQUIREMENT			
		IV	III	II	I
PERSONAL SKILLS					
Creativity	3	3	4	4	5
Decision Making/Crtitical Thinking	4	-	4	4	5
Presentations	4	3	4	4	5
Problem Solving/Troubleshooting	5	3	4	4	5
Verbal Communications	5	3	4	4	4
Written Communications	5	3	3	3	4
INTERPERSONAL SKILLS					
Conflcit Management	4	3	4	4	4
Flexibility	5	3	4	4	4
Influencing	3	-	3	3	4
Interpersonal Relations	4	3	4	4	4
Negotiating	4	-	3	3	4
Relationship Management	4	-	4	4	5
Team Management/Building	3	3	4	4	4

Figure 9.2 Olive Branch's personal and interpersonal skill profile.

	SELF-ASSESSED SKILL LEVEL	PROJECT COMPLEXITY REQUIREMENT			
		IV	III	II	I
BUSINESS SKILLS					
Budgeting	3	3	4	4	5
Business Assessment	2	-	4	4	5
Business Case Justification	2	3	4	4	5
Business Functions	5	3	4	4	5
Business Process Design	3	3	4	4	5
Company Products/Services	5	3	4	4	5
Core Application Systems	4	3	4	4	4
Customer Service	4	3	4	4	5
Implementation	4	4	5	5	5
Planning: Strategic and Tactical	2	3	4	4	5
Product/Vendor Evaluation	3	-	3	3	5
Standards, Procedures, Policies	5	2	3	3	4
Systems and Technology Integration	2	2	4	4	5
Testing	3	2	4	4	5
MANAGEMENT SKILLS					
Delegation	3	3	4	4	5
Leadership	2	3	4	4	5
Managing Change	3	3	4	4	5
Managing Multiple Priorities	5	3	4	4	5
Meeting Management	4	3	4	4	5
Performance Management	3	3	4	4	5
Quality Management	4	3	4	4	4
Staff and Career Development	3	3	4	4	5
Staffing, Hiring, Selection	2	4	4	4	4

Figure 9.3 Olive Branch's business and management skill profile.

Making Styles," that she is an accommodator and from her SDI profile in Chapter 8, "Conflict Management Styles and Strategies," that she is a people person, first and always. Her interpersonal skill profile suggests that she is rather passive, as noted from her low proficiencies in conflict management, influencing, and relationship management. She probably could use a dose of more aggressive behavior. Her business and management skills will be very complementary to whoever is the project manager throughout the project. She and the project manager should make a good, mutually supportive pair.

Figures 9.1 through 9.3 are a good way to present raw skill data, but they are a bit cumbersome for comparison and interpretation if we are interested in the skill profiles of two or more teams. Figure 9.4 is a template that uses a Kiviatt Chart to display the range of skill profile values for each project type. Such diagrams are very useful for displaying several variables on one diagram. In fact, the HBDI is also an adaptation of the Kiviatt Chart. Let's walk through how the upper and lower values of the shaded areas are calculated. For example purposes, I will show only the calculations for the project management skill area.

Recall from earlier in this chapter that the maximum proficiency level is 6. Because there are 18 skills in the project management area, the maximum total skill proficiency score for project management is 18 times 6, or 108. If we add the minimum proficiency level required for each skill in the project management area, we get 82; 82 is the 76th percentile of 108, and it is the minimum total project management skill proficiency required for Type I

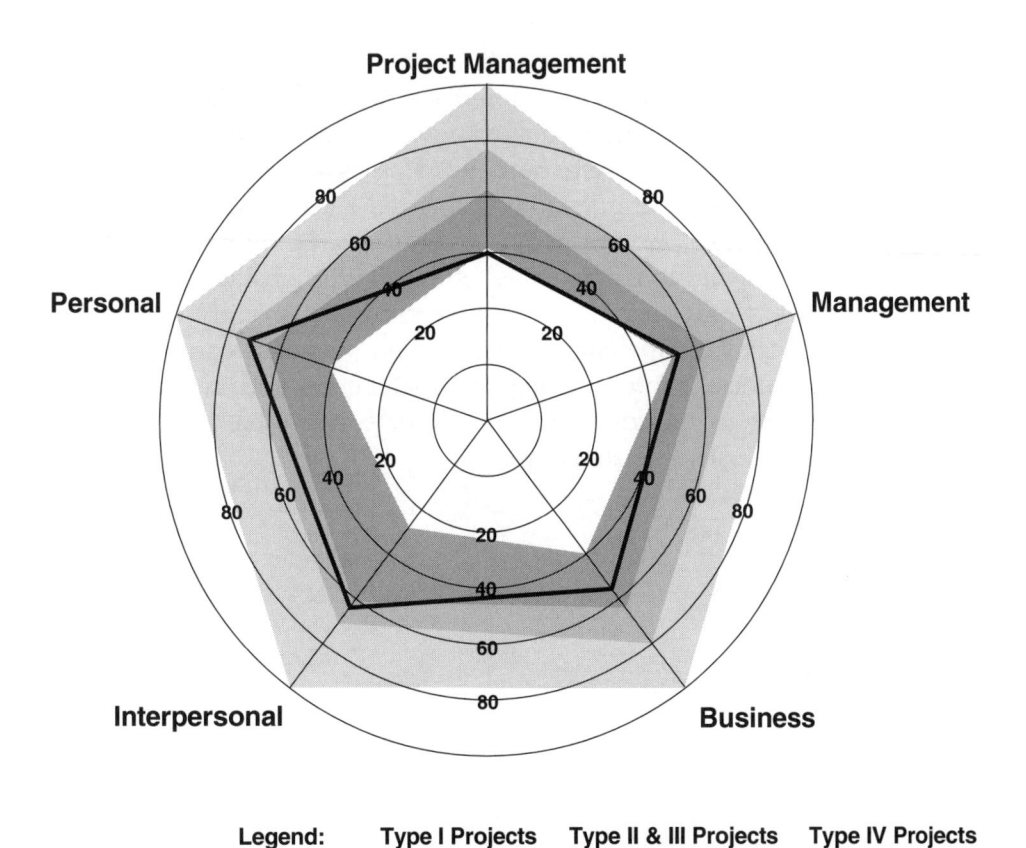

Figure 9.4 Olive Branch's skill percentile profile.

projects. That defines the lower value of the project management skill percentile.

The same type of calculation gives us the lower values for the other four skill areas for Type I projects. They are shown on the graph with the lightest shading. The lower values for Type II and III projects are the same and are shown on the graph in the medium shading. The lower values for Type IV projects are shown on the graph in the darkest shading. We will use this template to plot actual skill profile data for individuals, as shown next, and later for teams and the entire candidate pool.

Project Manager Competency Assessment

The PMCA is done only for the project manager. Unlike the skill assessment, which was a self-assessment done by every team member, the competency assessment is a 360-degree assessment that is done by subordinates, superiors, and peers. These individuals complete the competency survey in which they are asked to comment on observable behaviors of the project manager as they relate to one or more competencies. The project manager will also complete a self-competency assessment as well.

The PMCA consists of 72 questions formatted as semantic differential questions. For example, one of the questions is this: Develops innovative and creative approaches to problems when faced with obstacles or limitations. The answers range from "strongly agree" to "strongly disagree." There are four major competency areas profiled: business competencies, personal competencies, interpersonal competencies, and management competencies. Each of the four areas is further subdivided to produce a total of 18 competencies, as listed here.

Business Competencies

    Business awareness

    Business partnership

    Commitment to quality

Personal Competencies

    Initiative

    Information gathering

    Conceptual thinking

    Self-confidence

Concern for credibility

Flexibility

Interpersonal Competencies

Interpersonal awareness

Organizational awareness

Anticipation of impact

Resourceful use of influence

Management Competencies

Motivating others

Communications skills

Developing others

Planning

Monitoring and controlling

One of the more interesting features of the PMCA is the fact that the individual's self-assessment is shown along with the distribution of their assessors' data. There have often been some illuminating comparisons between the two. Often an individual will have an inflated perception of his or her competencies, and this becomes evident in the report that compares the individual's assessment with that of his or her peers. The resulting analysis will pinpoint areas where the individual needs some development. Left to his or her own assessment these development areas would never be identified. We will see some examples of this later.

The PMCA is a 360-degree assessment tool. The 360 comes from the fact that a person is assessed by his or her peers, subordinates, and manager. As many as 8 to 10 people may be involved as assessors. The report that is produced is merely a summary of their responses and the self-reported response of the individual being assessed. The report is graphical, as described later in this chapter.

Candidate Pool Members' PMCA

First, let me make some general comments about the report. Refer to Figure 9.5. The graphic associated with each of the 18 competencies needs a little explanation. The endpoints of the heavy line show the range. The

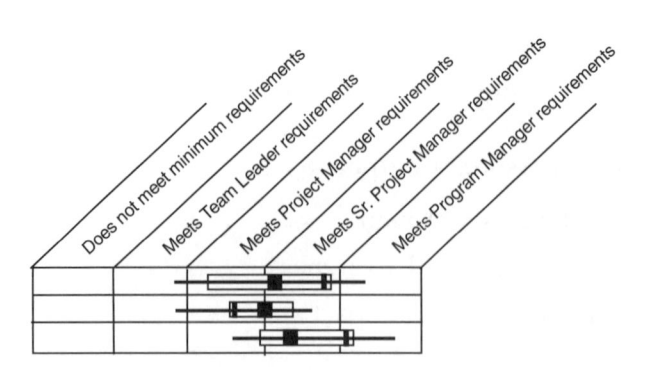

Business Competencies
- Business Awareness
- Business Partnership
- Commitment to Quality

(Rating scale: Does not meet minimum requirements / Meets Team Leader requirements / Meets Project Manager requirements / Meets Sr. Project Manager requirements / Meets Program Manager requirements)

Personal Competencies
- Initiative
- Information Gathering
- Conceptual Thinking
- Self Confidence
- Concern for Credibility
- Flexibility

Interpersonal Competencies
- Interpersonal Awareness
- Organizational Awareness
- Anticipation of Impact
- Resourceful Use of Influence

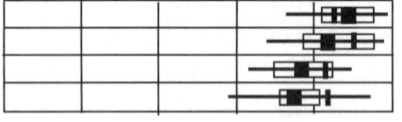

Management Competencies
- Motivating Others
- Communication Skills
- Developing Others
- Planning
- Monitoring & Controlling

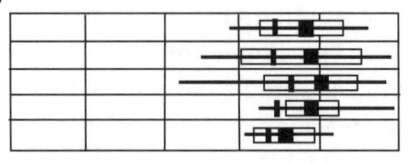

Figure 9.5 Hal's PMCA profile.

hollow rectangle is the interquartile range (a.k.a. middle half of the data). The narrower the interquartile range, the more agreement there is between the assessors. That is the case with several competencies, notably information gathering, interpersonal awareness, resourceful use of influence, and planning. The wider the interquartile range, the less agreement there is between assessors. That is the case with conceptual thinking. The filled square is the average response of the assessors. The narrow vertical bar is the individual's self-assessment of his or her competency.

The scale across the top tells us how the individual's competencies map to project manager roles. At the left-most column the individual does not meet minimum requirements to manage teams or projects at the lowest level. As you move across the columns the person's competencies map into higher and higher levels of project management responsibility. At the right-most column his or her competency level is sufficient to manage programs and hence the most complex types of projects the company might encounter. The position of the graphic with respect to these columns provides us with the necessary information to assess the individual's competency with respect to project management. Hal E. Lewya and Pearl E. Gates are the only two candidates for project manager. Let's take a look at their PMCA profiles and see what we can learn about them.

Hal E. Lewya's PMCA profile. Figure 9.5 is the result of the competency assessment for Hal. First, are there any glaring problem areas that Hal needs to address? Generally, he is very strong. His weakest area is in his personal competencies. He needs to work on his self-confidence. Note that his assessors also picked up on this, and although Hal is somewhat more positive about his self-confidence than his assessors, they are in pretty good agreement about this area. Conceptual thinking shows some interesting results. First, there are divergent opinions about Hal, as evidenced by the wide range of responses. The interquartile range spans the middle third of the grid, and the overall range spans nearly the entire range of possible responses. That would suggest that Hal doesn't appear the same to people across the organization. This is an area that deserves more introspection but is beyond the scope of our present assessment. Hal's interpersonal competencies and management competencies are exemplary, as evidenced by the narrow interquartile ranges for all nine of the competencies represented and the fact that they are positioned under the right-most columns.

Note that Hal has a more positive perception about himself than do his assessors in business awareness, commitment to quality, self confidence, flexibility, resourceful use of influence, and a few other competency areas. Hal should give some thought to the reasons for this variance. The same can be said about those competencies for which Hal has a lower perception of himself than do his assessors. None of the discrepancies between his self-assessment and those of his assessors are large enough to raise any serious concerns.

In summary, Hal is solid. Others see him as competent in all relevant areas. His interpersonal competency profile suggests that his colleagues view him in a very positive light. He is somewhat marginal in his personal competencies, especially in the conceptual thinking and self-confidence areas. There is no reason for concern, however. He has what it takes to be the manager of a mission-critical project.

Pearl E. Gates's PMCA profile. Figure 9.6 is the PMCA for Pearl. Note the differences as compared with Hal's profile. Pearl has a much higher self-image of herself than do the managers who provided the

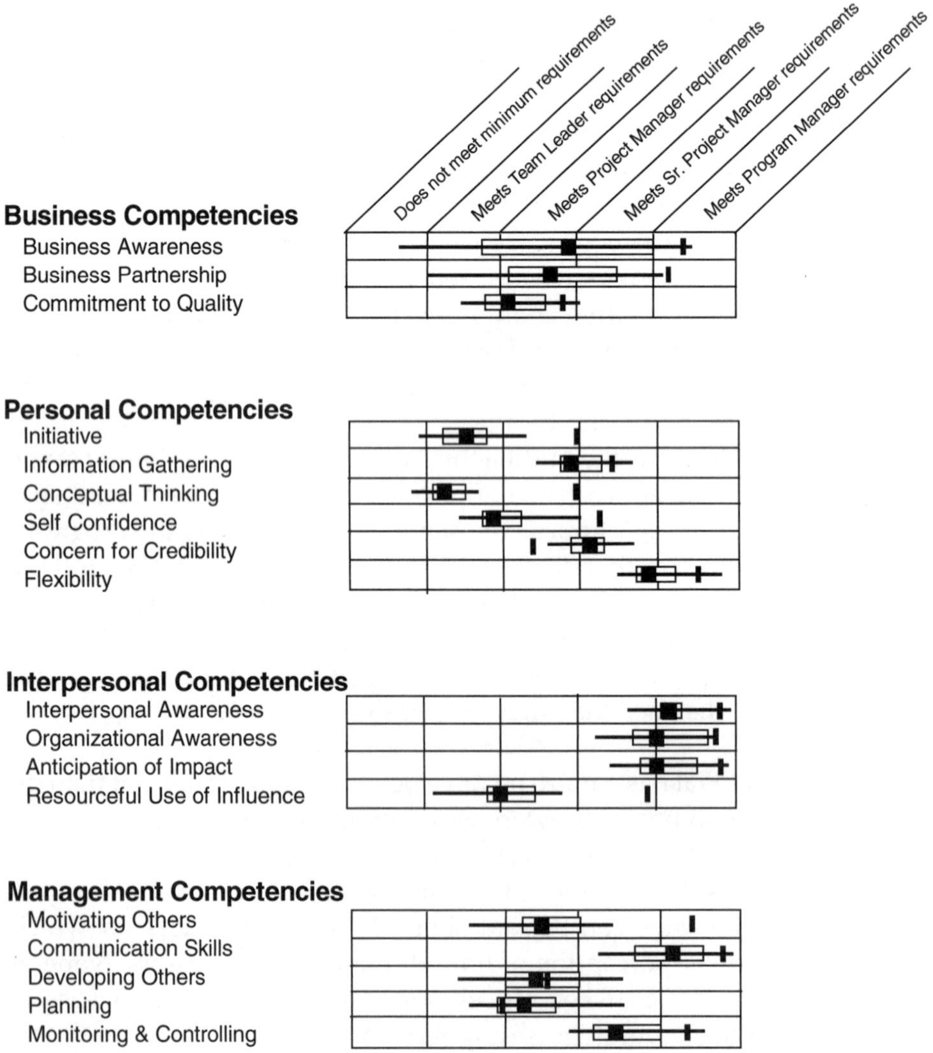

Figure 9.6 Pearl's PMCA profile.

competency data, as evidenced by her self-assessment data point lying to the right of the interquartile range of her assessors' data. This is especially evident in business awareness, business partnership, initiative, conceptual thinking, resourceful use of influence, and motivating others. Pearl needs to take a close look at how she sees herself relative to how others see her. This self-inflated phenomenon is not unusual. I have seen it time and again in many of these assessments. People are simply not aware of how they affect others. As a group, her interpersonal competencies are held in high regard by her fellow workers. Her personal competencies, especially initiative, conceptual thinking, and self-confidence, may be problematic if she is chosen as the project manager. In summary, Pearl's self-assessment of her competencies is not reflected by her fellow workers. She needs to seek professional help in planning a personal development program that focuses on the competency areas that have been highlighted in her PMCA.

Putting It All Together

This completes the toolkit. We now have the HBDI, LSI, SDI, PMSA, and PMCA data in our toolkit. These are the building blocks that we will use in the remainder of the book to build our project teams and assess the degree to which they are balanced. This also completes Part Two of the book. In the next chapter, we will introduce another use of the HBDI: to profile the project that our team is going to work on.

PART Three

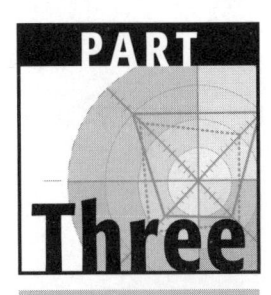

Formation

CHAPTER 10

Establishing the Profile of the Project

We know that projects come in all sizes and descriptions. Some, like process reengineering projects, will require extensive data collection and creativity on the part of the team. Others will involve very difficult and sensitive problem situations that must be resolved. Others will be straightforward applications of established procedures, and finally there will be projects that require exemplary communications and interaction between the customer and the developer.

These projects are all very different from one another, and, in order to maximize their likelihood of success; each should be staffed with teams that somehow have been formed on the basis of these project-to-project differences. As a result, the project and the team will be aligned for success. But how can we do that? The solution presented in this book is that to establish project and team alignment, we will need a single metric that measures the characteristics of the project and, at the same time, measures the characteristics of the project team. The key is to do so using the same set of characteristics for both the project and the team.

This impasse puzzled me for several years, and not until I attended an ASTD (American Society for Training and Development) conference in the mid-1990s did I discover a tool that held the promise of a solution. I recall that the booth on the exhibit floor had the word "brain" rather prominently displayed across its banner. I was interested in brain mapping, problem solving, and related topics, and so I stopped to find out more. I was introduced to Ned Herrmann, who invited me to sit with him and discuss my situation. Three hours later, after a great deal of exciting and revealing discussion, I knew I had found what I was looking for. That tool was the HBDI, which was introduced in Chapter 6, "Thinking Styles."

Ned Herrmann developed the HBDI to measure thinking styles as input to designing management education curricula and training programs. As a follow-on application Ned had also been using an adaptation of the HBDI to describe a company's annual report. He did that by establishing a relationship between words and combinations of words and the four HBDI quadrants. By counting the number of words in a document that fell into each of the four quadrants and then normalizing the counts, he could create a four-quadrant kite of the document. He called the resulting kite a *pro forma*.

He had had great success with this in his consulting practice and was able to portray such things as the degree to which senior management's thinking styles aligned with what they were saying in their annual report. Wow! The light went on immediately. If he could do that with annual reports, why couldn't I do that with project scope statements? I talked this over with Ned, and he didn't see any reason why not; although he had never tried it.

A few years passed before I was in a position to verify with actual test data that that could be done. This was a major breakthrough in my efforts to improve team effectiveness. It meant that I could superimpose the thinking styles of the project team on the HBDI profile of the project scope statement and assess the degree to which the two were in alignment with one another. Any significant misalignment could be corrected by team formation strategies, deployment, and training or by creating awareness on the part of the project manager and the project team members of potential problems that might result from that misalignment. Coupled with this awareness I could also offer proscriptive measures to mitigate the risks that might arise due to that misalignment.

Based on over 35 years of project management experience, both as a consultant and as a practitioner, I felt confident that I could offer corrective action plans for any situation that might be uncovered from such an analysis. That marked the beginnings of a journey that led me to the development of TeamArchitect and the writing of this book. *TeamArchitect* is a decision support system (DSS) primarily for use by project managers; it is designed to help them improve their project team's effectiveness.

My work with Herrmann International continues. We have jointly developed a system that we call the *Project Profiling System*. It accepts as input a project scope document and produces as output a four-quadrant graphic that maps the project to the four thinking styles. By purchasing this book you have the option of using the Project Profiling System for your projects. Appendix C, "How to Get TeamArchitect Tools," contains the details about how you can take advantage of this tool. If you are pleased with the results, Appendix C will also tell you how to arrange to use the Project Profiling System for other projects. I am furthering my research efforts with Herrmann International to incorporate the HBDI into the processes I have developed for team assessment, formation, development, and deployment. The Web-based project/team profiling system, which is part of TeamArchitect, is the first deliverable to come from this collaborative effort, and it is introduced for the first time in this book.

This chapter and the next two are the key to understanding why TeamArchitect is so powerful and insightful. In fact, TeamArchitect opens a number of new and innovative possibilities for significantly and positively affecting project success. In this chapter and the next two I will put these ideas together. This chapter focuses on profiling the project, and the next focuses on profiling the project team. The final chapter in Part Three puts the two profiles together and discusses the analyses and further team development and deployment strategies that logically follow from it.

Every Project Has a Profile

A *project profile* is a graphical representation of the project in the four quadrants of the Whole Brain Model of the HBDI. Every project profile is a mixture of all four quadrants, with some quadrants having a stronger representation than others. There is no correct profile.

TeamArchitect uses this project profiling technique as its project classification rule. It works in parallel with the project complexity model and the project classification rule introduced in Chapter 2, "The Project Environment." It is robust so that whatever model or scheme your organization uses, the TeamArchitect classification rule will complement it. It is not a replacement for those project classification rules, but an adjunct to them. You can think of it as a continuous classification model. That is, it does not describe a small number of classes as the others do, but rather a very large number of classes. (There are actually 81 distinct project classes that can be defined by the HBDI, but you don't need to worry about that bit of trivia because it will never come up again.) The reason for that large number is that it is based on the four separate but interdependent integer-valued scales that measure the inherent HBDI characteristics of the project. Every project exhibits some tendency toward each characteristic, and in extreme cases a single characteristic may dominate the project.

These four characteristics are as follows:

Analyze. Projects that score high on the analyze dimension are projects that are characterized by a high incidence of logical processing, formulae, and data analysis, probably associated with problem solving, diagnosing, explaining how things work, and clarifying issues. These projects will involve the design and development of new or revised processes and procedures. Engineering, information technology, and construction projects will score high on this quadrant.

Organize. Projects that score high on the organize dimension are projects that are characterized by having an ordered, planned, and controlled environment and that follow an established process and procedure to complete the work of the project. Implementation and business process reengineering projects are examples of projects that score high on this quadrant. Projects that are repetitive or follow a well-defined set of templates will also score high on the organize dimension.

Personalize. Projects that score high on the personalize dimension are projects that are characterized by a high degree of people interaction throughout the life of the project. Groups will be consulted at each phase of the project. It will be important to the success of the project that all affected parties buy in to the project. Such projects are further characterized by the need for a strong communications plan and its management. Projects whose scope and goal are not clearly defined or understood by all parties will require considerable interaction between the project manager and the customer and will therefore score high in the C-Quadrant. E-business companies will have projects that score high on the personalize dimension because, to be successful, these types of projects must be characterized by a shared vision and highly collaborative relationship with their clients.

Strategize. Projects that score high on the strategize dimension are projects that are characterized by stepping outside the box and taking risks, creating innovative solutions, being change oriented, and experimenting with and selling new ideas and new ways of doing things. Such projects are groundbreaking projects because they may involve using breakthrough technologies in challenging ways. Business process reengineering projects will score high on the D-Quadrant, as will Web design projects, especially those in the business-to-business and business-to-consumer spaces.

In Chapter 11, "Establishing the Profile of the Project Team," we'll see how the pattern of these characteristics will help us with team formation.

Let's take a look at two example project profiles. Figure 10.1 shows an example of a development project, and Figure 10.2 shows an example of an implementation project.

Each of these projects has some level of weighting in each quadrant. Projects may be dominated by a single quadrant, but all four quadrants have some representation on both projects. Let's compare the two in order to understand what the project profile tells us about the project.

If you saw these two profiles without the titles and were asked to describe the kinds of projects that might generate these plots, what would

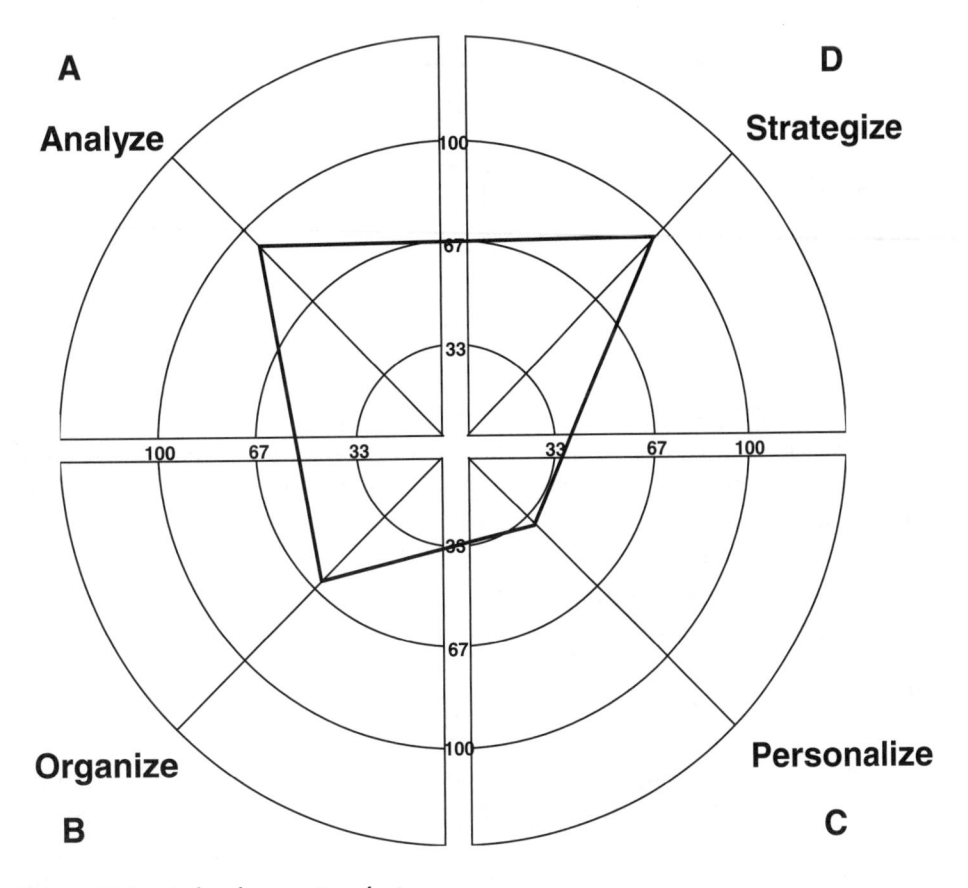

Figure 10.1 A development project.

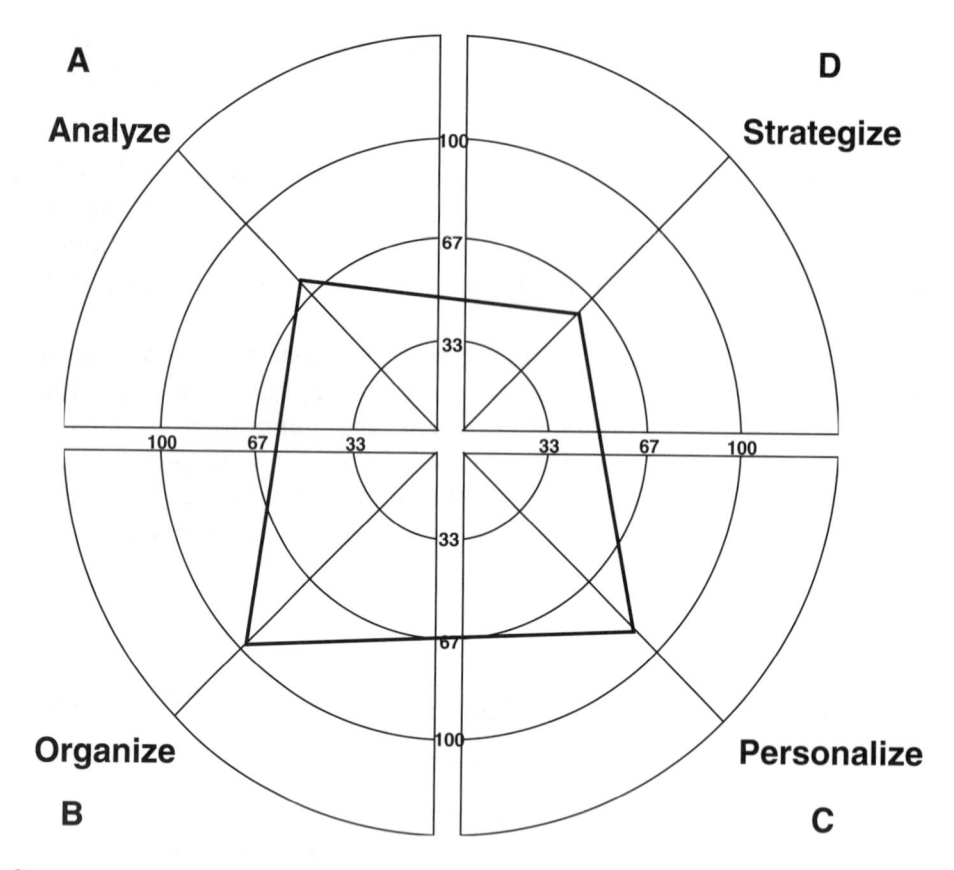

Figure 10.2 An implementation project.

you say? The project shown in Figure 10.1 describes a project that has a strong flavor of analytic and creative properties, as evidenced by high scores on the analyze and strategize quadrants. In other words, the project will require a good bit of analysis and creativity on the part of the project team to be successful.

The project shown in Figure 10.2 describes a project that has a strong flavor of organization and personal properties, as evidenced by high scores on the organize and personalize quadrants. That means that the project will follow process and procedure and will be sensitive to the needs of the people who will use the deliverables. One type of project that has these characteristics is the implementation project. Such projects have a high degree of involvement with the client because they are dealing with the transfer of project deliverables and processes into the client's environment. The client has to feel comfortable that he or she understands how the deliverables work and how he or she should interact with them. This means that the team must have strong interpersonal skills and styles. Implementation involves following a set sequence of steps that are designed to ensure an orderly transition to the client environment. In other words, the team must be attentive to process and procedure. This means that the team must have strong preferences for process and organization.

Profiling the Phases of a Project

You can take this profiling approach one step further and create profiles for each of the phases in a project. To do that you would need a narrative description of each phase of the project. The reason you would do this is that each phase can have a very different profile and hence require a team of different thinking style profiles to be successful.

Projects follow a sequence of phases such as design, build, test, and implement. Each phase has characteristics that differentiate it from the other phases. Figure 10.3 shows the profile of each of those phases for a project that involved creating a B2B Web site for one of my clients. Note that, even though the systems development methodology that was used for this project used an iterative, or spiraling, sequence, rather than the four phases in sequential order, we were able to profile the phases of this project. There is a lot of similarity to the prototyping approach to development, in which the four are repeated and each repetition produces more functionality until the final deliverable is produced.

The first thing to note from Figure 10.3 is how dramatically the profile of the project varies over the phases of the project. The design phase, because it displays a profile that is roughly evenly distributed across each quadrant, is a whole brain activity. Why is that? As a left-brain activity, design involves a good dose of analysis and problem solving, which are A-Quadrant characteristics, and must follow established process and procedure, which is a B-Quadrant characteristic. As a right-brain activity design calls on the team's creative energies and holistic thinking, which are D-Quadrant characteristics, and must meaningfully involve the customer in the entire process, which is a C-Quadrant characteristic.

What about the other phases? The build phase is a left-brain activity because it requires data collection and analysis as well as thoughtful use of design processes and procedures, which is evidenced by the high scores on the A- and B-Quadrants. The test phase is a triple-dominant phase, as evidenced by the high scores in the A-, B-, and C-Quadrants. Testing requires the following of very specific procedures for test data construction, unit testing, subsystem testing, integration testing, and several others. That

176 Building Effective Project Teams

Design Phase

Build Phase

Test Phase

Implement Phase

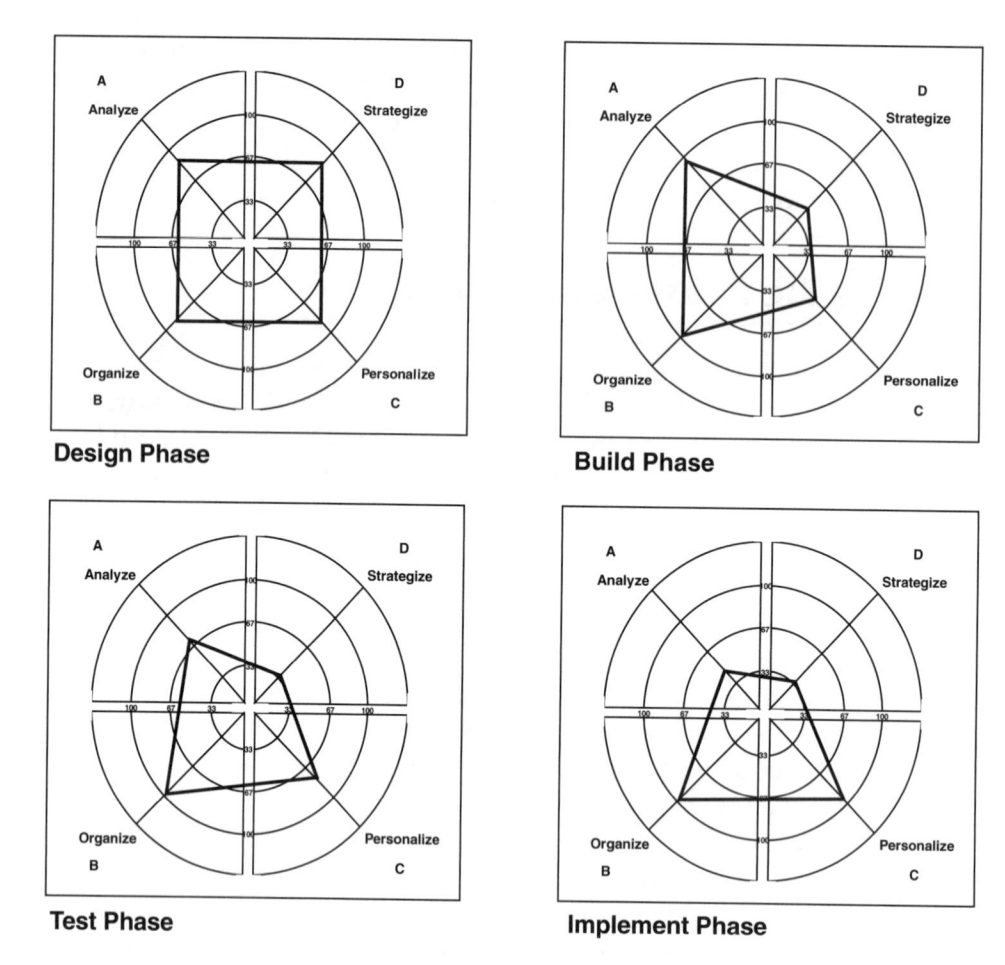

Figure 10.3 Project profiling at the phase level.

testing is followed by detailed analysis of test results and correction of problems encountered. These are A- and B-Quadrant activities. Testing is an activity that fully engages the client as well as the technical members of the project team. The client is involved in collaboratively designing test data as well as executing test procedures. All of this requires coordination between the project team and the client, which is a C-Quadrant activity. The final phase is the implementation phase. We have already discussed that phase with the example given in Figure 10.2.

In summary, we have seen how different each phase can be when viewed from the perspective of its HBDI profile. Those differences spill over into a consideration of the type of team (from the HBDI perspective) that would be best suited to work on each phase of the project. While we may not have the luxury of changing team membership to align with these profiles, we can talk about deploying project team members to those phases with which they are most closely aligned.

How do these differences affect team effectiveness? To say that one size fits all, that is, one team can accommodate these differences, may be a bit of an over-extension. The best approach would be to divide the phases into subprojects and have a different team assigned to each subproject. Each team would be chosen to minimize the gap between what the project phase requires and what the team can deliver. That is a common practice in B2B and B2C Web site development projects. In most other applications where there is just one team assigned to the entire project, another strategy is called for. This strategy involves developing and deploying team members to the assignments within phases that are in alignment with their capabilities. More will be said about this in Part Four.

Creating the HBDI Profile of the Gold Project

In collaboration with Herrmann International I am developing an automated version of the pro forma process to measure the project profile. It is called Project Profiling System, and it will be completed about the time this book is published.

The input to the Project Profiling System is a narrative description of a project. Even though I have a recommended format that I prefer for this narrative input, shown in Figure 10.4, it is not a requirement. Any narrative description of the project that consists of 200 to 500 words should contain sufficient information to produce the output, which is the project profile. Documents such as the Project Overview Statement (POS) or documents of understanding, scope statements, project charters, business case justifications, and statements of work, as well as other descriptive documents, will be equally as effective. The document is analyzed for word and phrase use and frequency. The resulting word counts are translated into scores on the four dimensions and normalized so that they can be mapped to the four quadrants of the Whole Brain Model. The current version of Project Profiling System, which we are using in this book, accepts only words as input. Graphics, figures, and tabular data are not recognized as valid input. Later releases will incorporate these other forms of input.

FOR YOUR REFERENCE See Appendix C for more details on how to arrange to use the Project Profiling System.

Figure 10.4 is the POS for the Gold Project. It is a narrative description, at a very high level, of what this project is all about. Note that there are five sections:

Problem/opportunity. This is the foundation of the POS. It is a brief restatement of a known problem or untapped business opportunity that is readily accepted by the organization. In other words, it is a statement of fact that does not need to be supported. If it is of high-enough priority, the person to whom it is sent will be encouraged to read on to see exactly what your project will do about the problem or opportunity.

Goal. This is a brief but definitive statement of what you intend to do to address the problem or opportunity identified in the problem/opportunity section. It is intended to raise the interest of the person reading it to get him or her to read on for more specific information about how you intend to do that. If the reader views your goal statement as significant he or she will read on.

Objectives. This is a more detailed explanation of the goal statement. These objectives will clarify the boundary of what the project will entail. Together the goal statement and the objectives provide a high-level scope statement for your project.

Success criteria. This section answers the question about why you want to do this project. It is stated in quantitative terms so that the person reading it knows exactly what business value will result from the successful completion of the proposed project.

Assumptions, risks, obstacles. This section is intended to raise the awareness of senior management as to the conditions under which this project is proposed and the conditions that exist that may hinder or block the successful completion of the project. If senior management views the risks as too extreme or as risks that they cannot mitigate, they may render the proposed project inappropriate, and their approval will not be forthcoming.

While it is not necessary for the high-level description to have this format, I have found that this gives the more accurate picture of the project and results in a more reliable HBDI profile than any other form of input I have tried. In one engagement all I had was a memo from the requester to the IT department stating what he wanted. I was able to produce a meaningful project profile from that document, but I wouldn't want that to be the practice. I would rather have a Project Overview Statement like the one shown in Figure 10.4.

Problem/Opportunity
- Drop off in business due to market price sensitivity
- Perception on the part of the market that our products are too traditional
- By using current technology, we can create the perception of offering greater value while holding our price line
- Need to appeal to young emerging musical artists that are technology oriented
- Does not require a major redesign of the core organ
- Can create a new model line with only incremental development costs
- Can enhance the image of the company
- Could gain marketing data via on-line diagnostics

Goal
Increase our market share with young, emerging, upwardly mobile artists by 50% within two years by launching a new, enhanced technology product line known as the Gold Medallion Organ. This line will use the latest in computerized touch screen technology to replace the traditional pulls and stops thus appeal to that part of the market that has grown up with video games and the internet. Product launch will be within one year of the project start date.

Objectives
- Increase market share by 50% with the target market, within two years of launch.
- Design, develop and produce first example of product within one year.
- Use this project to convince the "old guard" in O&P of the need to incorporate new technology in the product line.
- Gain corporate knowledge of how to operate in a modern technology environment

Success Criteria
- Industry critics and press give strongly positive reviews
- Market share with the target market is increased by 50%, within two years of launch
- The corporation gains significant technology knowledge that can be leveraged for future products

Assumptions, Risks, Obstacles
- The target market is interested in blending musical artistry and technology
- There is a large enough customer base in the target market to justify the cost of the project
- This product can spawn a new product line for O&P
- The touch screen technology can be integrated tastefully with old time woodworking craftsmanship
- The O&P corporate leadership will continue to support the project and the product

Figure 10.4 Gold Medallion Organ Project Overview Statement.

FURTHER READING For a detailed discussion of how to construct a valid Project Overview Statement, consult *Effective Project Management, Second Edition* by Wysocki et al. (Wiley, 2000).

The actual process of translating the POS into the project profile is the proprietary property of Herrmann International. What I can say about it is that Ned Herrmann created a lexicon of terms for each of the four quadrants. My company, Enterprise Information Insights, then worked in collaboration with Herrmann International to translate the lexicon and the normalizing process into an automated process for generating the project profile from the POS, or from any narrative description of the project for that matter. To create the project profile using the manual process, all we had to do was count the number of terms in the POS that fall in each quadrant. The resulting counts were then normalized to produce the quadrant score for each quadrant. The normalized scores were the data that defined the project profile (or kite, if you prefer). Figure 10.5 follows from the Project Overview Statement in Figure 10.4.

This project is mostly a computer numerical control type of project. We start with the traditional pull-and-stop organ and are required to replace the mechanical process with an electronic process. That is, we are going to integrate computer technology into the organ and replace its mechanical processes with computer processes. Using the Gold Medallion Organ, the organist will now configure the organ using a touch screen rather than

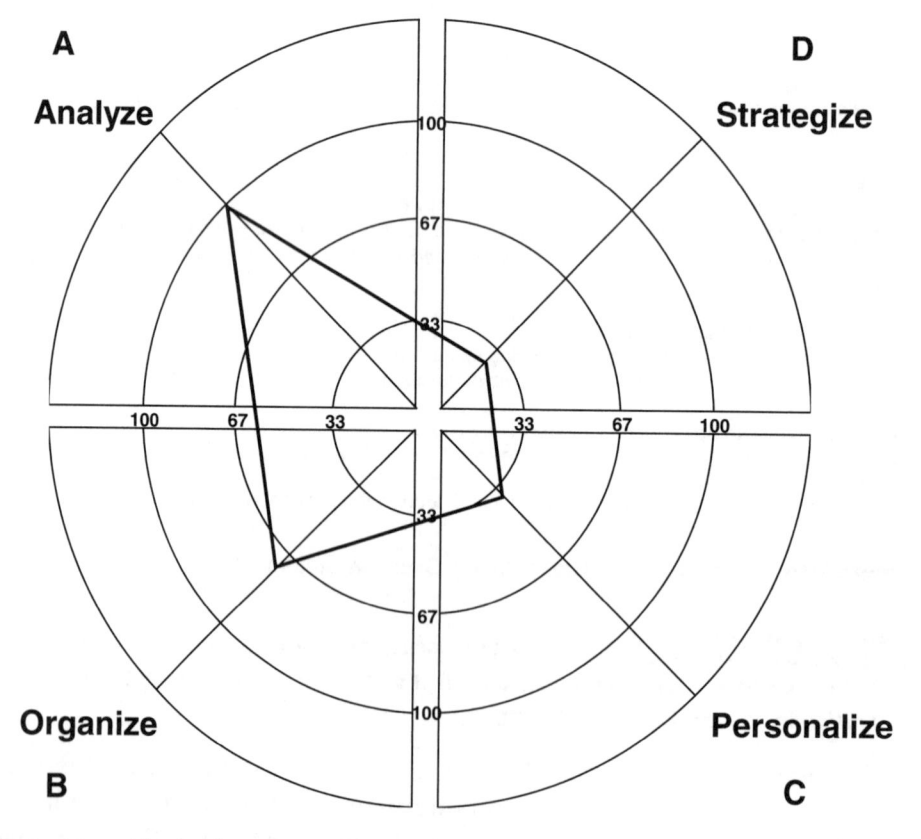

Figure 10.5 The Gold Project profile.

physically setting a number of pulls and stops. All of this speaks of technical analyses, solving interface and process control problems, dealing with the physical constraints on space and location of functions, solid planning of technical design and fabrication, and a host of other process and procedural matters. All of these are typical left-brain characteristics.

On the other hand, there is not much representation of right-brain characteristics in this project. Yes, there is consideration for product acceptance and testing, which will involve musicians. These are C-Quadrant characteristics and are weakly represented in the profile. The D-Quadrant is not a factor in describing the characteristics of this project. Whatever creative and imaginative characteristics you might have expected to see are overshadowed by the technical and process control aspects of the project.

Putting It All Together

This is a key chapter in that it describes the major tool that will be used to examine the alignment of the project team to the project. We saw in Chapter 6 how the HBDI can be used to measure the thinking styles of the individual and hence of the team; in this chapter we saw how the HBDI can be used to profile the project. In the next chapter we will merge these two analyses to see how the project team and the project align with one another.

CHAPTER 11

Establishing the Profile of the Project Team

In this chapter we switch our focus from the project to the team that will work on the project. I have discussed how to profile the project, and in this chapter, in parallel fashion, I will discuss how to form the project team using the profile data available to us.

In the best-case scenario, you'll be able to pick and choose your team members. In reality, you may have little freedom to form the team. It may have been formed for you, and you have had no say in who is on it. In either case, a team will be formed.

Before we get down to the work of forming the Gold Team, I want to take a look at the pool of people from which the members of the Gold Team will be chosen. For the purposes of this discussion, let's call this pool the candidate pool. My analysis of the candidate pool, which is given in the next section, is similar to an analysis that you should do as a matter of course. This is an analysis of the supply side of the equation—project teams represent the demand side. Once we have a better understanding of what we have (supply side) we can do a more informed job of forming the Gold Team (demand side). More generally, however, an analysis of the relationship between the supply side and the current and forecasted demand side will give you insight into the development and training needs of your organization with respect to the portfolio of projects it is, or will be, working on.

Analyzing the Candidate Pool

Just as a project has a profile, so also does a team. The team profile is a composite of the profiles of the individual team members. When presented in the aggregate, the individual profiles give us an insight into the true characteristics of the team that are not evident from the individual profiles. I'm not sure what the long-term effects of this finding will be, but I do know that this is a major breakthrough in improving project team effectiveness. Time will tell exactly how significant this contribution will be. As unusual as this all may seem to you, the team profile gives you the ability to assess the extent to which a project team is aligned with their project. That means you have a way of assessing a specific team's fit with a project or the further development of an existing team.

Our analysis will include using the HBDI to describe the alignment between the project and the project team. We'll also use the SDI and LSI to assess the balance in the project team with respect to its ability to solve problems, make decisions, and resolve conflicts. Finally, you'll use the PMSA and PMCA to assess the degree to which the project team is technically prepared to manage the work of the project. In most cases the PMSA and PMCA as well as other skill profiling data is used to "select" team members. The HBDI, SDI, and LSI are used to assess the team once it has been formed.

Candidate Pool HBDI Profile

The significant feature of TeamArchitect is that it can profile projects and teams on one four-quadrant graphic that can be interpreted. For the project, TeamArchtect describes the thinking styles needed to be successful with the project. For the team (or its individual members) it displays their thinking styles. We can superimpose the two, and—voila—we have a way of comparing what the project needs with what the team provides.

Figure 11.1 shows a composite team profile built using the individual profiles of all 16 members of the candidate pool. The bold lines are the project profile (I will show that from now on, on every HBDI profile) and the narrow lines are the team members' profiles. There are 16 HBDI kites on this diagram and, while it may look cluttered to you, certain patterns do manifest themselves in this type of plot. In fact, for small teams (5 to 10

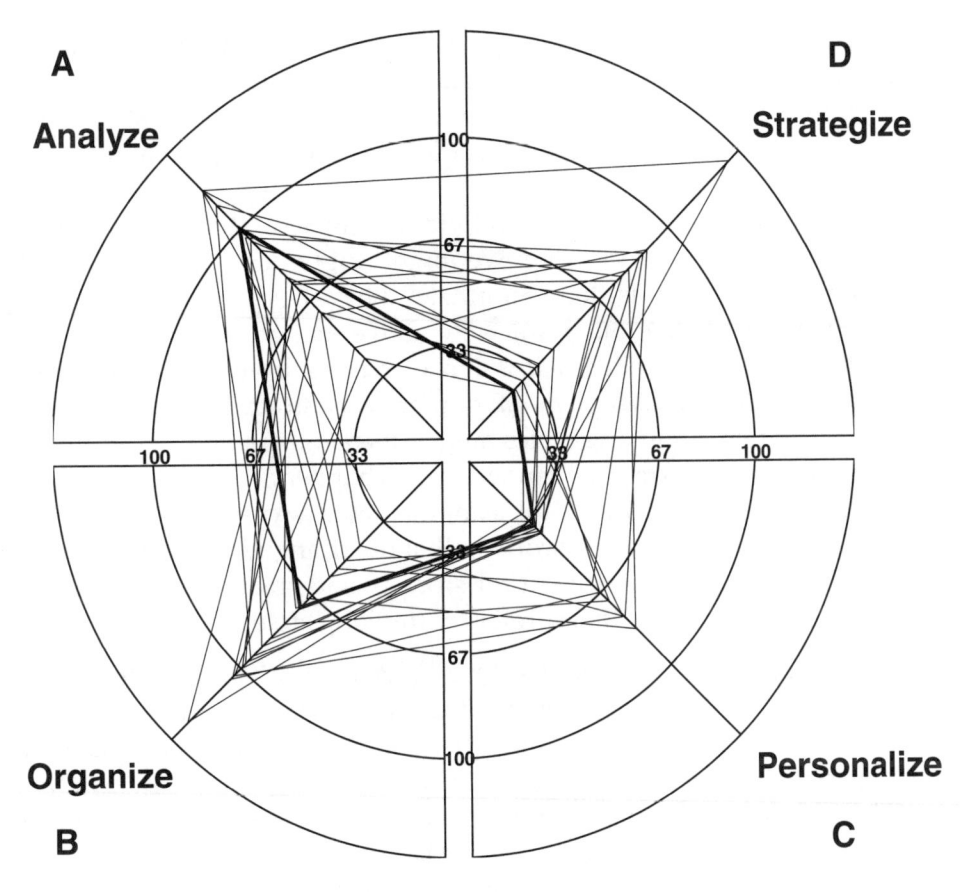

Figure 11.1 HBDI profile of the candidate pool.

members) this may be the way you prefer to see that data. The important thing to remember is that we are not so much interested in picking out an individual's HBDI kite as we are in seeing what the team, as a whole unit, looks like. That is, the pattern that is displayed by the entire team is the focus. The individual in these types of plots is not of interest.

What does this plot tell us about the candidate pool and specifically the degree to which it aligns with the project? Let's look at the plots in each quadrant. This will give us some insight into any staffing problems we will have to deal with. The more out of alignment the candidate pool is to the project profile, the more difficulty we will have building an effective team.

A few general comments are in order before we proceed to analyze the candidate pool. If we had an ideal team in mind for this project, what distribution pattern of individual thinking styles would we expect to see? While there isn't an ideal or best distribution, I think we would like to see the scores of one quadrant to be equally distributed above and below the quadrant score of the project. That would mean that the team would have some members that could lead the team in using that thinking style while it would have other members who would temporize the team in its use of that thinking style.

On the other hand, if all of the individual scores on the quadrant were above or below the project score, we might not be too comfortable with that arrangement. Why is that? First, take the case where all of the team members' scores on one quadrant were above that of the project on that quadrant. Recall the earlier discussion of having a very strategic team when the project was an implementation project and really needed little in the way of strategic thinking styles among its members. As we discussed, that situation would be a problem waiting to happen.

The reverse situation, where all team members' scores on the quadrant were below that of the project score on that quadrant, would also be problematic. Here the project cries out for strategy and creativity, and none of the members have that as their preferred thinking style.

A-Quadrant. The Gold Project A-Quadrant score is 100. That means that the project will require a good deal of analysis in order to be successful. While some of the members of the candidate pool have A-Quadrant scores above 100 (Sal Vation, Terri Tory, Mike Rowtoys, and Barry deBones) the preponderance have scores that range all the way down to 42 (Pearl E. Gates) and 45 (Mack N. Tawsch). It would be very easy to end up with a team whose members all had A-Quadrant scores that were all below, even significantly below, 100. This could become a problem.

B-Quadrant. The Gold Project B-Quadrant score is 73. This means that the project will require the following of process and procedure, but that it is not a major characteristic of the project. Ten of the members of the candidate pool have B-Quadrant scores that lie above the B-Quadrant score of the Gold Project, and six have scores that lie below. It should not be difficult to generate a project team whose B-Quadrant scores will be equally distributed around 73, the Gold Project B-Quadrant score. While this is not a serious situation it will require some attention as we begin to form the Gold Team. The risk is that the team will religiously follow process and procedure and become its own obstacle to open and creative problem solving.

C-Quadrant. The C-Quadrant score of the Gold Project is 36, and most of the members of the candidate pool have C-Quadrant scores above that number. Recall that the C-Quadrant is the personalize quadrant, and high scores in that quadrant mean that the individual tends to be interpersonal and thinks about how others will react to whatever is done or being contemplated. The danger for us is that we will create a Gold Team whose C-Quadrant scores are high. That will be a team that is overly concerned about others to the point where it becomes an obstacle to progress for the project team. Remember this is a technical project that involves applying technology to automate a manual process. Because 10 of the 16 candidate pool scores are clustered tightly around the Gold Project C-Quadrant score of 36, this thinking style preference will not be an issue in most teams that can be formed from this candidate pool.

D-Quadrant. The D-Quadrant score of the Gold Project is 25, and all 16 D-Quadrant scores of the candidate pool lie above that number, with many of them significantly higher. This project does not require strategic or creative thinkers. It is a very straightforward technical project. It is a certainty that the resulting Gold Team will have a D-Quadrant profile that is significantly above that of the project. This will require close attention when we choose the Gold Team. The risk is that we will form a very creative Gold Team for a project that does not require a high level of creativity. The result is a team that is bored and will go out of its way to find problems just so that it will be able to rise to the challenge of working on exciting problems. That is not something we want to encourage, so we will have to pay particular attention to the D-Quadrant score of the team we finally choose. While this thinking style may be offset by a strong B-Quadrant (a team that has a preference for following process and procedure), we will need to pay attention to that balance in whatever teams are being considered.

Alternative Presentations of HBDI Profiles

There are three other ways to represent the HBDI profile of a group. You may find one of these formats more useful than the raw data displayed in Figure 11.1.

Team average profile. A more intuitive and less cluttered presentation of the team profile is to show only the average score on each quadrant and plot a single kite, as shown in Figure 11.2. Note how the kite for the team profile aligns with the project profile. This figure is simply the average of the data shown in Figure 11.1. Averages can be misleading because they hide information that may be relevant, such as the distribution of data around the average and extreme data points.

188 Building Effective Project Teams

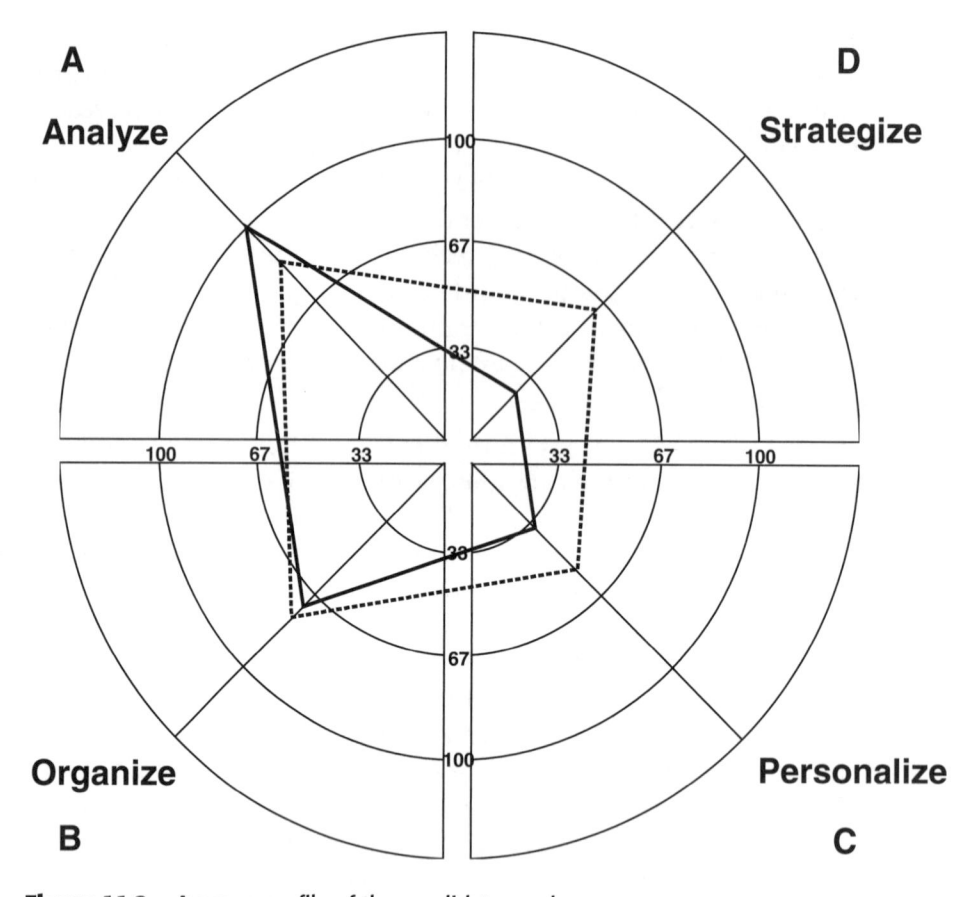

Figure 11.2 Average profile of the candidate pool.

The team average format may have more application in presentations that the project manager will make to managers outside the project, while the raw data format may be more useful for internal analysis by the project manager.

Team midrange profile. A compromise to displaying the team average profile is to show some of the data distribution by displaying the midrange of the data. The midrange (a.k.a. interquartile range) is simply the middle half of the data. In Figure 11.3, the shaded band is the midrange of the team profile data. One further modification would be to add the range statistics, as shown in Figure 11.4 by the light dashed lines. Adding the range statistics completes a summary of the entire data set for the candidate pool and means the summary can be used for the team-level data as well.

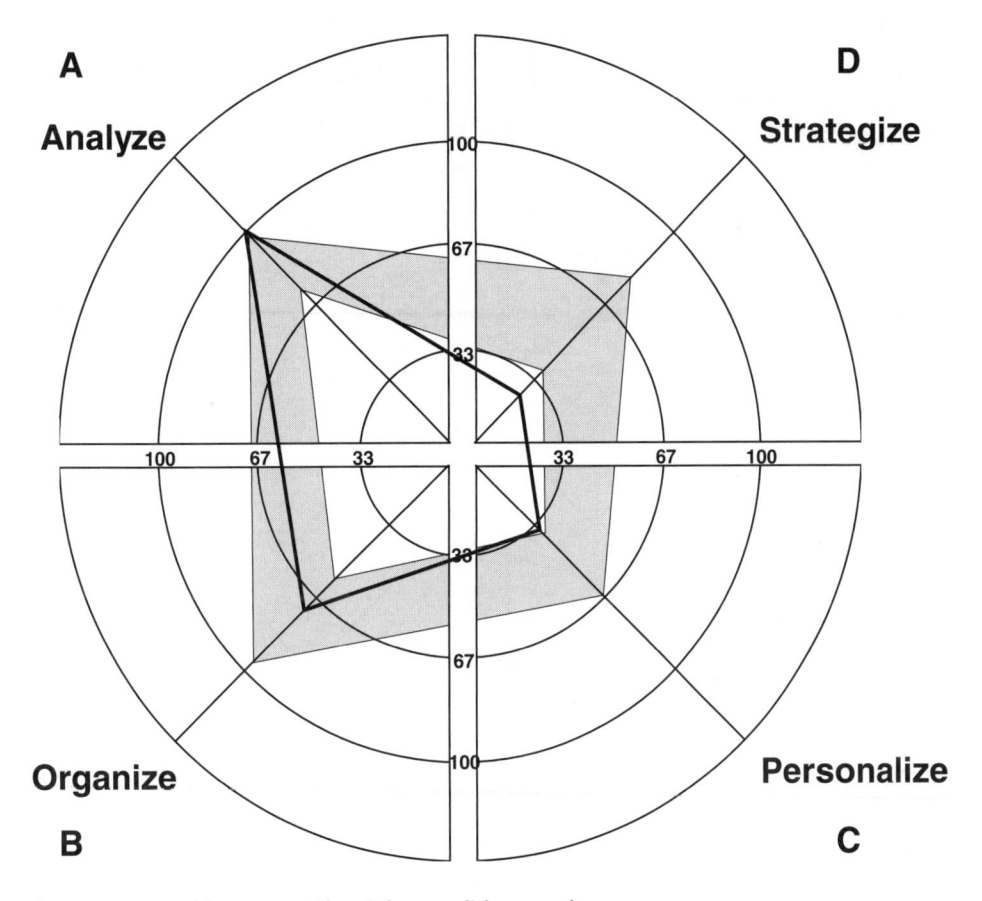

Establishing the Profile of the Project Team 189

Figure 11.3 Midrange profile of the candidate pool.

Team profile using individual kite distribution. A third way to display team profile data is to use the individual profiles and display them as small icons near the coordinates defined by A-C-Quadrant scores, B-D-Quadrant scores. This is the form preferred by Herrmann International when it displays team member data. Let's take a closer look at how it arrives at this format.

First, two coordinates must be defined in order to locate the position of the icon on the graphic. The first coordinate is calculated by taking the difference (A-Quadrant score minus C-Quadrant score). The second coordinate is calculated by taking the difference (B-Quadrant score minus D-Quadrant score). By way of example, let's use the Gold Project quadrant scores. They are 100, 73, 36, and 25 for the A-, B, C-, and D-Quadrants, respectively. Therefore, the A-C coordinate is

190 Building Effective Project Teams

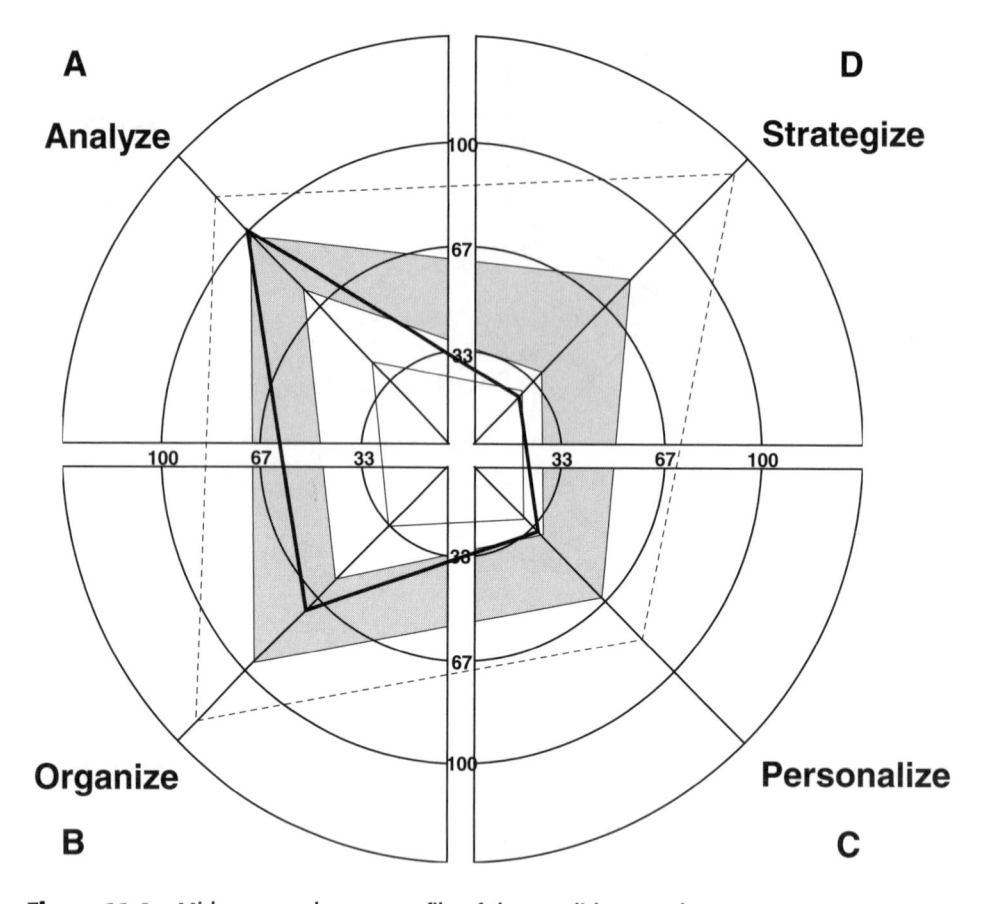

Figure 11.4 Midrange and range profile of the candidate pool.

100 − 36 = 64, and the B-D coordinate is 73 − 25 = 48. An example using the candidate pool data is shown in Figure 11.5. Once you get comfortable interpreting HBDI profile data you will find this format to be a more useful and crisper presentation of the data.

I have shown you five ways to represent the team's HBDI data. In the final analysis, the choice is a matter of preference. Different situations may call for you to use different formats. For example, when working with the team itself, you may prefer to use the format shown in Figure 11.1. When reporting to senior management or in situations where simplicity is called for, you may use the format shown in Figure 11.3 or Figure 11.5. I have had occasions to use all five formats. There are no hard and fast rules. It really boils down to a matter of taste and comfort level.

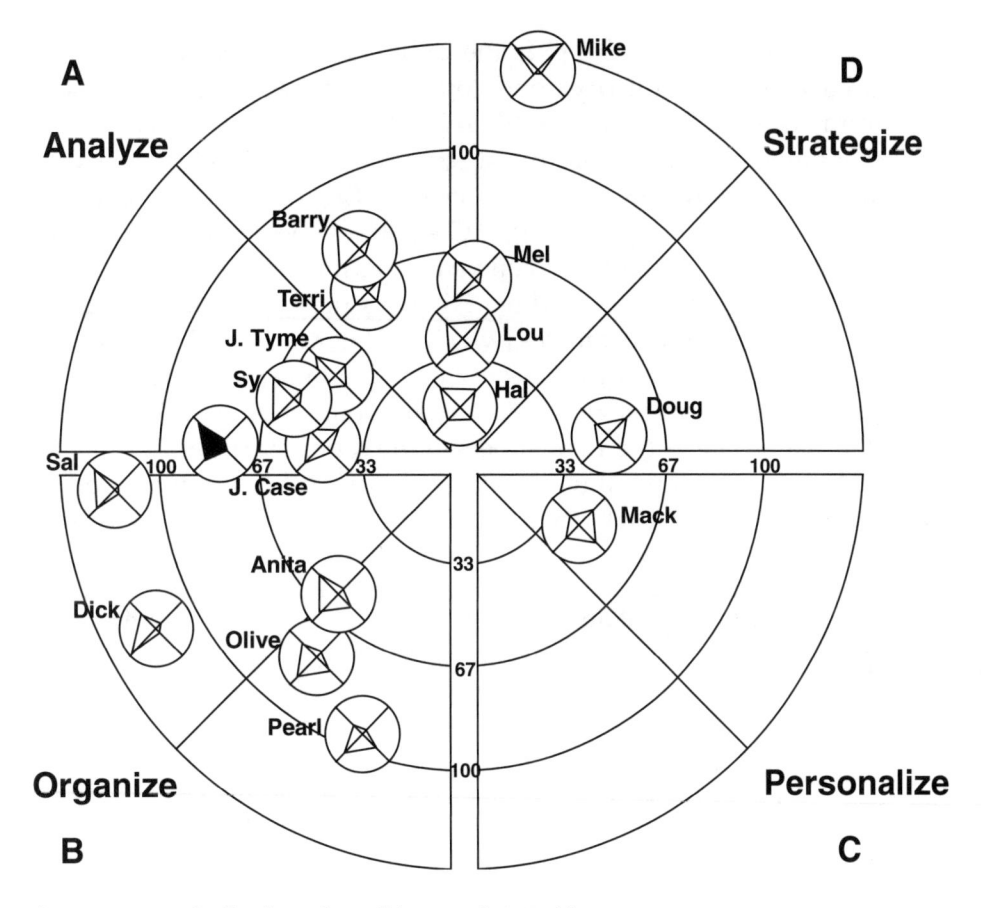

Figure 11.5 Distribution of candidate pool HBDI kites.

Candidate Pool LSI Profile

The LSI kite is the best way to portray an individual's learning preferences, but it doesn't describe the team's learning styles very well. In order to explain the team's learning style patterns and preferences, the four quadrant scores for each team member are transformed into a single data point and displayed on one graph. Each team member is represented as a single data point.

To get your scores for learning style types compute the following for each team member:

(AC-CE) score = AC score − CE score
(AE-RO) score = AE score − RO score

The vertical dimension (AC-CE) is the difference between the scores on abstract conceptualization (AC) and concrete experience (CE). The horizontal dimension (AE-RO) is the difference between the scores on active experimentation (AE) and reflective observation (RO). Let's take an example to illustrate exactly how this works. Pearl's LSI scores are 29, 36, 16, and 30 for AE (active experimentation), AC (abstract conceptualization), RO (reflective observation), and CE (concrete experimentation), respectively. Hence her AC-CE score is –5, and her AE-RO score is 15. I have superimposed the raw numeric coordinates (which are not linear) on Figure 11.6 as well as the percentile coordinates (which are linear). Using the raw numeric scores you can see how Pearl's data point is plotted. Figure 11.6 shows the LSI profile of the 16 members of the candidate pool.

What does Figure 11.6 tell us about the ability of the candidate pool to solve problems? Recall that whatever Gold Team we choose to form, it

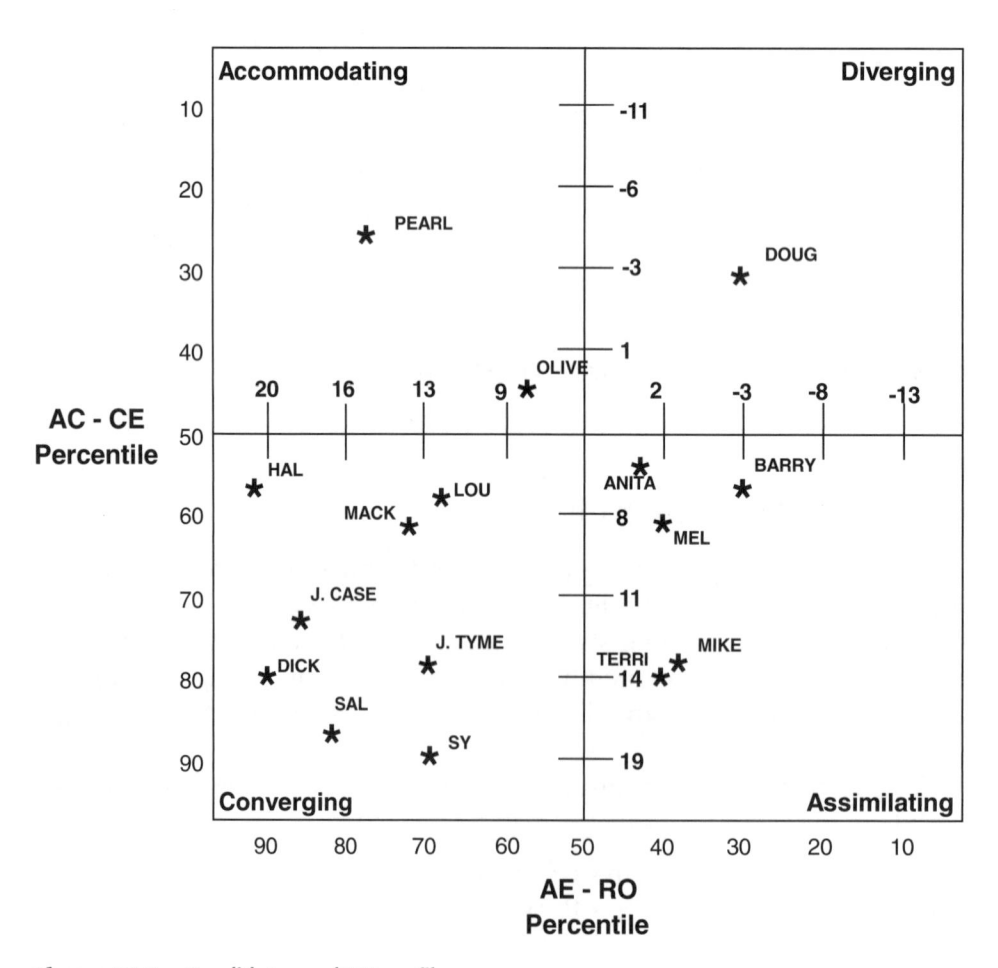

Figure 11.6 Candidate pool LSI profile.

must be balanced with respect to its problem-solving capabilities. That means we should look for a team that has representation in all four of the quadrants shown in Figure 11.6. Such teams would, as a minimum, consist of Doug deGrave because he is the only team member in the diverging quadrant and either Pearl E. Gates or Olive Branch because they are the only two team members in the accommodating quadrant. The remaining quadrants have several team members in each, and so there will be several choices for the remaining two quadrants.

I have used the LSI for several years in a variety of consulting situations. Most of these have been with high-tech professionals whose LSI data is distributed very much like the data in Figure 11.6. The LSI data from engineers and computer professionals is usually clustered in the lower-left quadrant with some scattering into the lower-right quadrant. Doug deGrave, a systems analyst, is an anomaly. People like Doug are rare and, if you are fortunate to have a Doug on your team, keep him challenged and motivated. Losing him would be unfortunate because he would be difficult to replace with a systems analyst of like persuasion.

Candidate Pool SDI Profile

Recall that the SDI assesses motivational values, valued-relating styles and conflict management strategies. Figure 11.7 shows the distribution of the SDI profiles of the 16 members of the candidate pool. I have labeled each person's arrow. It is somewhat cluttered, but I think it will help with the following discussion. The question is this: Can this pool produce a team that is balanced with respect to its ability to handle conflicts between and among the team members as well as with others outside the team?

I think we are on safe ground to answer in the affirmative. Note, however, that there are a lot of green arrowheads (Analytic-Autonomizing)—8 to be exact, 11 if you include Mack N. Tawsch, Pearl E. Gates, and Mel Otious. These folks will try to resolve conflict by first adopting an analytic position. While this may not be an obstacle to resolving within-the-team conflicts (most of the team is Green anyway), it may be an obstacle to resolving outside-the-team conflicts. To diffuse these potential obstacles and create some balance with respect to conflict strategies, the Gold Team might include members with Red arrowheads (Terri and/or Sy) as well as members with Blue arrowheads (Olive and/or Mel). Hal E. Lewya's arrowhead is right in the middle of the hub. Recall that this is the flexible-cohering conflict sequence (RGB). That means that Hal can be a pivotal person on the Gold Team because he will always take all points of view into consideration and use any one of several strategies for resolving conflict. These types of people are generally very good diplomats because of their adaptive styles.

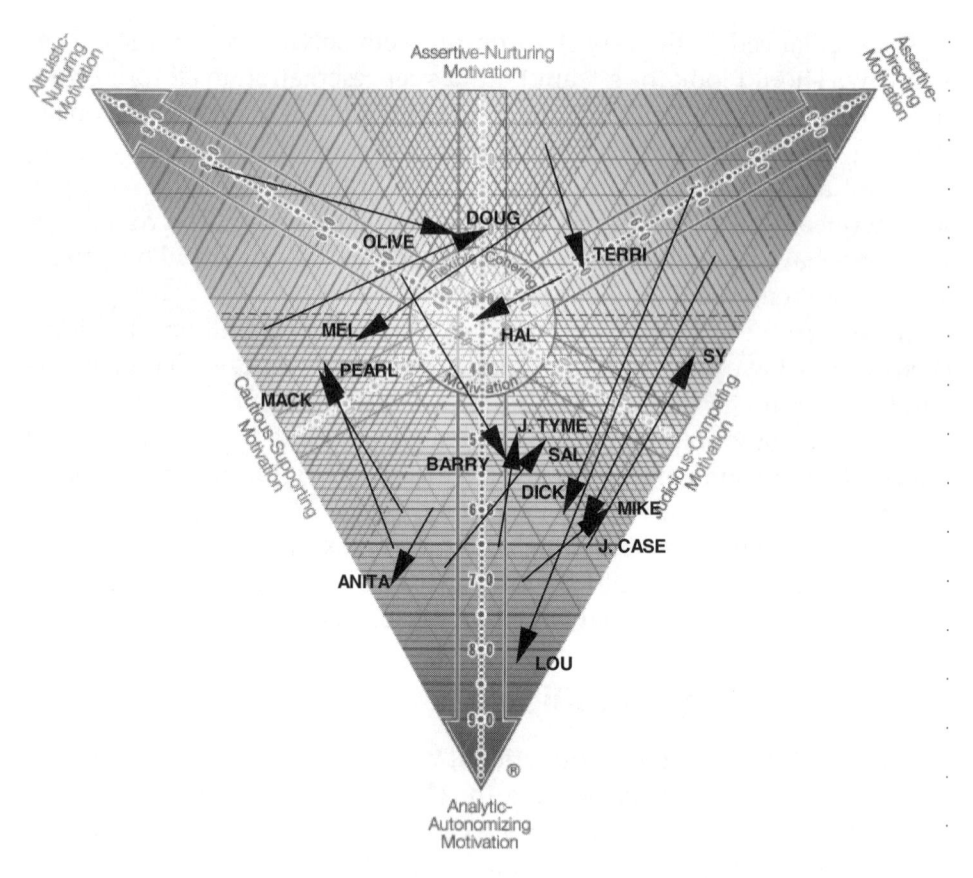

Figure 11.7 Candidate pool SDI profile.

Regardless of the final composition of the team that is chosen, an analysis of the team's SDI data will indicate the degree to which their valued-relating and motivational styles are balanced as well as their need to use borrowed behavior in compensating for any lack of balance.

Candidate Pool Skills Profile

A number of organizations already do something similar to skills assessment and reporting. The data may be collected through self-assessment or some form of 360 process. It can be used by the Training Management staff to decide on how to spend the training budget. I have always thought that skills data is most useful when it is mapped into the types of projects that the organization is or will be working on. To that end I have modified the skills reports to show how many folks are qualified to work on projects of a certain classification. The candidate pool skills profile is reported that way in Tables 11.1 through 11.5.

Establishing the Profile of the Project Team 195

Table 11.1 Candidate Pool Project Management Skill Profile

PROJECT MANAGEMENT SKILL	\multicolumn{7}{c}{NUMBER AT EACH SKILL LEVEL}	\multicolumn{4}{c}{NUMBER QUALIFIED BY PROJECT TYPE}
	0	1	2	3	4	5	6	IV	III	II	I
Charter development	0	1	4	7	4	0	0	11	4	4	4
Complexity assessment	6	1	1	7	1	0	0	10	8	8	1
Cost estimating	0	0	2	7	6	1	0	14	7	7	1
Cost management	0	0	3	9	2	2	0	13	4	4	2
Critical path management	0	0	5	9	2	0	0	11	2	2	2
Detailed estimating	0	1	2	6	6	1	0	13	7	7	1
Project closeout	2	0	6	5	3	0	0	8	3	3	0
Project management software	2	0	0	6	7	1	0	8	8	8	8
Project notebook construction	2	0	5	8	0	1	0	9	1	1	1
Project organization	0	0	6	6	4	0	0	16	10	10	0
Project planning	0	2	2	8	4	0	0	12	4	4	4
Project progress assessment	0	1	4	10	1	0	0	15	11	11	1
Resource acquisition	0	0	3	8	4	1	0	16	5	5	1
Resource leveling	1	0	8	3	4	0	0	15	4	4	0
Resource requirements	0	0	3	8	3	2	0	16	5	5	2
Schedule deployment	0	0	2	9	4	1	0	14	14	14	5
Scope management	0	0	8	3	5	0	0	8	5	5	0
Size estimating	1	1	1	8	3	2	0	13	5	5	2

Table 11.2 Candidate Pool Personal Skill Profile

PERSONAL SKILL	\multicolumn{7}{c}{NUMBER AT EACH SKILL LEVEL}	\multicolumn{4}{c}{NUMBER QUALIFIED BY PROJECT TYPE}
	0	1	2	3	4	5	6	IV	III	II	I
Creativity	0	0	0	8	4	4	0	16	8	8	4
Decision making/critical thinking	0	0	0	2	14	0	0	16	14	14	0
Presentations	0	0	1	4	9	2	0	15	11	11	2
Verbal communications	0	0	1	5	5	5	0	15	10	10	10
Written communications	0	0	2	4	4	6	0	14	14	14	10

Table 11.3 Candidate Pool Interpersonal Skill Profile

	NUMBER AT EACH SKILL LEVEL							NUMBER QUALIFIED BY PROJECT TYPE			
INTERPERSONAL SKILL	0	1	2	3	4	5	6	IV	III	II	I
Conflict management	0	2	2	6	6	0	0	12	6	6	6
Flexibility	0	0	5	4	3	4	0	11	7	7	7
Influencing	0	0	3	9	4	0	0	16	13	13	4
Interpersonal relations	0	1	3	3	9	0	0	12	9	9	9
Negotiating	0	0	4	7	5	0	0	16	12	12	5
Relationship management	0	0	3	7	6	0	0	16	6	6	0
Team management/building	0	1	4	5	6	0	0	11	6	6	6

Table 11.4 Candidate Pool Business Skill Profile

	NUMBER AT EACH SKILL LEVEL							NUMBER QUALIFIED BY PROJECT TYPE			
BUSINESS SKILL	0	1	2	3	4	5	6	IV	III	II	I
Budgeting	0	0	1	9	5	1	0	15	6	6	1
Business assessment	0	2	5	7	2	0	0	16	2	2	0
Business case justification	0	2	3	6	2	3	0	11	5	5	3
Business functions	0	0	1	5	4	6	0	15	10	10	6
Business process design	0	0	4	6	4	2	0	12	6	6	2
Company products/services	0	0	0	5	4	7	0	16	11	11	7
Core applications systems	0	0	1	6	8	1	0	15	9	9	9
Customer service	0	0	2	10	3	1	0	14	4	4	1
Implementation	0	0	1	7	8	0	0	8	0	0	0
Planning: strategic and tactical	0	0	7	3	3	3	0	9	6	6	3
Product/vendor evaluation	0	0	1	10	1	4	0	16	15	15	4
Standards, procedures, policies	0	0	0	10	1	5	0	16	16	16	6
Systems and technology integration	0	0	3	6	3	4	0	16	7	7	4
Testing	0	0	1	7	4	4	0	16	8	8	4

Table 11.5 Candidate Pool Management Skill Profile

MANAGEMENT SKILL	\multicolumn{7}{c	}{NUMBER AT EACH SKILL LEVEL}	\multicolumn{4}{c}{NUMBER QUALIFIED BY PROJECT TYPE}
	0	1	2	3	4	5	6	IV	III	II	I
Delegation	0	1	5	5	4	1	0	10	5	5	1
Leadership	0	1	9	4	0	2	0	6	2	2	2
Managing change	0	0	3	9	2	2	0	13	4	4	2
Managing multiple priorities	0	0	3	7	3	3	0	13	6	6	3
Meeting management	0	1	2	7	5	1	0	13	6	6	1
Performance management	0	0	7	3	5	1	0	9	6	6	1
Quality management	0	0	5	6	4	1	0	11	5	5	5
Staff and career development	0	4	4	3	5	0	0	8	5	5	0
Staffing, hiring, selection	0	4	6	0	6	0	0	6	6	6	6

The left third of the reports lists the skills. The middle third of the reports shows the distribution of skill levels for the 16 members of the candidate pool. The right third of the reports contains the most valuable summary of the skills data. For each of the project types (four in our case) I have shown how many members of the candidate pool have the required skill level to work on a project of that type.

The most glaring deficiency in the candidate pool is in the business skill area. The implementation skills of the candidate pool members are very weak, as evidenced by the fact that most of the members of the candidate pool are qualified at the Type IV project level but very few at the more complex Type III, II, and I levels. The Gold Project is a Type I project, the most complex and business-critical type of project. The most glaring deficiencies are in implementation—only 8 are qualified for Type IV projects and none at any higher level of complexity. That means that regardless of the team that is formed from the candidate pool, its implementation skills will be an area of great concern.

Again, rather than show the raw team skill data, you might prefer to summarize it at the percentile level. Recall that this format was introduced in Chapter 9, "Project Management Skills and Competencies." Rather than show averages or midranges, I prefer to show the range. The reason is simple. The project manager's concern is that someone on the team possesses a skill at a proficiency level needed by the project. The Gold Project is a Type I project—the most complex type of project the company will undertake. Figure 11.8 depicts the percentile profile.

198 Building Effective Project Teams

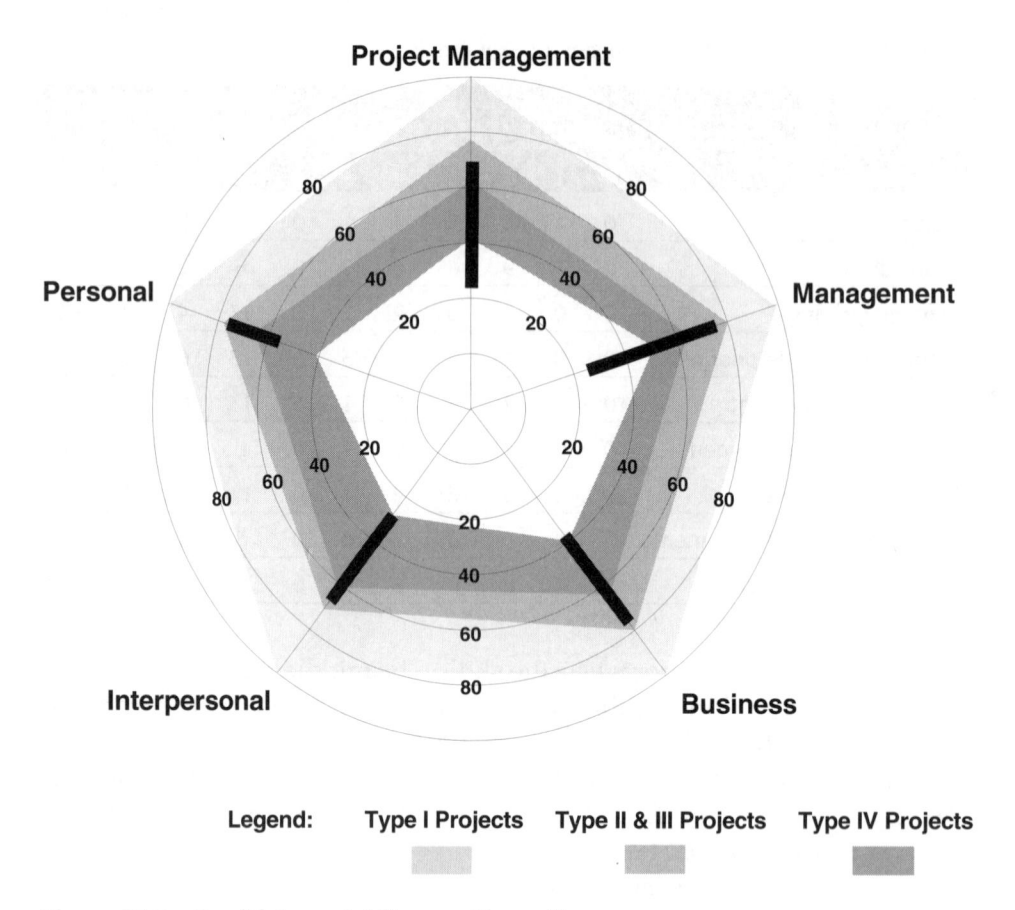

Figure 11.8 Candidate pool skill percentile profile.

Even though this type of presentation shows the data at a high level of aggregation, it tells us a story about the quality of our professional staff and their ability to handle a Type I project. What does this tell us about the skill profile of the candidate pool with respect to its preparedness for the Gold Project, which is a Type I project? Are you concerned about their skill preparation or not? You should be, and here is why.

The range data shows that the candidate pool does not have the minimum necessary proficiency levels in any of the five skill areas. The minimum proficiency level for a Type I project is shown in the outermost band (the lightest of the gray shaded areas). It is possible that a number of staff may each contribute one or more of the skills within a skill area so that as a group they cover all skills in that area at the proficiency level required for a Type I project. For the project manager, that means the skill area is covered but only with a lot of coordination between the members of the team.

They will share those duties that require their collective proficiency. It can work, but it is clumsy!

Remember, people are chosen for the team primarily on the basis of skills and competencies. In the case of this Candidate Pool there are deficiencies and that will become problematic regardless of who is on the team.

Steps to Forming a Project Team

Now that we have a good picture of the pool of talent we have to work with, it's time to assemble our Gold Team. First, some general comments are in order. What are the general steps one usually follows in building a project team? I'll answer that question, and then we will move on to the task at hand—forming the Gold Team.

Populating the Project Team

Putting together a project team may involve less choice than most project managers would find comfortable. In any case, let me walk you through a series of questions that the project manager will need to answer. These are the kinds of questions that you might try to answer if you do have the luxury of choosing your team members.

What Do I Need?

Balance! Above all else, you need balance, and I mean that in the most expansive and comprehensive way. That balance extends beyond the technical to all of the areas we have been talking about in this book: thinking styles, decision making, problem solving, and conflict management.

What Do I Have Available?

What do you have and what do you have available for the project being staffed are two very different questions. At some level in the management structure of your company anything that you have can be made available. It's only a matter of priorities. That involves managing the project portfolio of your organization, staying on top of the needs of the business, adjusting priorities accordingly, and finally managing the resources assigned or available to your project portfolio. These are all very relevant concerns, but they are beyond the scope of this book. Your staffing alternatives for the project being staffed are constrained by what you have available.

Availability is an interesting concept. How often have you chosen a team member simply because he or she was available? In this day and age, when the demand for certain kinds of professionals far exceeds the supply, we will take whatever we can get and be happy for that. It may not be what we would have chosen, but we have to make the best of it in any case. Availability is not a skill, but in many cases we sure treat it like it is.

Who Should I Choose?

If you do happen to have a choice, what do you do? Do you bother to look at the kinds of psychometric data covered in Part Two and try to make an informed decision about which of two or more teams will be a better choice? Or do you go with your gut and base a decision on what you can recall or what others are telling you about the alternatives you have? It is easy to choose the latter, and that in fact may be what you do in almost all situations, but now that you know how simple it is to collect and analyze the HBDI, LSI, and SDI data at the team level, why not give it a try? You can only win!

But don't get too fixated on the data and ignore common sense. You need to take people's preferences into account as well. People who have an opportunity to work on something they prefer will often do better than people with a better skill preparation for the task but who have little or no interest in the task for which they are being recruited. Last but most importantly, remember that we are measuring only preferences, motivational values, learning preferences, not skills. It is true that when someone prefers a particular style it is likely that they will exceed at practicing that style, but don't get too carried away with the data. Consider situations in which you have been. You like to share responsibility with your team, but your organization is very heavy-handed and the chain of command is sacred. You have two choices: either leave the company or hide your true values and feelings and conform to the culture of your organization. To do otherwise is simply asking for trouble.

What Will They Do?

Sooner or later you reach the point where the team is chosen. You may have participated in the choosing, or you might simply inherit the team members because they were available or they were the only choice. As project manager, you will have some choices to make regarding specific assignments of each team member. Part of their assignment will, of course, be related to the technical skills they bring to the project. After all, that is the main reason they are on your team. Beyond their technical assignment there will be other assignments for which you will consider them. In this book, you should have collected data on the HBDI, LSI, and SDI assessment tools from each team member. That data is a gold mine and will tell you quite a bit about the work preferences and styles of each member. It will be invaluable to you as you work with each team member to find the best fit for them on your project team. Not only will you utilize the skills they bring to the project but you will also use project assignments as on-the-job training and development opportunities for them to help them develop additional skills and competencies. The project can be a rich source of career and professional development opportunities, if you will only look.

Several years ago I was managing a project for one of my clients. On my team was a woman, call her Mary, who took me aside after our first team meeting and asked if she could take minutes at all of our team meetings. She went on to say that she really liked doing it and felt that she did an excellent job. "Please let me demonstrate by taking minutes at our next team meeting." How could I say no? A strange request because professionals do not often seek out responsibility for this particular task. As it turned out, she was very good at the job, and the job became hers for the duration of the project. I think there must have been a sigh of relief from the rest of the team knowing that they would not have to be burdened with minute taking!

The larger point that I want to make again is this—find out what people like to do and give them a chance to do it. More to the point—find out where people are going in their career and professional development and give them every opportunity to work toward it as part of their project responsibilities. You can't always do that, but just be cognizant of it. I have found it to be a great morale booster for my team members. If people are given those opportunities, the chances are good that they will remain on your project and have a sense of commitment to you and to your project as well.

Building Effective Project Teams

Now that we have taken a brief look at the candidate pool and how it is configured for a selection of the Gold Team, we can turn to the task of choosing the team to assign to the Gold Project. There are many ways to do this. In fact, for the 16 members of the candidate pool and the 8 positions to be filled, there are 384 possible teams! You can check all 384 if you like by visiting www.teamarchitect.com. I am not going to do that.

As an alternative, in actual practice you may have had previous experience with many of the candidates and have identified likely candidates and team members already. On the other hand, some of the team members may be already chosen based on availability or some other criteria, and you need to fill only a few of the remaining vacancies. I would guess that this is the most likely situation.

For the purposes of this exercise we'll assume the best scenario—you get to choose all the team members, and all of the candidates are available to you. To help you hone your newfound skills at team formation, we will build the team one role at a time. The purist would argue that this will not ensure that the best team is formed because to ensure that you have the best you would have had to consider every possible team and then pick the one that meets all requirements. Therefore, picking team members one at a time does not ensure that you have found the best. They are right, but the optimal solution—considering all 384 teams and choosing the best—is simply not feasible.

Early in my career as a systems consultant I made a proposal to my manager on how I could find the optimal solution for a particularly thorny reliability engineering problem that we had been trying to solve. He immediately responded, "I have never paid anyone to find an optimal solution to anything, and I never will. I will pay you to improve our current situation by 5 percent, that's all." Filling the team, one member at a time, may not be optimal, but who cares?

Even though we have profiled the project and every team member on a number of dimensions, choosing the members for the Gold Team is not a science. The data we have collected is not sufficient, nor should it be, for choosing team members. That is not their purpose. There is no quantitative measure that will allow us to compare one choice against another and determine which among those choices is best. It is very unlikely that there will ever be a best choice. There will be a number of judgment calls, and many will be very subjective. In the case study, some of our choices will seem rather arbitrary. That will not be the case in a real situation. In those cases you will have additional information that will assist in your decision making. My purpose here is to show you how you can use these tools to make better use of the people that you do have on your team. In the final analysis, we will choose a particular team because we can handle the deficiencies it presents better than we can handle the deficiencies of any other team that was available to us.

In Chapter 5, "The Case Study," I presented the Gold Team organizational structure shown in Figure 11.9. Keep it in mind as we proceed to choose the team members.

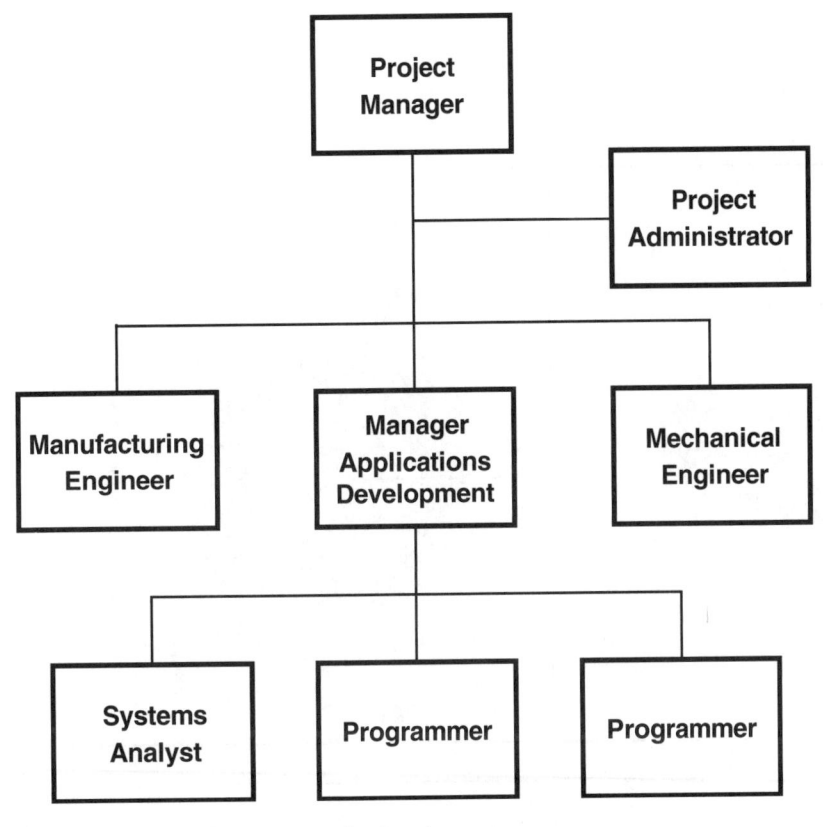

Figure 11.9 Gold Team organizational structure.

Choosing the Team Members

Let's start at the top of the organizational chart and describe the choices we have for project manager first. Then we'll work our way down through the project positions one at a time. Figures 11.10 and 11.13 through 11.18 display the HBDI, SDI, and LSI data for each candidate for the position. Figures 11.11 and 11.12 show the Project Manager Competency Assessment data for each of the two candidates for the project manager position. You will also need the individual skill profile data, that information is stored on the CD-ROM. Given this data, who would you choose and why?

I'll give you the analysis of the HBDI, SDI, and LSI data. Remember, that data is not used for selection. It is used for assessment of the final outcome of our choices. We'll follow this same format for all eight positions, and when you are done, you will have formed your Gold Team. Then go to www.teamarchitect.com and generate the team reports and analyze the balance on your team.

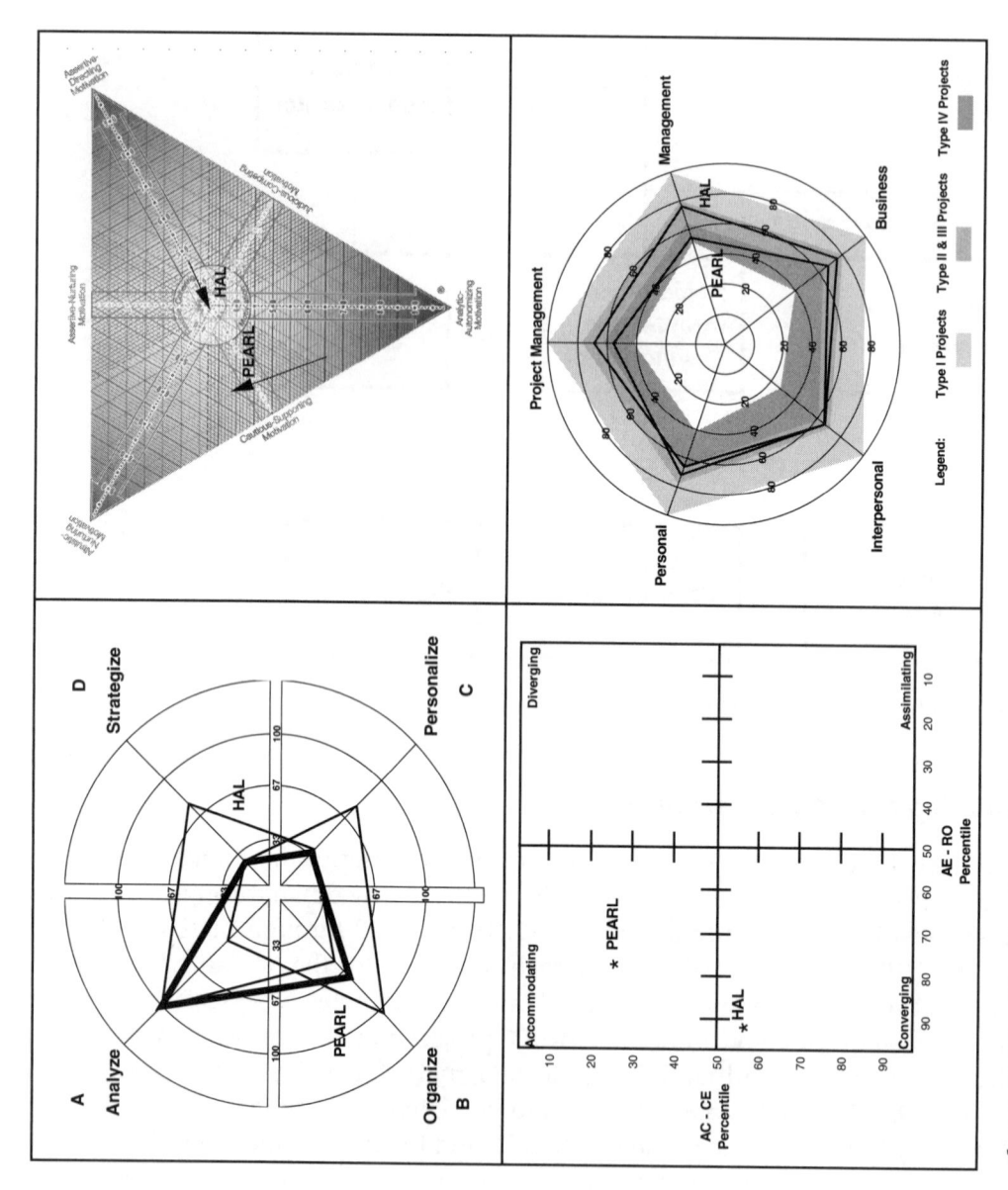

Figure 11.10 Choosing the project manager.

Before we start, a word of caution is in order. None of the assessment instruments (HBDI, SDI, or LSI) were developed as selection tools. They describe motives, behaviors, and styles, not skills. Every one of us can adjust our behaviors to fit a given situation. Every one of us exhibits different behaviors and styles at different times. Every one of us is multidimensional. To depend on one assessment tool to select a team member is nonsense. Rather, we try our best to understand the whole individual and based on that understanding choose the best course of action for the given situation. Some of our inputs will come in the form of assessments. Some of our inputs will come from our first-hand experiences with people, what others say about them, what track record they have established for themselves, how they interact with others we are considering, and a host of other experiential and behavioral inputs. The exercise that I will lead you through in the next section is hypothetical. It is designed to give you some experience and practice in interpreting the data we have been talking about in this book. It is purely that and nothing more.

Project Manager

If Pearl has been chosen as project manager, her weak analytic thinking preferences as evidenced by her low A-Quadrant score will have to be compensated for by others on the team. If Hal has been chosen as project manager, his creative and strategic styles, because they far exceed the Gold Project characteristics (87 for Hal versus 25 for the project), may lead to frustration on his part. Based on his SDI profile (flexible-cohering), Hal would appear to be an excellent fit for project manager. His motivational values and valued-related style are a natural fit for project management. Because he is flexible-cohering he readily adapts to a variety of situations and will be even-handed and take all factors into account in settling conflict situations. Hal is a good problem solver and will be results oriented. Pearl, on the other hand, works well with people and will be a good asset when it comes to implementation.

The PMCA reports (Figures 11.11 and 11.12) show a marked difference between the two project manager candidates. We discussed those differences in Chapter 9. Hal's PMCA showed that he was seen as strong by his assessors in all areas significant to the Gold Project and that he had a realistic self-awareness of his competencies. Pearl, on the other hand, had a number of deficiencies. Most notably, she had a very inflated view of herself, and although her interpersonal competencies were excellent her management competencies were lacking.

206 Building Effective Project Teams

Business Competencies
 Business Awareness
 Business Partnership
 Commitment to Quality

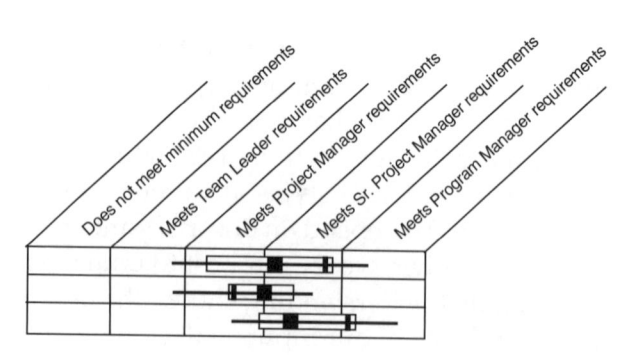

Personal Competencies
 Initiative
 Information Gathering
 Conceptual Thinking
 Self Confidence
 Concern for Credibility
 Flexibility

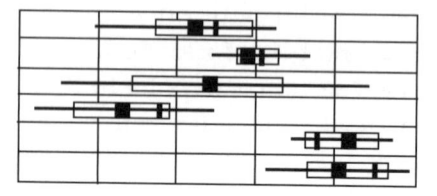

Interpersonal Competencies
 Interpersonal Awareness
 Organizational Awareness
 Anticipation of Impact
 Resourceful Use of Influence

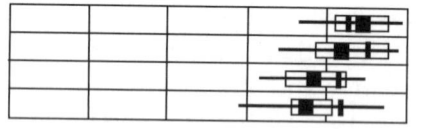

Management Competencies
 Motivating Others
 Communication Skills
 Developing Others
 Planning
 Monitoring & Controlling

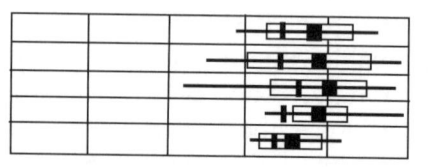

Column headers: Does not meet minimum requirements | Meets Team Leader requirements | Meets Project Manager requirements | Meets Sr. Project Manager requirements | Meets Program Manager requirements

Figure 11.11 Hal E. Lewya's PMCA profile.

Project Administrator

Dick is most effective in getting results by the book. He prefers to follow process and structure as evidenced by his high B-Quadrant score, but he can be abrasive in so doing, as evidenced by his low C-Quadrant score. Olive, on the other hand, deals effectively with people in getting results, as evidenced by her C-Quadrant score and her Blue SDI arrow. The only observable HBDI difference between the two is their interpersonal thinking styles. As far as conflict situations are concerned, Olive, because of her Blue arrow, would appear better equipped than Dick, because of his Green

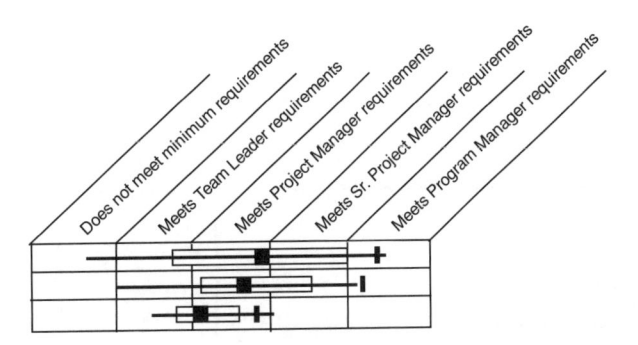

Business Competencies
  Business Awareness
  Business Partnership
  Commitment to Quality

Personal Competencies
  Initiative
  Information Gathering
  Conceptual Thinking
  Self Confidence
  Concern for Credibility
  Flexibility

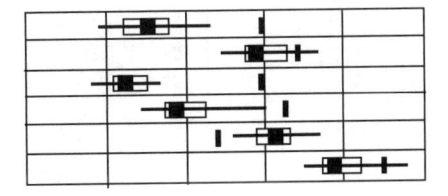

Interpersonal Competencies
  Interpersonal Awareness
  Organizational Awareness
  Anticipation of Impact
  Resourceful Use of Influence

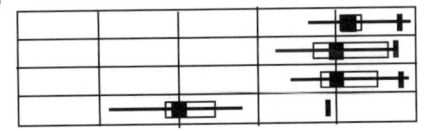

Management Competencies
  Motivating Others
  Communication Skills
  Developing Others
  Planning
  Monitoring & Controlling

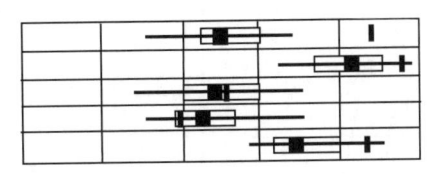

Figure 11.12   Pearl E. Gates's PMCA profile.

arrow, to deal with conflict that involves people outside the team. Their problem-solving styles are quite different. Olive prefers moderation (she is an accommodator) while Dick prefers a more direct style (he is a converger). Both styles are effective, however.

Applications Development Manager

Sal and Anita's thinking preferences are very similar to one another and match well to the thinking characterization of the Gold Project. Based only on the HBDI profiles, either person would be a good fit. Their conflict

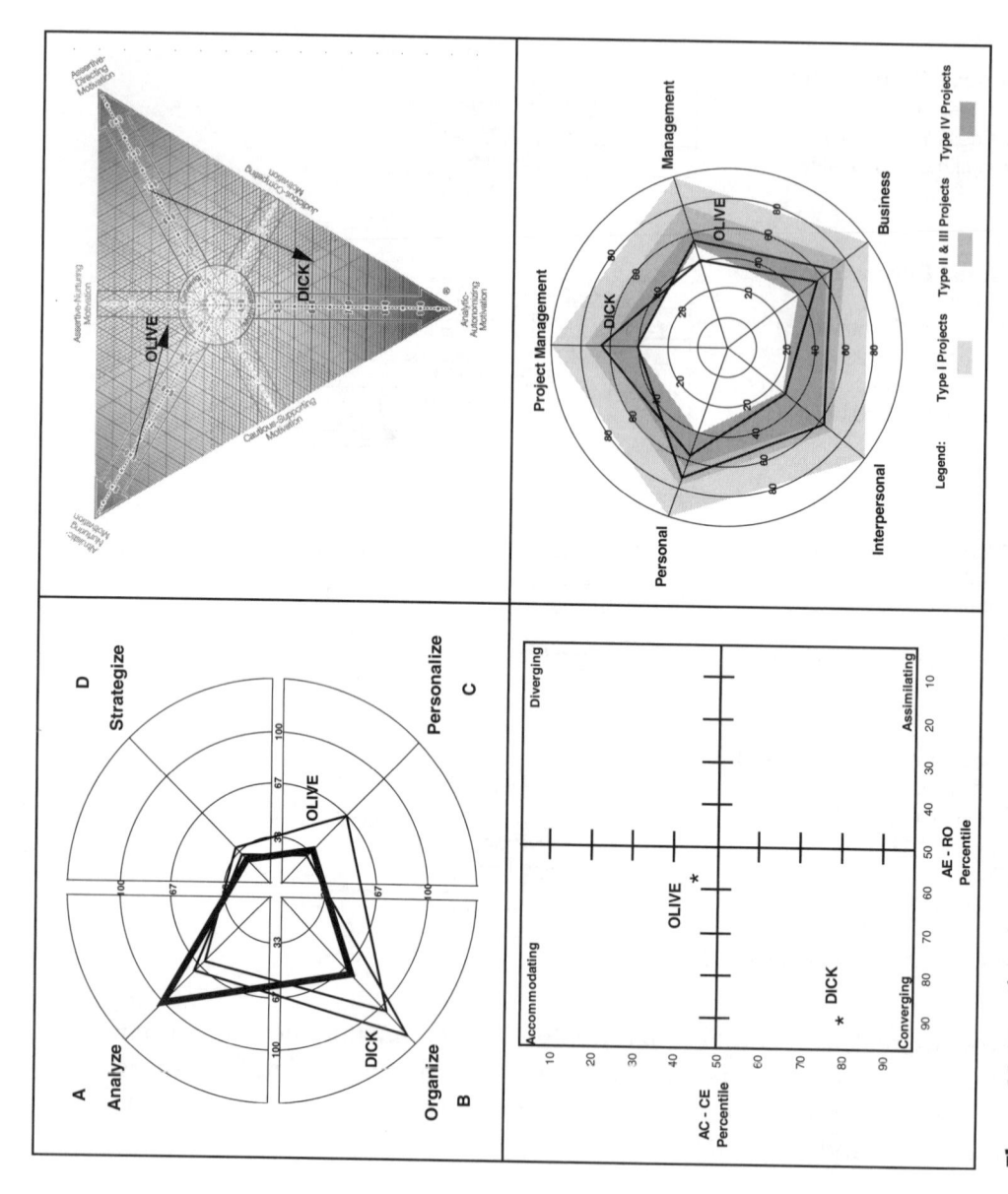

Figure 11.13 Choosing the project administrator.

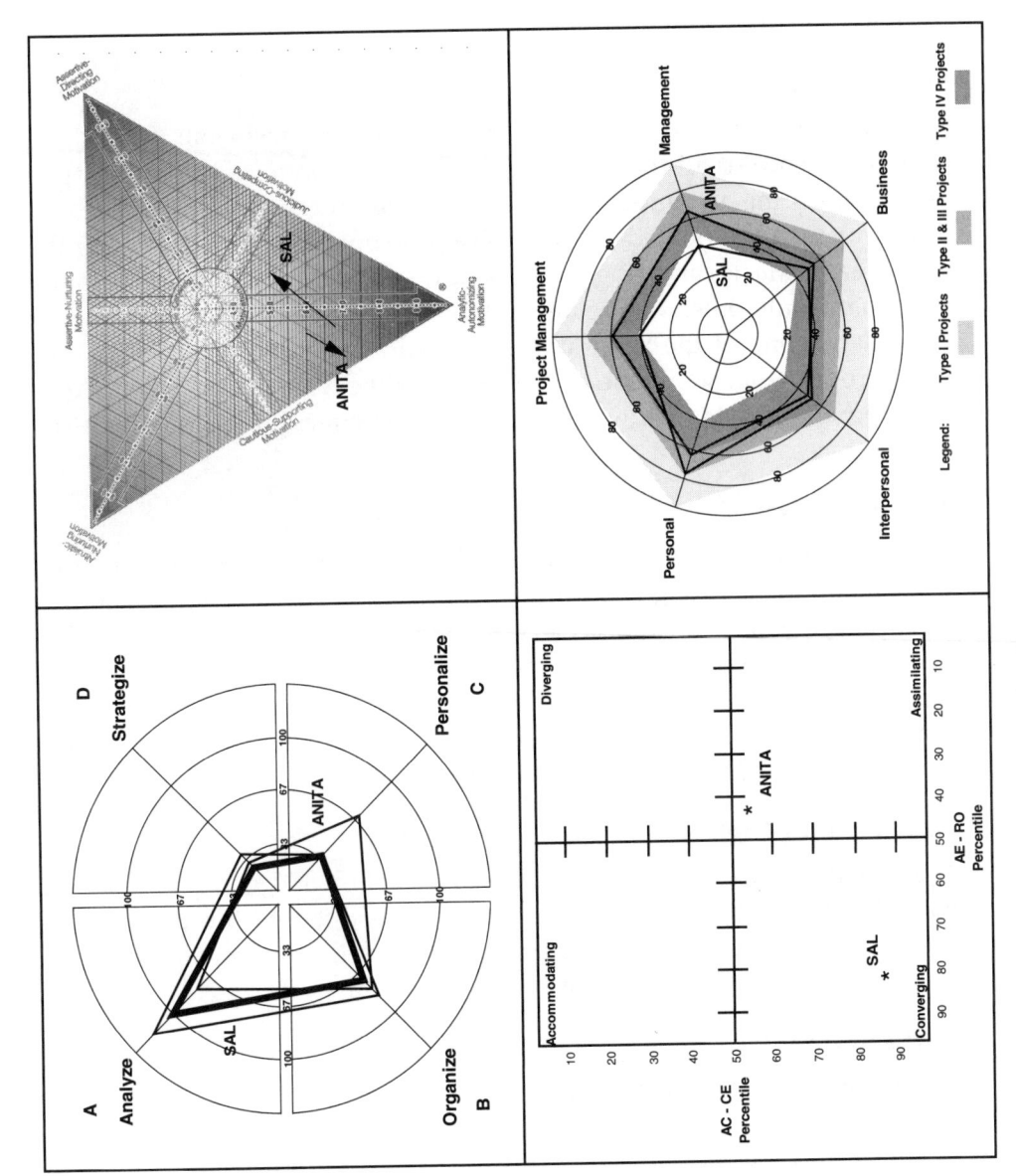

Figure 11.14 Choosing the applications development manager.

resolution sequences will not be distinguishable in practice. Both have Green arrows. Anita's problem-solving skills are more balanced than Sal's, which is evidenced by her LSI data point near the center of the four quadrants. Sal brings stronger closure (he is a strong converger, as measured by the LSI) than does Anita.

Programmers

Mike Rowtoys presents a dilemma. He has the strongest analytic thinking style preference of all the programmers, but his preferred thinking style would also bring an almost unbridled creative energy to the team. He and Sy are not people-oriented and may be a problem if both are chosen for the Gold Team. Mack can bring some people orientation to a programming team that would otherwise be insensitive to others in any kind of situation. For balance one of the programmers should be either Sy or Mack. The other programmer should be either Terri or Mike. This strategy would give the programming team a wider range of problem-solving skills than any other choices.

Systems Analyst

Barry is a strong left brain, as evidenced by his high A- and B-Quadrant scores; Doug is a strong right brain, as evidenced by his high C- and D-Quadrant scores. The Gold Project is a left-brain project. From a conflict management perspective, both candidates share the same valued-relating styles. Doug is more likely to offer multiple perspectives on a situation (he is a diverger) than is Barry (he is an assimilator), but again the two are not that different when it comes to their learning styles.

Manufacturing Engineer

The two Justins are very similar on their HBDI, LSI, SDI, and PMSA scores. Basically, you can flip a coin. Both are well-suited to the project. The remarkable similarity in their profiles suggests that they were probably classmates and spent a lot of time studying together.

Mechanical Engineer

Mel's thinking styles are more closely aligned to the Gold Project than are Lou's, who has a high D-Quadrant score as compared to Mel. In view of the integration of the computer with process control aspects of the new organ design, Lou (because he has a Green arrow) may be a better choice to have in your corner during conflict situations. Mel's valued-relating style is far more people-centered (his arrow is Blue).

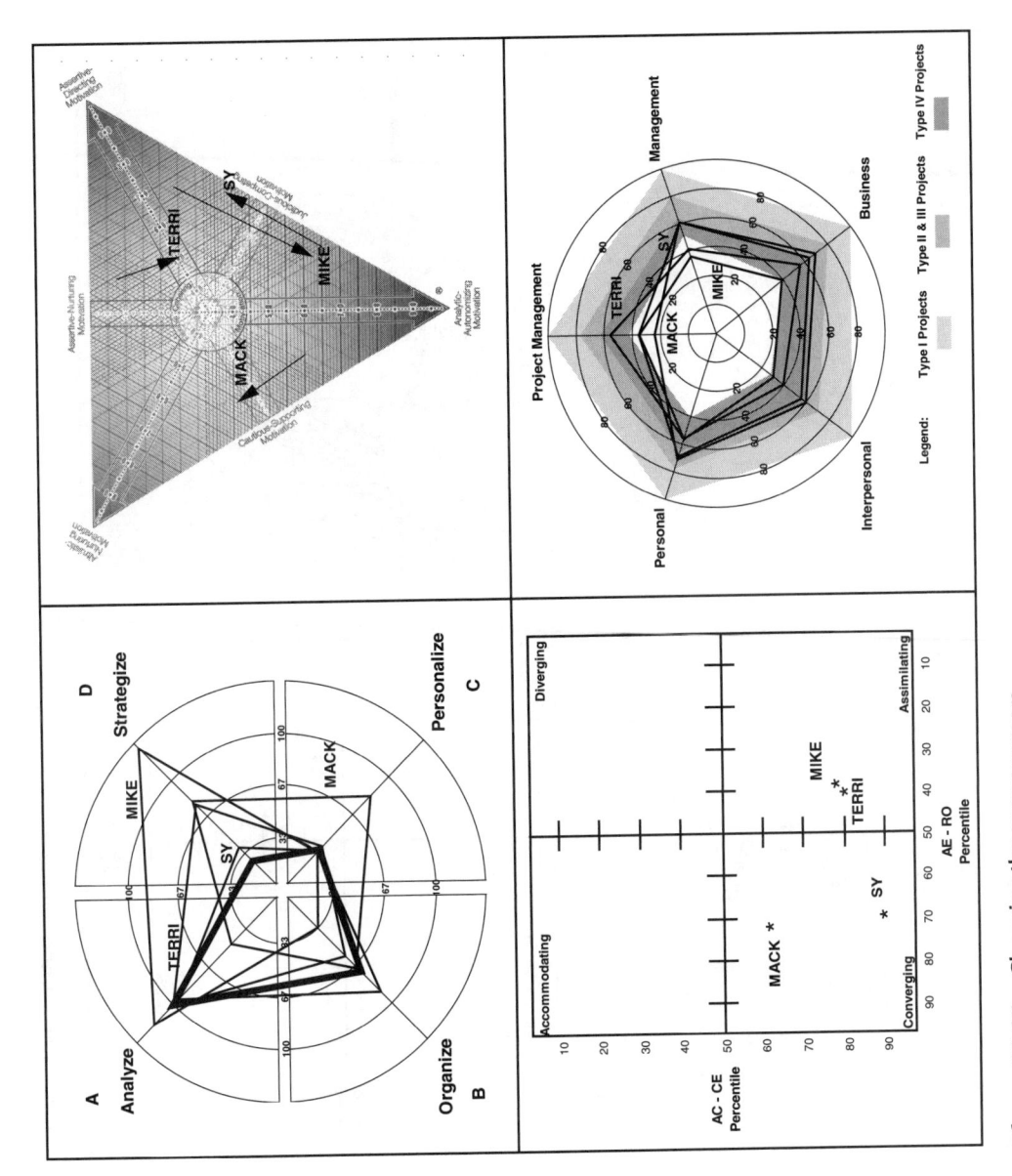

Figure 11.15 Choosing the programmers.

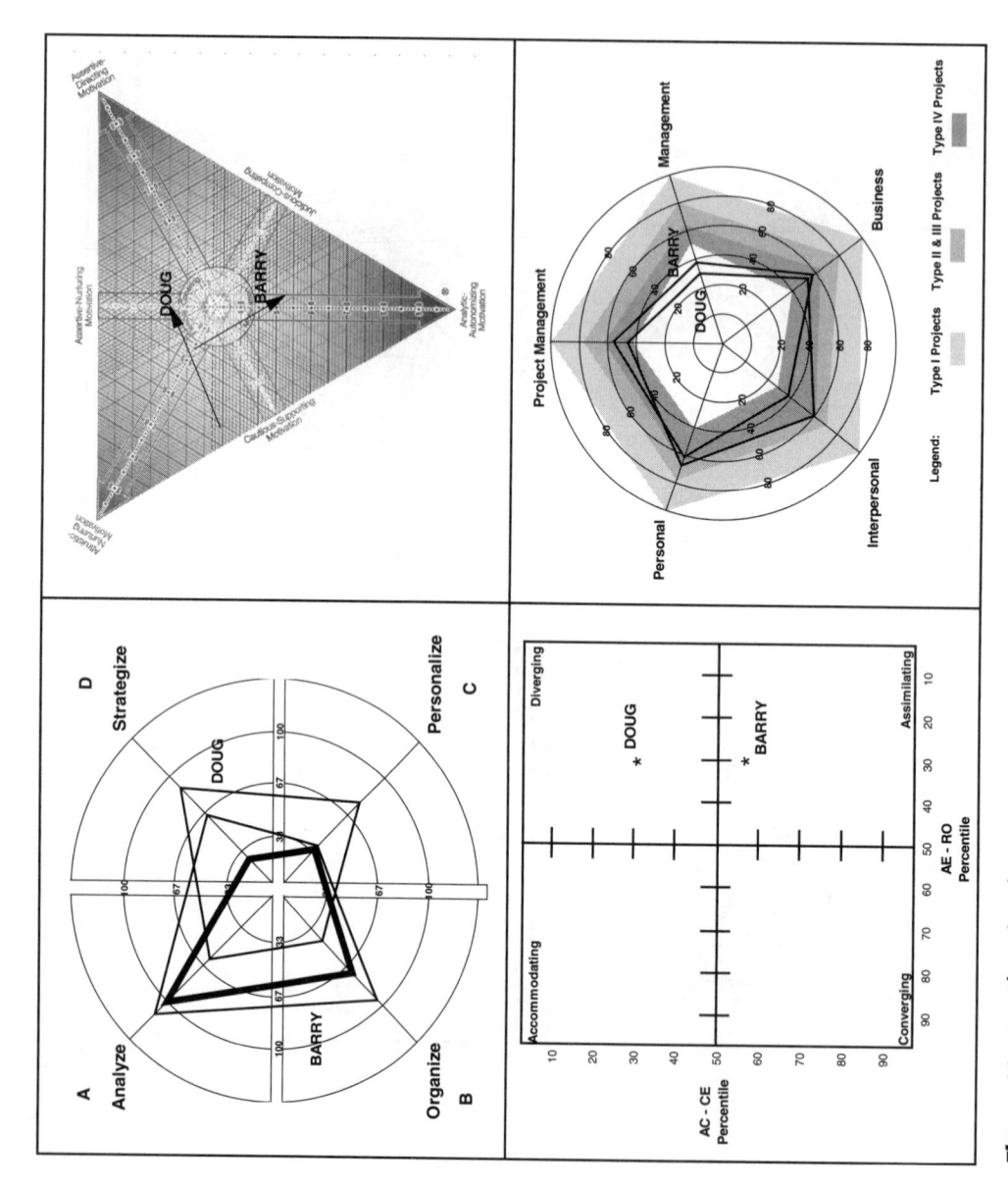

Figure 11.16 Choosing the systems analyst.

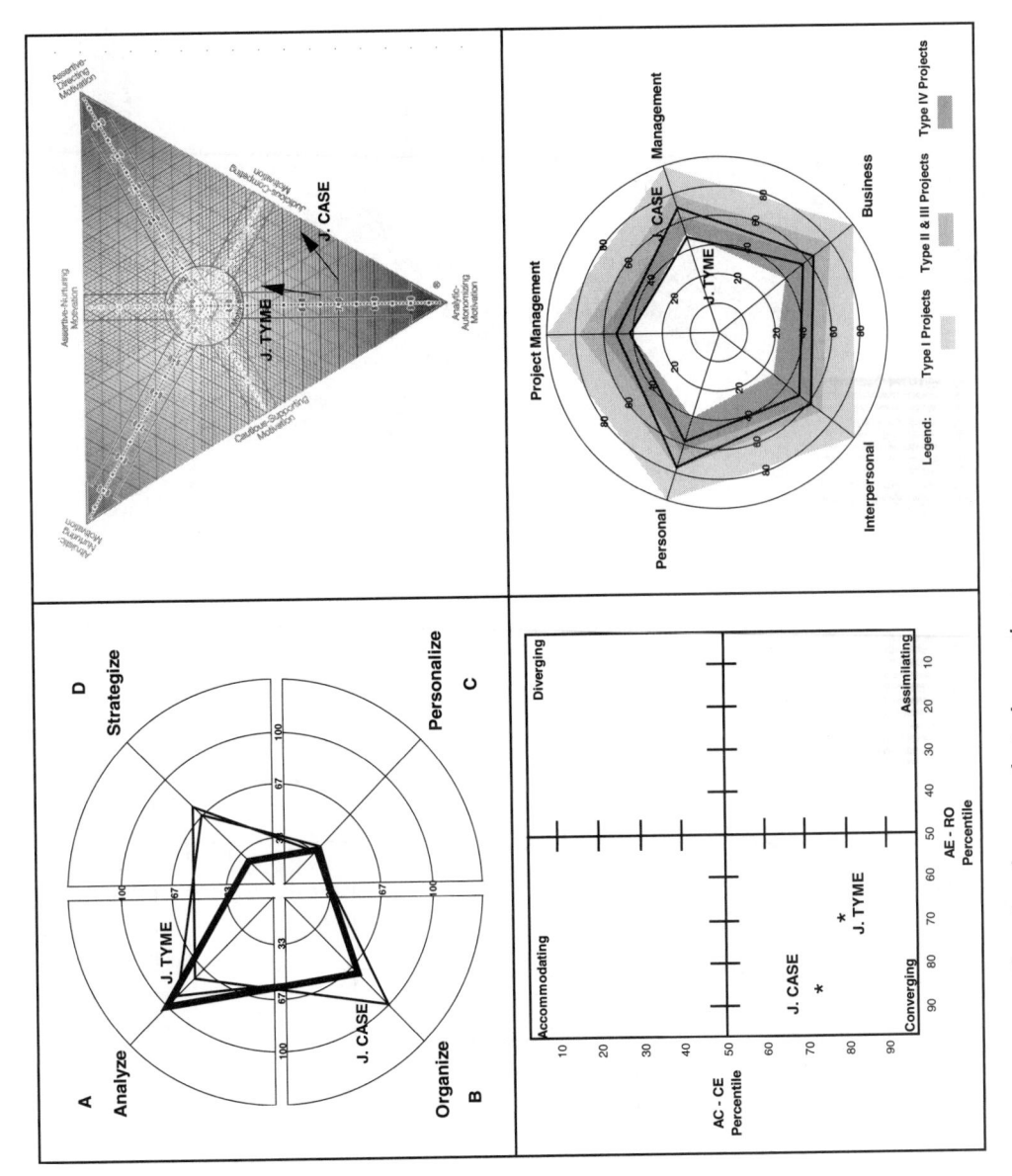

Figure 11.17 Choosing the manufacturing engineer.

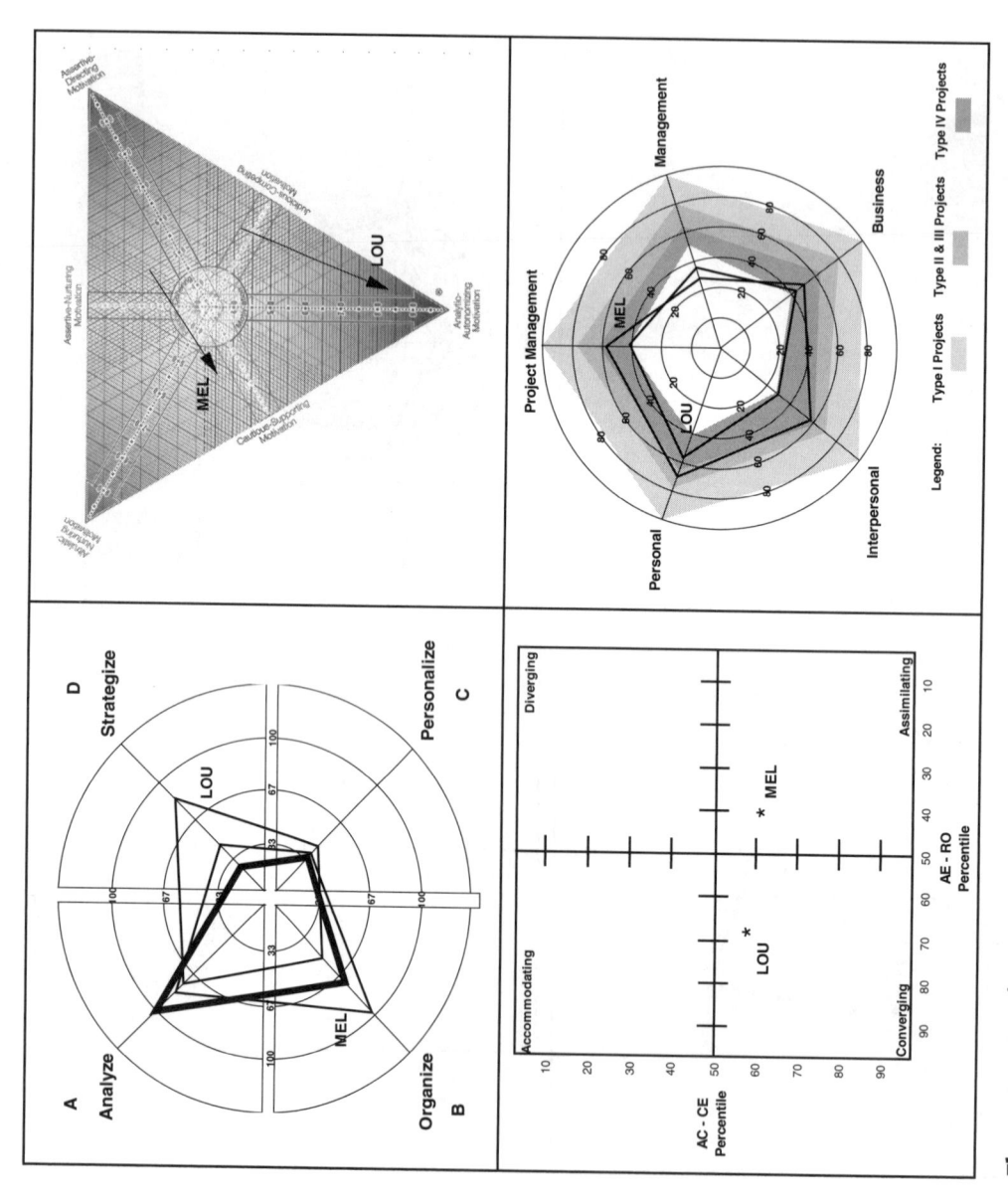

Figure 11.18 Choosing the mechanical engineer.

Putting It All Together

I hope that you did the exercise and have formed a team. Now go to www.teamarchitect.com. You can access it from the CD-ROM. Define your team, and generate the reports. Print the reports and turn to Chapter 12, "Assessing Team Alignment and Balance," where we will analyze the alignment gaps between the team and the project and determine the appropriate corrective action.

In the next chapter we will further analyze the team's profile and discuss what we can do to improve its effectiveness. One of the profiling tools we have at our disposal is the HBDI. As we have learned, it is significant because it allows us to use the same four-quadrant characterization for both the project and the project team. This is the only metric that I am aware of that has this property. It is unique! It is significant! It is powerful! It will be the foundation on which much of the remainder of this book is based.

CHAPTER 12

Assessing Team Alignment and Balance

Welcome back! You should have used the CD-ROM to run the profile reports on the members you picked for your team. Were you surprised by any of the reports? Are there any decisions you would like to change now that you see the results of your earlier decisions? If so, go ahead and make them now.

You have now reached the point where you have formed your project team. How you got here really doesn't make any difference to the assessments that will shortly follow. You may have had the luxury of recruiting each and every one of your team members. If you used the tools we talked about, your team is as good a team as you can form—at least within reason. At the least, it is as ideal as the pool of available candidates will allow. It is unlikely that you will be able to hand pick each and every team member very often, if at all.

In 35 years of practicing project management, I have had only one occasion where I was able to recruit each and every member of the team. I am living proof that project management can be a lot of fun when you get to pick the entire team. I used all of the tools I have talked about in this book to help me develop my 30-person team. The team was actually four separate teams that worked on four projects that made up the program. The program was completed in 27 months (it was planned for 36), it cost $2.7 million (it was budgeted for $5 million), and the customer was satisfied.

On a more realistic note, you probably reached this point and have a team for which you had no opportunity to adjust its membership. You may not even have had the opportunity to work with any of your team members in the past. You may know some of the team members by reputation or by what others have said about them. You simply have to make the best of it. As desperate as this situation may be, this book equips you with a pretty powerful set of tools that will help you make the best of it. We'll put them to use in this chapter.

The third path to this point is the one where you have been able to choose some, but not all, of your team members. The ones you did choose were people you have had previous success working with and who were available. Others that you would have chosen were not available, and those team positions were filled by people who were available but with whom you had no previous experience working. They were unknowns to you. Your team is therefore made up of people you were familiar with and people who were new to you. The dynamics in this situation can be uncomfortable. For example, how will you integrate the new people into the team? Will they feel like outsiders who are trying to gain membership into your club, or will they be treated as equals? Think about that the next time this situation comes up. Once you have a strategy for handling that it's time to move on to the assessment of the full team and how you are going to handle any alignment problems that that assessment uncovers. That is the topic of this chapter.

Regardless of the path you took to get the team you have, your next task is to assess the team you have and to figure out the best way to develop and deploy them to the work of the project. The assessment has three parts: team-to-project alignment (we'll use the HBDI), team balance (we'll use the LSI and SDI), and team skills profile (we'll use the PMSA and PMCA). All three will be covered in this chapter.

Team-to-Project Alignment

The HBDI is the tool that will help us measure and analyze the team-to-project alignment. Regardless of the manner in which the team was formed, there will be differences between the profile of the project and the profile of the team. The two may be closely aligned because we had the opportunity to recruit all or most of the team members. They may not be at all aligned because the team was formed in a rather haphazard fashion, such as by simply assigning anyone who happened to be available who had the needed technical skills. The project team may possess more or less of particular thinking styles than the project calls for. If it is less, the project manager will have to support training and development to overcome that shortfall, or the team will have to find workarounds to minimize the negative impact of that skill shortage on the project. If it exceeds the requirements of the project, the team will have some relief because the thinking styles profile of the team exceeds that of the project.

Don't get too comfortable, though. If the team greatly exceeds the requirement, your team may still be at risk. Too much of a good thing will have a negative effect on the project.

Definition of an Alignment Gap

An *alignment gap* is any variance between what the project requires and what the team provides. It can be either a positive or a negative alignment gap. A *positive alignment gap* arises when the team provides more of a skill or characteristic or style preference than the project requires. At first glance, you might ask: "Why worry about a positive alignment gap?" There are at least two reasons that I can think of for worrying about a positive alignment gap. The first has to do with wasting resources. Why buy a Cadillac when a Ford will do just fine? Perhaps there is some other project that needs a higher dose of that skill. Save it for places where it is needed. The second, and more important, reason is that too much of a good thing is not good. If I don't need a lot of analytical thinking on my team but I have a lot of analytical team members, what do you think will happen? My guess is that they will be looking for things to analyze that don't really need analyzing. That's what they like to do, and that is what they will try to do.

A *negative alignment gap* arises when the project requires more of a characteristic than the team possesses. The development and implementation projects discussed in Chapter 10, "Establishing the Profile of the Project," are a good example. Suppose the project team has a B-Quadrant profile score that is very low; say most of the team members' scores are between 30 and 50, and the project D-Quadrant profile is 80. This creates the negative alignment gap. This team would rather avoid the organized thinking style, yet the project requires that style. Unless something is done to correct this negative alignment, the team may be heading for trouble.

Interpreting Alignment Gaps

Here are some guidelines that I have used. Small alignment gaps, less than 10 points on any one of the four quadrant scales of the HBDI, of either type will be of little concern to the project manager. Any variance greater than

10 points will be considered worthy of attention. A gap of more than 10 points signals an out-of-control situation to which the project manager will have to respond with some corrective action or strategy.

Figure 12.1 shows a project and project team profile that I will use as an example for this section. Figure 12.2 gives us the rule that we use to decide whether the gap is significant. If the magnitude of the gap is greater than 20 (positive or negative), it is significant and some corrective action is required. If the magnitude of the gap is between 10 and 20 (positive or negative), some monitoring of the situation is called for. If the magnitude of the gap is less than 10 (positive or negative), it is considered marginal and not likely to cause any alignment problems.

The alignment gaps in this example are: A +9, B –22, C –14, and D +39. The particular situation will suggest the appropriate actions, but we can offer some general comments. The negative gap in the B-Quadrant might be handled by having an outside agent monitor and enforce compliance to

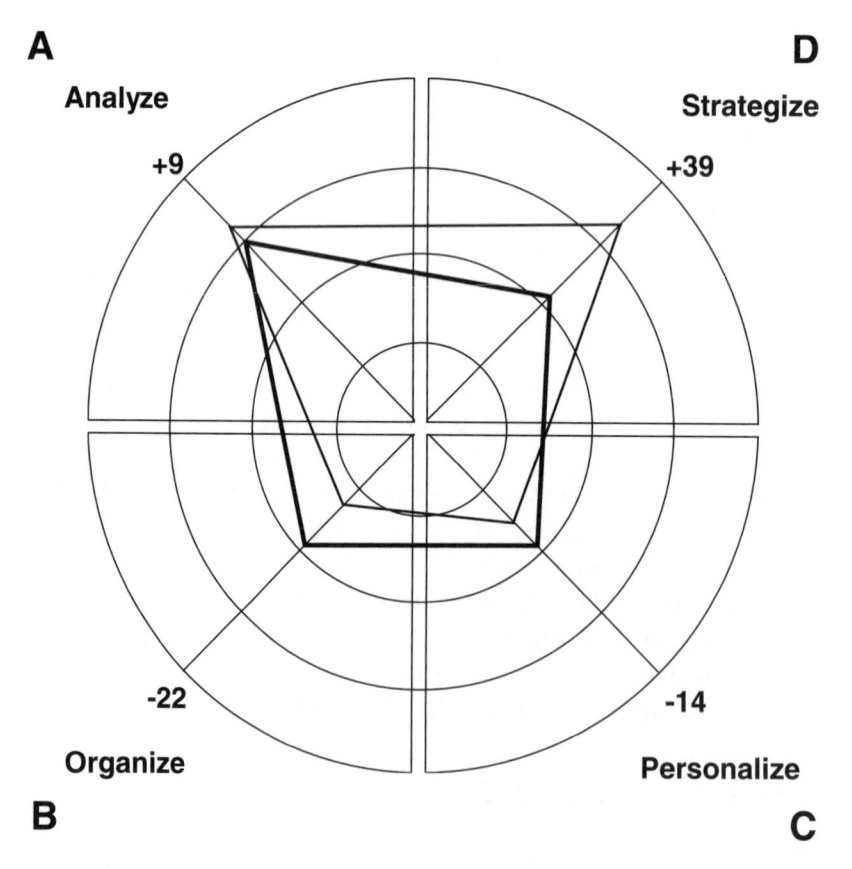

Figure 12.1   An example project and team profile.

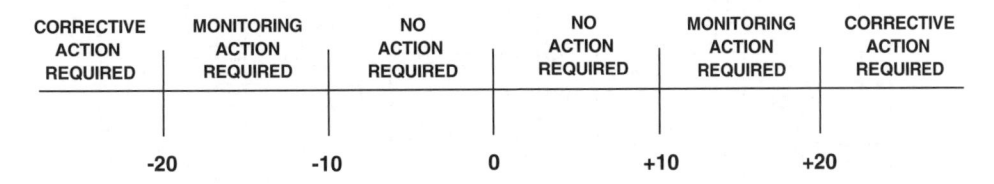

```
CORRECTIVE    MONITORING    NO           NO           MONITORING    CORRECTIVE
ACTION        ACTION        ACTION       ACTION       ACTION        ACTION
REQUIRED      REQUIRED      REQUIRED     REQUIRED     REQUIRED      REQUIRED
   |             |             |            |             |             |
  -20           -10            0           +10           +20
```

Figure 12.2 How to handle the size of the gap.

standards. If your company has a project office, someone from that office might act in that capacity. The negative gap in the C-Quadrant could be handled by designating someone on the team to be responsible for reminding the team to think about people's reactions to a pending action or decision being considered by the team. Role playing can be an effective corrective action. The large positive alignment gap in the D-Quadrant must be addressed. We have seen several examples of this in the five teams formed in Chapter 11, "Establishing the Profile of the Project Team." The project manager is going to have to be a strong leader and keep the team focused. There will be a constant effort to build a fully equipped Jaguar when a low-end Ford is called for.

The best way to apply these rules is to assess some actual project teams.

Assessing a Project Team

Your next assignment will be to analyze your chosen team. But before I turn you loose on that, I'll run you through a few analyses of my own. To do so, I have created five teams, which we will analyze. The data and team membership for each of the 16 members of the candidate pool is shown in Figure 12.3. The last five columns on the right identify the members of each team (A = Team Alpha, B = Team Beta, G = Team Gamma, D = Team Delta, E = Team Epsilon). Each team was created using a different formation strategy. You should be able to discern what those strategies were based on the reports that are reproduced here.

First some observations, which apply to all of the teams, are in order. These were deduced from our analysis of the candidate pool. All of the D-Quadrant scores were above the project's D-Quadrant score. That means each team will have to be alert to the tendency of team members to get more creative than the project calls for. The candidate pool has a serious deficiency in several skill areas. While that is observable from the percentile graphic shown in each of the figures that follow, a more detailed analysis is required. That can be found in Table 12.1.

GOLD MEDALLION ORGAN CANDIDATE POOL DATA

NAME	TITLE	ROLE	HBDI A	HBDI B	HBDI C	HBDI D	SDI (BRG) normal			SDI (BRG) conflict			LSI AE	LSI AC	LSI RO	LSI CE	SKILL % PM	MG	BU	IP	PE
Hal E. Lewya	VP Mfg	PM	98	54	63	87	26	46	28	35	32	33	38	36	16	30	69	76	76	67	67
Pearl E. Gates	VP Dev	PM	42	105	80	26	28	7	65	50	10	40	29	36	14	41	55	54	68	67	72
Olive Branch	Admin Asst	Proj Admin	60	107	67	36	78	9	13	43	35	22	24	41	16	39	40	54	56	64	72
Dick Tator	Admin Asst	Proj Admin	74	123	30	30	21	60	19	10	30	60	43	34	23	20	66	41	55	29	56
Sal Vation	IT Mgr	Mgr App Dev	116	86	37	37	22	11	67	16	33	51	47	30	30	13	41	43	49	52	75
Anita Kaskett	Mgr Appl Dev	Mgr App Dev	80	80	74	30	27	13	60	27	3	70	41	23	38	18	59	67	54	48	64
Terri Tory	Sr Pgmr	Pgmr	100	58	40	78	37	54	9	25	50	25	40	28	38	14	55	41	56	40	56
Mack N. Tawsch	Pgmr	Pgmr	45	69	84	82	30	8	62	50	9	41	27	44	14	35	24	61	68	60	72
Sy Yonara	Pgmr	Pgmr	93	90	35	40	4	31	65	4	58	38	35	40	17	28	34	61	65	55	69
Mike Rowtoys	Jr Pgmr	Pgmr	118	33	34	128	9	67	24	6	33	61	41	26	40	13	34	37	39	31	56
Barry deBones	Sr Analyst	Analyst	110	93	41	65	47	27	26	21	27	52	15	46	19	40	55	37	58	38	61
Doug deGrave	Analyst	Analyst	60	43	80	90	61	5	34	40	40	20	29	28	32	31	46	31	53	60	67
Justin Case	Sr Mfg Engr	Mfg Engr	78	100	35	80	10	20	70	4	35	61	36	39	24	21	52	69	65	62	75
Justin Tyme	Mfgr Engr	Mfg Engr	90	74	41	68	15	21	64	21	29	50	32	41	20	27	42	48	56	52	58
Mel Otious	Mech Engr	Mech Engr	83	97	38	46	32	50	18	48	15	37	27	38	25	30	41	35	44	29	56
Lou Neetoon	Mech Engr	Mech Engr	76	50	45	86	12	48	40	5	14	81	35	34	24	27	57	28	50	57	69
Project			100	73	36	25															

Figure 12.3 Gold Medallion Organ candidate pool data.

Team Alpha Assessment

Team Alpha's HBDI profile is reasonably well distributed around the project profile in the A- and B-Quadrants. Except for two members (Pearl and Anita) the rest of the team has C-Quadrant scores that are very close to the project's C-Quadrant score. The D-Quadrant is another story. As already pointed out, the candidate pool scores very high on the D-Quadrant relative to the project. Team Alpha is no exception. That high positive gap will be a continuing problem for most, if not all, of the teams. The SDI plot shows that Team Alpha is well balanced with respect to its conflict management strategies. Except for the assertive-nurturing valued-relating style and conflict strategy, all other situations are covered by at least one team member. The altruistic-nurturing valued-relating style is somewhat lacking in Team Alpha. Justin Tyme is the closest to this style, but he is more of a hub person because of the central location of the base of his arrow.

The LSI plot shows slight imbalance with respect to the diverger quadrant, but we knew that this quadrant would be problematic because only one member of the candidate pool, Doug, is a diverger and he is not a member of Team Alpha. All other quadrants are covered by at least one team member. That means that Team Alpha will do reasonably well in solving problems as long as the team members remind themselves to look for alternative solutions rather than going with the first one suggested. They don't have Doug to remind them to seek other solutions. Because Doug is not on the team there will be a slight tendency toward groupthink. That is what can happen when there is no diverger on the team.

Team Beta Assessment

Team Beta is a left-brain team, as evidenced by the high A- and B-Quadrant score distribution. That means that Team Beta is very analytic and process-oriented. The HBDI profile suggests two potential problems arising from this misalignment. The distribution of the B- and D-Quadrant scores of the team are skewed well above the project scores on those two quadrants. Hal is the project manager, and his B-Quadrant score of 54 should be a moderating factor if the team gets too wrapped up in process and procedure to the extent that it becomes an obstacle to progress.

The positive gap in the D-Quadrant is a much more serious problem for Team Beta than it was for Team Alpha. Hal will have his hands full keeping the more creative members of his team (Mike, for example) focused on the deliverable. While the positive gaps on both the B- and D-Quadrants are present these may counter-balance one another to some extent, caution

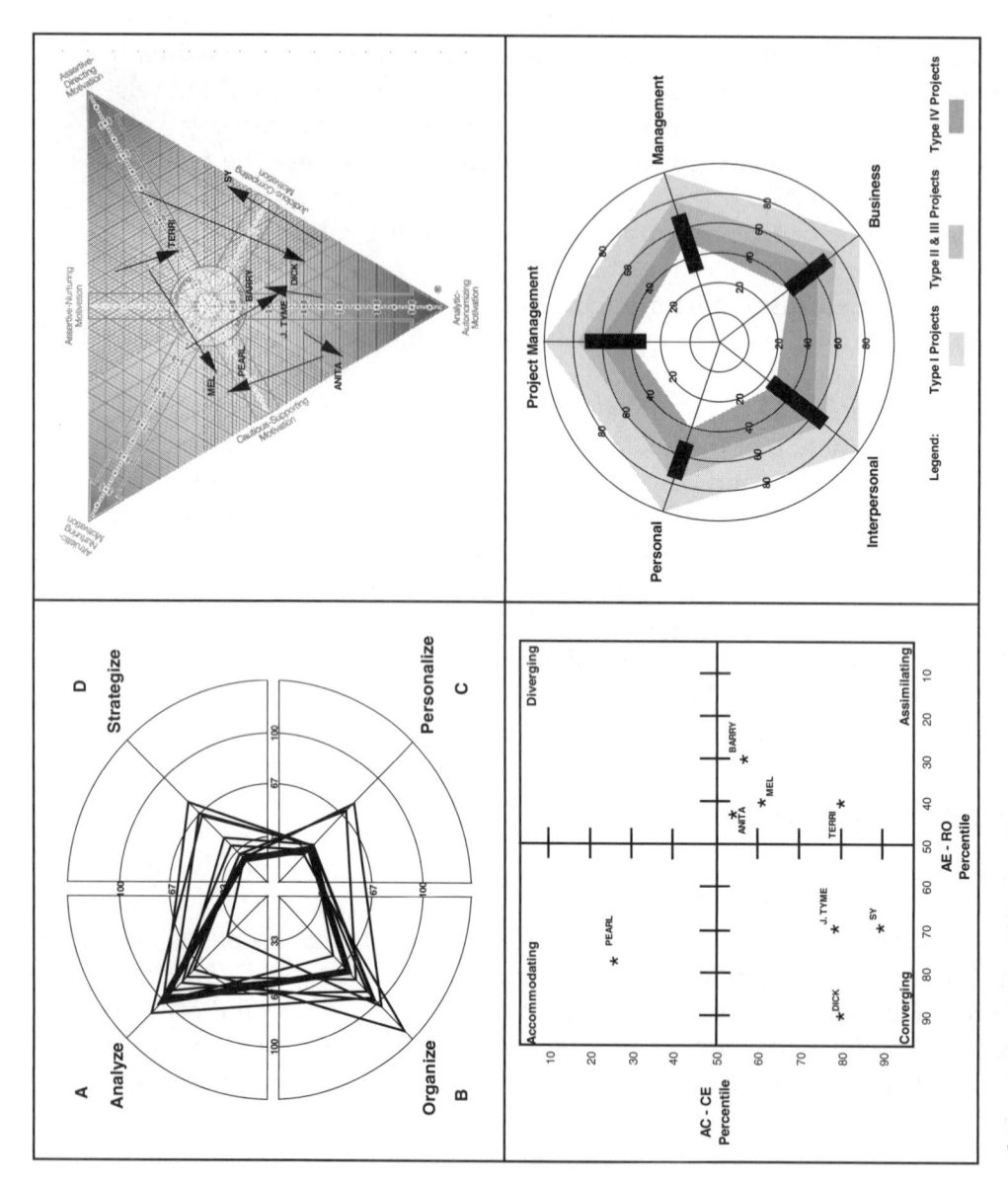

Figure 12.4 Team Alpha profile.

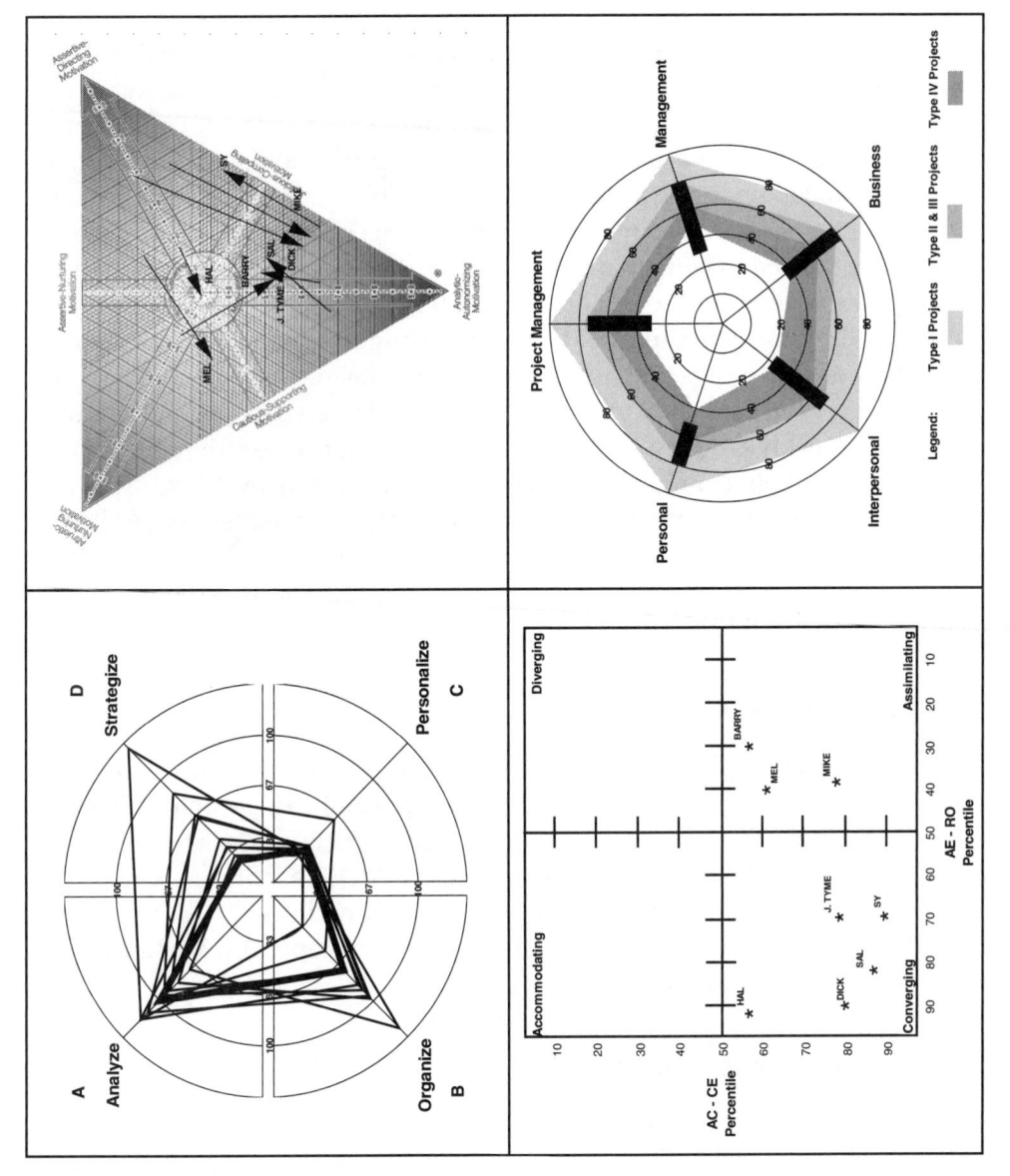

Figure 12.5 Team Beta profile.

225

needs to be exercised so that the team doesn't fall into the trap of creating problems just to have problems to solve and doesn't get too wrapped up in following process and procedure and forget the nature of the task at hand.

The SDI plot further reinforces the analysis of the HBDI profile. We already learned from the HBDI profile of the team that they are analytic and process-oriented, and the preponderance of Green arrows in the SDI is a further reflection of that observation. The team is very strong left-brain and as such may have a penchant for the analytic and get very comfortable just because they are a team of like-minded professionals. Any conflicts that they have among themselves will be highly charged as each tries to inject his or her own analysis of the situation. In the end, the strongest argument will be the one that cannot be refuted by even the most analytic among them. Logic will prevail over emotion.

The LSI plot is consistent with the preceding observations. The team is made up of convergers and assimilators. That means that they will assemble the relevant data, explain it from an analytic perspective, and get to a decision quickly. It may not be the best decision (they do not have a diverger on their team), and it may not be accepted by those who are affected by it (they do not have an accommodator on their team), but it will be sound from an analytic point of view. With this type of team membership, groupthink is a very likely outcome. Hal may need to intervene to counter-balance this tendency.

Team Gamma Assessment

Team Gamma displays some of the same attributes as Team Beta (left-brain with a high positive gap in the D-Quadrant). Its structure is even more analytic than that of Team Beta, however (note the strong Green arrow profile of the team). The team has the added benefit of having Pearl E. Gates on the team. Because she is an accommodator she brings some implementation strength to an otherwise very conceptual team (a team of convergers and assimilators).

Team Delta Assessment

Team Delta offers the best balance across all assessments of all of the teams described previously. Its HBDI, SDI, and LSI profiles are all balanced with respect to the project, valued-relating styles, conflict management strategies, and learning styles. The A-Quadrant profile is skewed below the project's A-Quadrant profile, but the team is a left-brain team (moderate to high A- and B- Quadrant scores), so this negative A-Quadrant gap

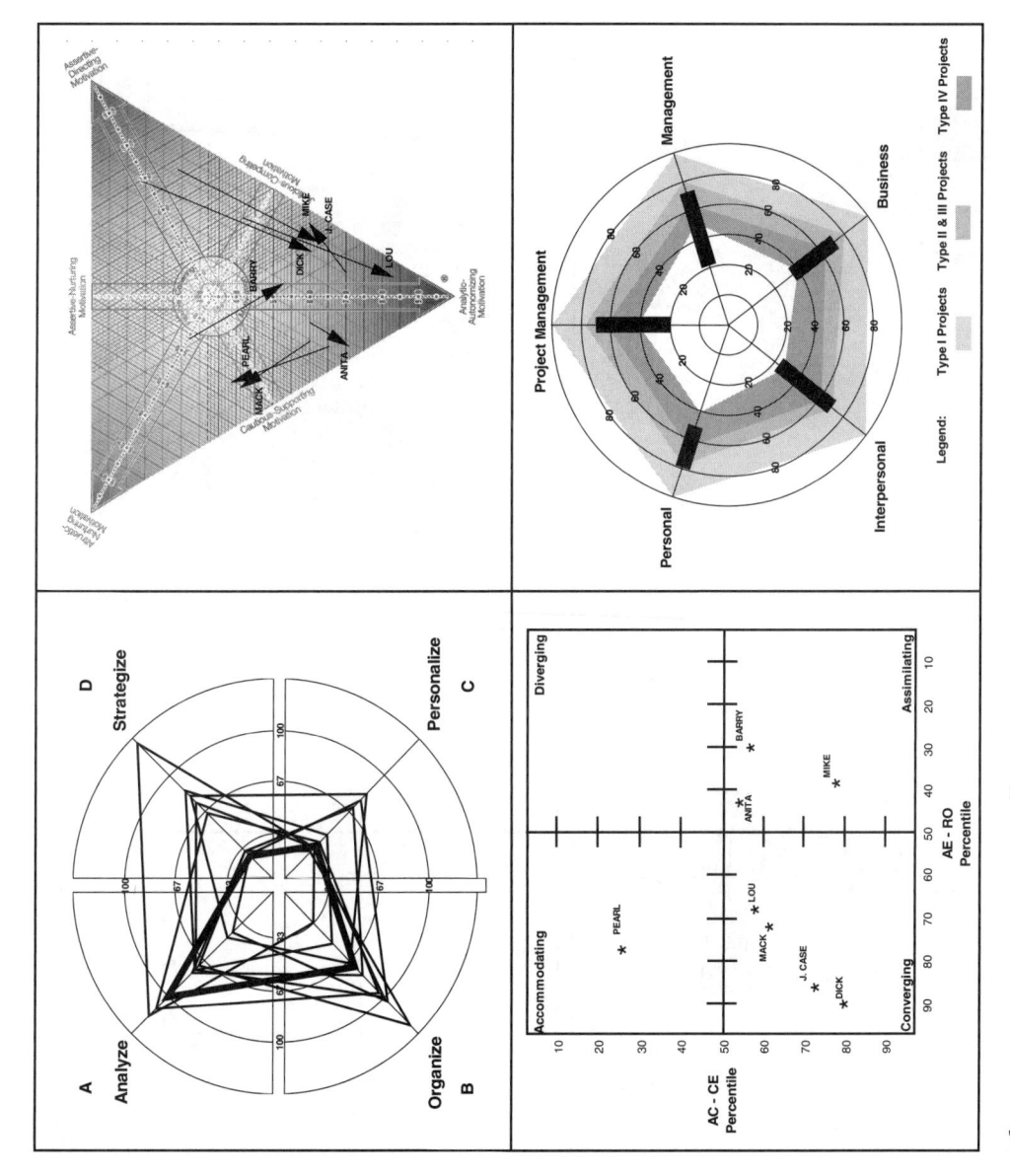

Figure 12.6 Team Gamma profile.

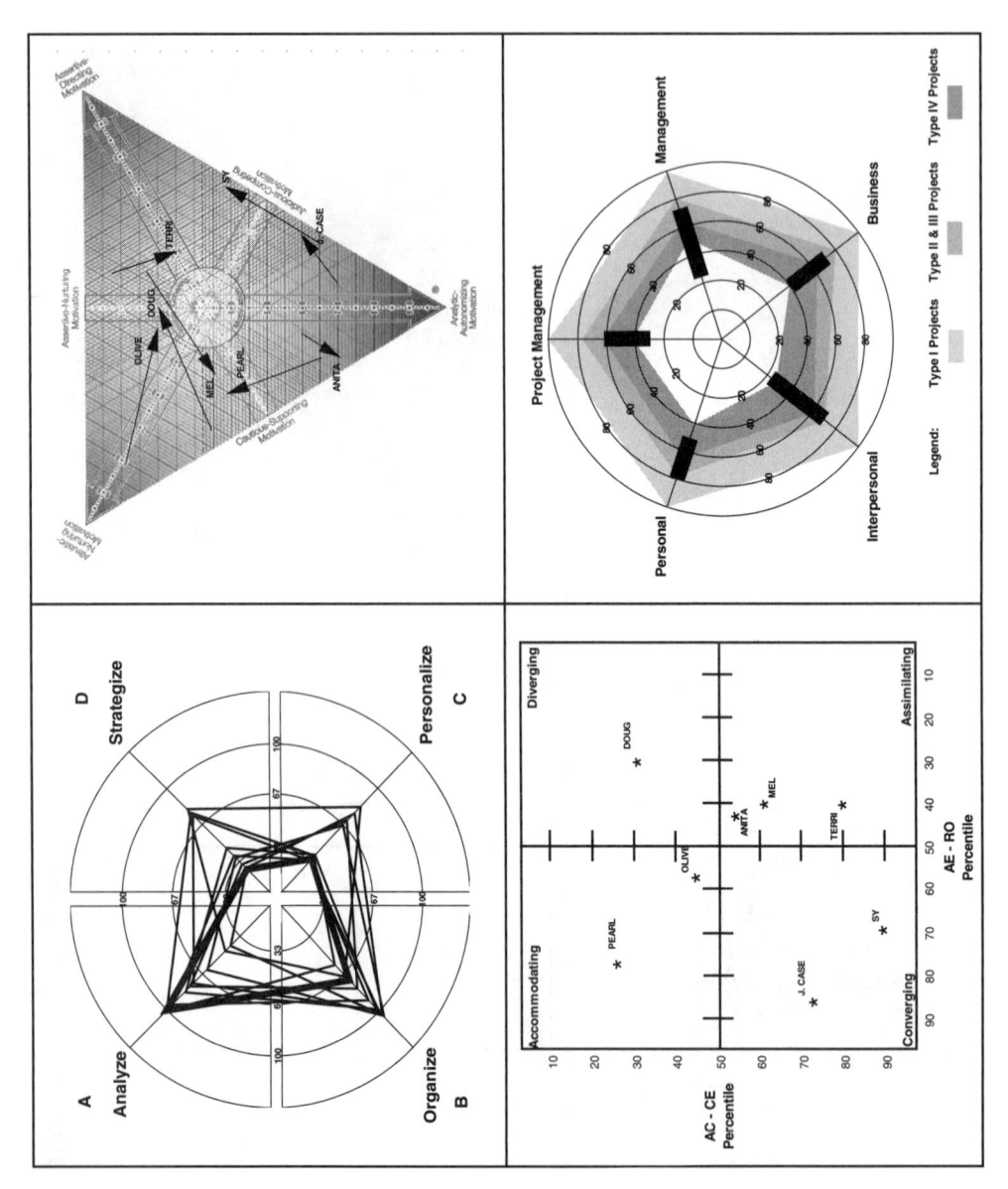

Figure 12.7 Team Delta profile.

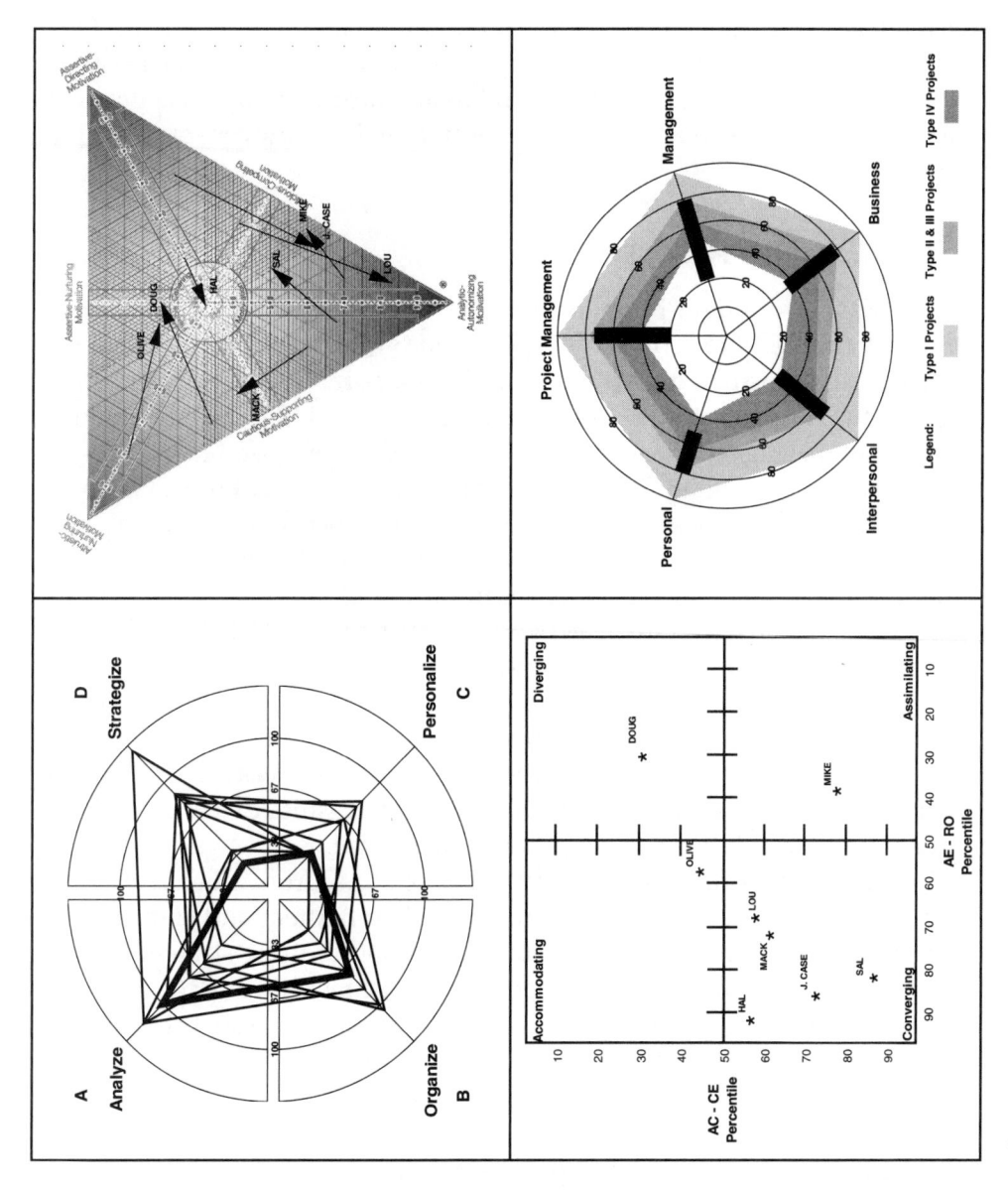

Figure 12.8 Team Epsilon profile.

should not be of major concern. The team can expect to resolve conflicts within and without the team with ease because all seven value–relating styles and conflict management sequences are represented in their SDI profile. They are well represented in every problem-solving quadrant. The team has Doug (the only diverger in the candidate pool), Pearl and Olive (the only two accommodators in the candidate pool), and at least two members in each of the converger and assimilator learning style types. As a result, the team should have great confidence in whatever solutions they develop.

Team Epsilon Assessment

Team Epsilon is a right-brain team (high C- and D-Quadrant profile) trying to work on a left-brain project (high A- and B-Quadrant profile). That presents a large positive gap in the C- and D-Quadrants and a high negative gap in the A-Quadrant. From the standpoint of the HBDI, Team Epsilon is seriously misaligned with the project. The SDI profile of Team Epsilon is somewhat encouraging. The arrows are mostly Green and Blue. Except for Hal (whose arrow is in the hub) there is a distinct lack of the assertive-directing valued-relating style. Hal is the only semblance of leadership on the team. Team conflict situations will pit the Blue arrows (Mack, Olive, and Doug) against the Green arrows (Lou, Justin Case, Mike, and Sal). Hal, because of his hub valued-relating style, will be the go-between.

From a problem solving perspective, Team Epsilon is reasonably well distributed. It has one diverger (Doug), one accommodator (Olive), one assimilator (Mike), and the balance are convergers. Because of its strong converger profile, we can expect the team to be results-driven and able to generate good solutions because of its LSI balance.

Team Epsilon presents an interesting case study from a behavioral perspective. When they see the task they have before them and compare it to their own preferences and styles they have one of three strategies. Bring someone onto the team who is a better fit for the task at hand; change team composition (temporarily or permanently); or simply adjust their behaviors and preferences to accommodate the situation. The strategy they choose should be a decision made by the team.

PMSA Assessment for All Five Teams

The final piece to the puzzle is the PMSA (Project Manager Skill Assessment). Recall that there are 54 project manager skills (18 in project management, 6 personal, 7 interpersonal, 14 business, and 9 management).

Each member of the candidate pool self-assessed his or her proficiencies on each of these 54 skills using Bloom's Taxonomy. The results of those self-assessments are analyzed next for each of the five teams.

Table 12.1 lists all of the deficiencies of each of the five teams at the skill level. A skill deficiency was assigned to the team if the team did not have a member whose proficiency level matched or exceeded the requirements of a Type I project. These requirements were given in Table 9.2 through 9.6. The data shown here is merely the deficiencies ranked within each team based on how serious the deficiency really is. I have set the major deficiencies in bold. These must be corrected if we are to use the team. That means you will choose a team based on your ability to provide corrective action plans to address the deficiencies.

Table 12.1 Ranked Team Skill Deficiencies

SKILL	ALPHA	BETA	GAMMA	DELTA	EPSILON
Project Management					
Complexity assessment				15	8
Cost estimating	22		12	17	
Cost management	8				
Critical path management				**4**	
Detailed estimating	20		10	**16**	
Project closeout	5	2	3	**6**	3
Project notebook construction				2	**1**
Project organization	23	12	13	18	**9**
Project progress assessment				19	**11**
Resource acquisition	10	7			
Resource leveling	10	7	6	7	**6**
Resource requirements	10				
Scope management	19	11	7	8	**4**
Size estimating	10				
Management					
Delegation	5		7	11	
Leadership	1			**1**	
Managing change	**7**				

(Continues)

Table 12.1 (*Continued*)

SKILL	ALPHA	BETA	GAMMA	DELTA	EPSILON
Management					
Meeting management	**10**	6			
Performance management	**18**		5	**11**	
Staff and career development	**17**	2	4	**11**	**5**
Business					
Budgeting	**10**		11	**9**	
Business assessment	3	7	**2**	5	**7**
Business process design	8	5			
Customer service	4	4		9	
Implementation	**2**	**1**	1	**2**	2
Interpersonal					
Relationship management	**10**	**7**	7	**14**	10
Personal					
Decision making/critical thinking	**23**	**13**	14	**20**	12
Presentations	**20**				
TOTAL SKILL DEFICIENCIES	24	13	**14**	20	**12**

This data is not an anomaly. Expect to see skill deficiencies just like these in many of the projects you are trying to staff. We simply have to have a way to deal with deficiencies. My suggestion is to take a closer look at the project and ask how important each skill really is for the project at hand. Then take a look at which skill deficiencies are most easily removed or mitigated. For example, staff and career development ranked high on all five teams. Is that a significant deficiency for this project? Probably not, and so you might choose to ignore it. Business assessment was also high on all teams' lists. Could a consultant be of some help here? Implementation also is high on all five lists. Some very focused training may be called for here. By taking the list one skill at a time, it can be managed and a decision on choice of team will follow. It may not be a great decision, but it will be the best one you can make given the situation.

Putting It All Together

Now that we have looked at all the relevant data and tried to assess how well one team versus another would fit, it's time to pick our team. For the sake of this exercise, I will limit our choices to the five discussed here. That may or may not be the situation you find yourself in, but I think it will be instructive nevertheless. The team we pick will be the topic of the next chapter.

Now it's your turn. Repeat the analysis in this chapter with the team you have formed. If you would like to email me your analysis (rkw@eiicorp.com), I will be happy to offer my critique.

FOR YOUR REFERENCE If you are interested in doing this same analysis on one of your projects and its team members, see Appendix C, "How to Get TeamArchitect Tools," for details.

PART Four

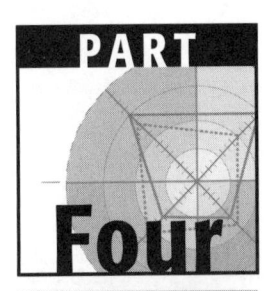

Development and Deployment

CHAPTER 13

Developing and Deploying the Project Team

The die has been cast. Based on our analysis, Team Delta has been chosen to be the Gold Team. It seems to be more balanced than any other of the choices available to us. Actually, we could have chosen any one of the five teams to illustrate the approach to developing and deploying the team regardless of the balance or lack thereof.

The focus of this chapter is the newly appointed Gold Team. You now have all of the assessments necessary to manage the team and the project. We'll begin with a discussion of the initial development and deployment of the team. The two are not independent of one another, and, as you shall see, they are best done with the collaboration of the entire team. The more development opportunities you can take advantage of, the easier will be the task of deployment.

Later in the chapter, we'll talk about changes to that development and deployment as events surrounding the project occur and change the situation. You'll recognize that what we are doing is really risk management, but our approach is limited to mitigation strategies that arise because of the nature of the team as compared to its assigned task.

General Strategies

We need a strategy for approaching development and deployment. I have used an analysis tool quite extensively and effectively in strategic planning engagements called *SWOT* (*Strengths, Weaknesses, Opportunities, Threats*). SWOT analysis adapts very well to the situation where we have to evaluate the state we find ourselves in and adopt a strategy for going forward. Each part of a SWOT analysis fulfills a specific need.

Let's briefly look at each part of a SWOT analysis and then apply it to our specific situation. *Strengths* relates to the characteristics of the situation that directly address the strengths that we bring to the situation. For example, if the project requires a very creative team and we have a team that has a high score on the D-Quadrant, that would be a strength that our team brings to the project. On the other hand, if for that same situation the team had a very high score on the B-Quadrant and a very low score on the D-Quadrant, we would conclude that that represents a *weakness* of the team with respect to its working on the example project.

To understand *opportunity*, consider the following. The project is mission critical and requires all the creativity the organization can muster. While the project profile may suggest a team that has mediocre preferences for creativity, senior management recognizes that by loading the team with members whose thinking preferences are high D-Quadrant they may create an opportunity for instilling more creativity in the project than its profile would suggest is needed.

Threats and risk are different points of view on a topic with a lot of commonality between them. Suppose the team has the only assimilator available from the candidate pool and that person leaves the team. The team's ability to develop good solutions to the problems it faces will be compromised. The potential loss of that person is a threat to the project, and its mitigation borders on risk management. On balance, SWOT is my tool of choice for building strategies for managing the development and deployment of the project team to the work of the project. The following sections briefly describe each part of the analysis, followed by the SWOT analysis of the Gold Team.

Strengths

In a project/team profile gap analysis, strengths are meaningful only in the context of the relationship between the team and the project on each of the four dimensions (analytical, organizational, personal, and visual). What might be a team strength in one project could be a team weakness in another project. What might be a team strength in one phase of the project could be a team weakness in another phase. It's all relative. Identifying the positive gaps (one or more dimensions on which the team average profile exceeds the project profile) gets the analysis started. The other data (LSI scores, SDI scores, and the skills assessment) available on each team member will be an added source of information for any decisions that will come from this part of the analysis.

This should be an analysis conducted by the team rather than just the project manager. I strongly encourage the team analysis because it helps create a shared vision and commitment from each and every team member. This is not the time for the project manager to harbor secrets and subterfuges from the team. Information that is not visible in the data may come to light in the ensuing discussions. For example, a team member might have a great affinity for a particular assignment, which could offset any measured weakness. A team member may have had prior experience with the customer and can leverage the good relationships that were established at that time and are still maintained.

The deliverable from the SWOT analysis will be a deployment strategy—which team member will be assigned what roles and responsibilities. That deployment will take advantage of the team's strengths and, as we shall see in the next paragraph, will avoid the team's weaknesses.

Weaknesses

Remember that these are team weaknesses on one or more of the four dimensions. They will have negative gaps. That is, they are dimensions on which the project profile exceeds the average team profile. Because we are dealing with averages, there are two cases to consider. The first is the situation where no team member has a score that exceeds the project profile on that dimension. Unless there is some counter-balancing factor at play, this could be a serious deficiency of the project team. Training one or more team members, adding another team member, or recruiting an outside consultant may be a way out. Less serious is the case where one or more team members have scores that exceed the project profile even though the team average falls below the project profile. These individuals will be assigned those activities that require the strength that they possess. The project manager needs to protect that assignment to that individual because there may not be an acceptable alternative if he or she should lose that team member.

The other areas of weakness arise from a lack of balance for problem-solving, decision-making, or conflict resolution situations. These will be discovered by an analysis of the team profile on the LSI and SDI. In some cases, the imbalance can be neutralized by adopting some form of borrowed behavior. In other, more extreme cases, intervention or team training may be required.

The deliverable from this part of the analysis will be to make assignments of team members to project activities that avoid or minimize the weaknesses as much as possible.

While it is beyond the scope of this book, it is worth mentioning how strengths can in fact become weaknesses. That occurs when an area of strength is overdone. For example, Sal is a very analytic person. If he were to take that skill to the extreme, his team might suffer from analysis paralysis. His strength would therefore have become a weakness. Personal Strengths Publishing, as part of the SDI, has done considerable work in this area of overdone strengths. The interested reader should consult them for further information.

Opportunities

Carpe diem or, in our case, *carpe opportunitas*. Are there any hidden gems among the team? A past relationship with the customer and an accomplishment or skill heretofore unnoticed in one of the team members are examples of opportunities that may positively affect the work of the project. How can we take advantage of them? What parts of this project can benefit meaningfully from our strengths? Find them, and try to make the assignments needed to take advantage of those opportunities. Finding these opportunities is not the result of a deliberate plan to uncover the diamonds in the rough. Rather, they are discoveries that occur as the team goes about its business. In the context of a team meeting the project manager may discover that a team member knows one of the parties involved in the situation under discussion or perhaps a team member says that he or she once had a situation quite similar to the one under discussion and he or she has a suggestion for a good way to handle it. This isn't something you can anticipate or plan for. It just happens.

Threats

Take a close look at the three environments shown in Figure 13.1. Where are the risks to your project? What strategy will you employ to mitigate the consequences? For example, is the business climate unstable, and how

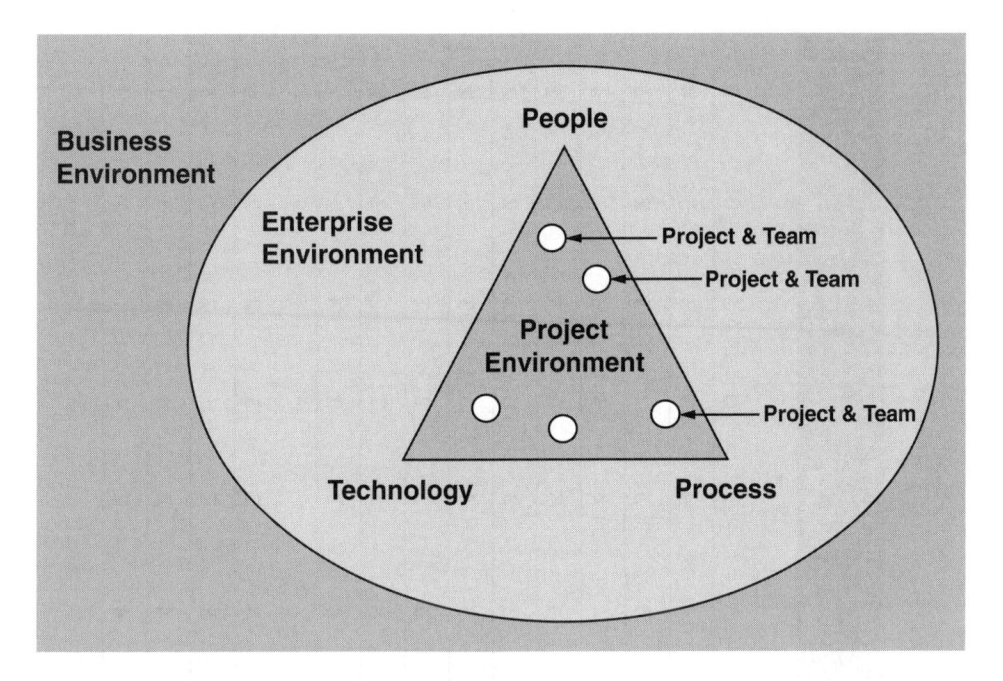

Figure 13.1 The project/team environment.

might changes in it affect the project? Turnover among professional staff is a common occurrence. Does this concern you? What is your contingency plan if the events associated with those risks should occur? You have done this type of planning before. It is nothing but a straightforward risk analysis and risk management planning. The difference is that you are now looking at different variables (the four HBDI quadrants, for example) and determining how to protect the positive gaps and contain the negative ones.

SWOT Analysis of the Gold Team

To conduct this analysis, let's revisit the Gold Team data on all four of the assessment tools discussed earlier and then summarize it in the form of a SWOT analysis.

PMSA Team Profile

Let's start with the PMSA data for the Gold Team, which is shown in Table 13.1. The PMCA data is also part of the SWOT analysis. We discussed that

Table 13.1 Gold Team Skill Deficiency Profile

SKILL	RANK	REQ'D PROF.	PEARL	OLIVE	ANITA	TERRI	SY	DOUG	MEL	J. CASE
Project Management										
Complexity assessment	15	4	3	3	3	3	0	2	0	0
Cost estimating	17	5	4	3	4	4	3	3	3	4
Critical path management	4	4	3	3	3	3	2	3	2	3
Detailed estimating	16	5	4	2	4	4	3	3	3	4
Project closeout	6	5	4	2	3	3	0	3	2	2
Project notebook construction	2	4	3	3	3	3	0	3	2	2
Project organization	18	5	4	2	3	4	3	3	2	2
Project process assessment	19	4	3	3	3	3	2	2	3	3
Resource leveling	7	5	2	2	4	3	2	2	2	2
Scope management	8	5	4	2	4	3	2	3	2	2
Management										
Delegation	11	5	4	3	4	2	3	2	2	4
Leadership	1	5	2	2	3	2	3	2	3	3
Performance management	11	5	3	3	4	2	4	2	2	4
Staff and career development	11	5	4	3	4	2	4	1	1	3

Business

Budgeting	9	5	4	3	3	3	3	3	3	4
Business assessment	5	5	3	2	2	2	3	3	1	3
Customer service	9	5	3	4	3	3	4	3	3	3
Implementation	2	5	4	4	3	4	4	3	3	4

Interpersonal

Relationship management	14	5	4	4	3	2	3	3	2	4

Personal

Decision making/critical thinking	20	5	4	4	4	4	4	4	3	4

report in Chapter 9, "Project Management Skills and Competencies," and will not repeat that analysis here. Recall that Hal was seen as solid in every one of the four areas and had a self-perception quite similar to the perceptions of his assessors. Pearl, on the other hand, was seen as deficient by her assessors in several areas and had a tendency to inflate her competency in a number of areas that could prove harmful to the project should she become the project manager.

Table 13.1 lists only those skills where none of the team members has the proficiency level required for a Type I project. By displaying the data in this way, deployment strategies will often emerge. Let's take a look at a few skill areas and decide how to best handle them.

Leadership. Leadership is the top-ranked skill deficiency for the Gold Team. This is quite obvious by noting that the distribution of the team's proficiencies in leadership is farther away from the required proficiency than any other skill. Something must be done. There is really nothing that can be done in the short term to instill strong leadership characteristics in Pearl, the project manager. We have to look to the alternatives available to the team. For example, do any of the leadership models discussed in Chapter 2, "The Project Environment," suggest a strategy? If you answered "Yes" and chose either the shared leadership or self-managed models, you understand how the team can deal with its lack of a strong leader. For this project, leadership will be a collaborative activity involving the entire team.

Project notebook construction. This one is easy. Olive is the project administrator, and the construction and maintenance of the project notebook will be her responsibility. While she does not possess the requisite proficiency she is reasonably prepared to do this. This is not a difficult skill to acquire, and a little training or use of an example from a completed project may suffice.

Implementation. You might argue that Pearl, because she is the project manager, should assume this responsibility. It is, in fact, a common assignment for the project manager. That might not be a bad strategy, but in light of the fact that we decided to use either a shared or self-managed team leadership model, might it not make good sense to do the same with the implementation phase of the project? Based on the balanced distribution of Team Delta's LSI scores in all four quadrants and a proficiency level of 3 or 4 for all eight members its implementation skills are rather uniformly distributed across the entire team. Pearl's proficiency at implementation is not any different from that of others on the team, and this strategy is as likely to succeed as any other.

Each team member should have something of value to contribute to project implementation, and the leadership model we are using can take advantage of the team's proficiencies in implementation.

Critical path management. Critical path management (ranked fourth on the list) and resource leveling (ranked seventh on the list) can be assigned to Anita. She has the strongest project management skills of any of the team members, as evidenced by her proficieny levels being at or above those of most team members on all of the project management skills listed in Table 13.1. She should be able to rise to the occasion in these two skill areas. Some minimal training may be advisable as well.

Business assessment. Overall, the team is weak in all of the listed business skills. With few exceptions their proficiency levels are at 3, whereas the project requires that they be at 5. Outside intervention may be the only course of action.

HBDI Profile of the Gold Team

Figure 13.2 is the HBDI profile of the Gold Team.

I have shown the gaps for each of the four quadrants, and the team has some serious alignment issues to manage. As noted in Chapter 11, most of the candidate pool has D-Quadrant scores that exceed the project's D-Quadrant score. That may foreshadow problems. The team will need to moderate its tendencies to be creative and innovative. The best choices for the moderators would be Pearl and Anita because their D-Quadrant scores are the lowest of all the team members. Both occupy management roles on the project and may have to continually refocus the team to keep it in line with the scope of the project.

The next most serious gap is the A-Quadrant. On average, the team does not prefer an analytic thinking style and should defer that type of work to Terri, Sy, Justin, and Mel, who have strong preferences in that quadrant. The large positive gap in the C-Quadrant is due mostly to Pearl, Doug, Anita, and Olive. The remainder of the team, specifically Terri, Sy, Justin, and Mel, will have to keep the team focused on the technical aspects of this left-brain project and not be distracted by its preference for right-brain thinking styles.

SDI Profile of the Gold Team

Figure 13.3 is the SDI profile of the Gold Team. As pointed out earlier, the team displays a great deal of balance with respect to its conflict management

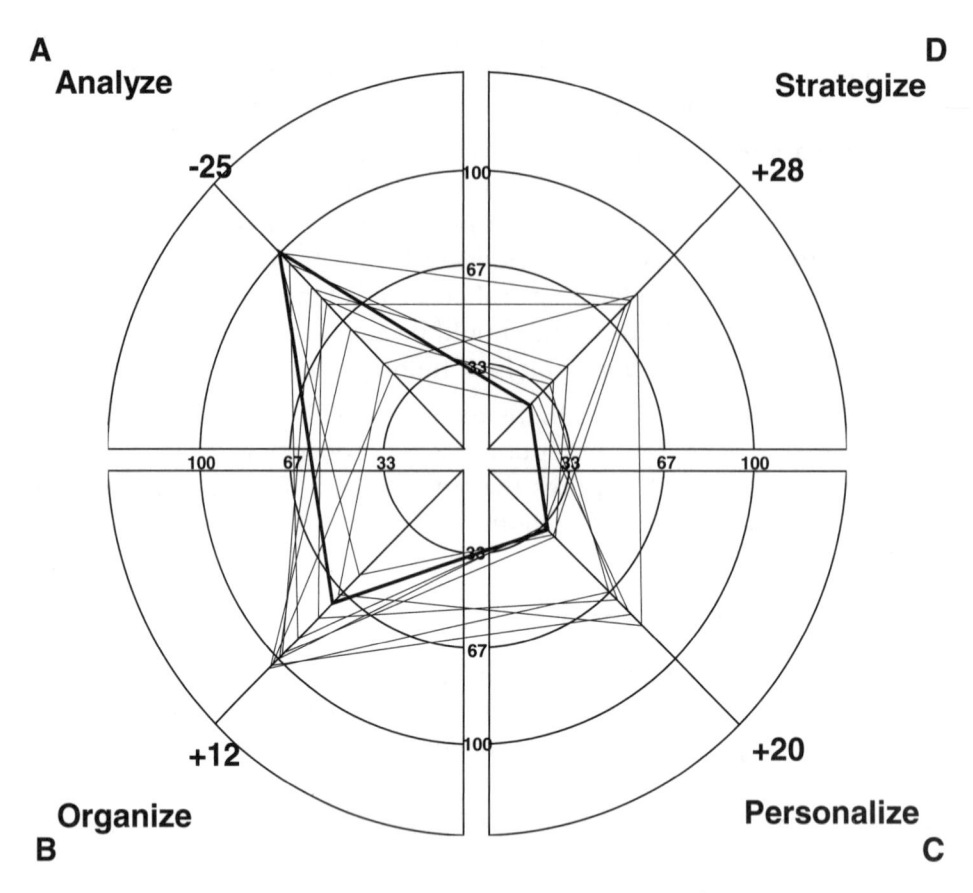

Figure 13.2 HBDI profile of the Gold Team.

style. Recall that all valued-relating and conflict sequences are accounted for by the team. This fact, coupled with the decision to use a shared or self-managed leadership model, means that the team should be able to resolve both internal and external conflict situations with ease. In practice, the project manager should refer to this profile. It can be useful in deciding the specific strategy to use for a given conflict situation. In particular, it may offer the project manager an approach to use or a person to use for a given conflict situation.

LSI Profile of the Gold Team

Figure 13.4 is the LSI profile of the Gold Team. Of all the teams we could have chosen as our Gold Team, this team has the greatest balance with

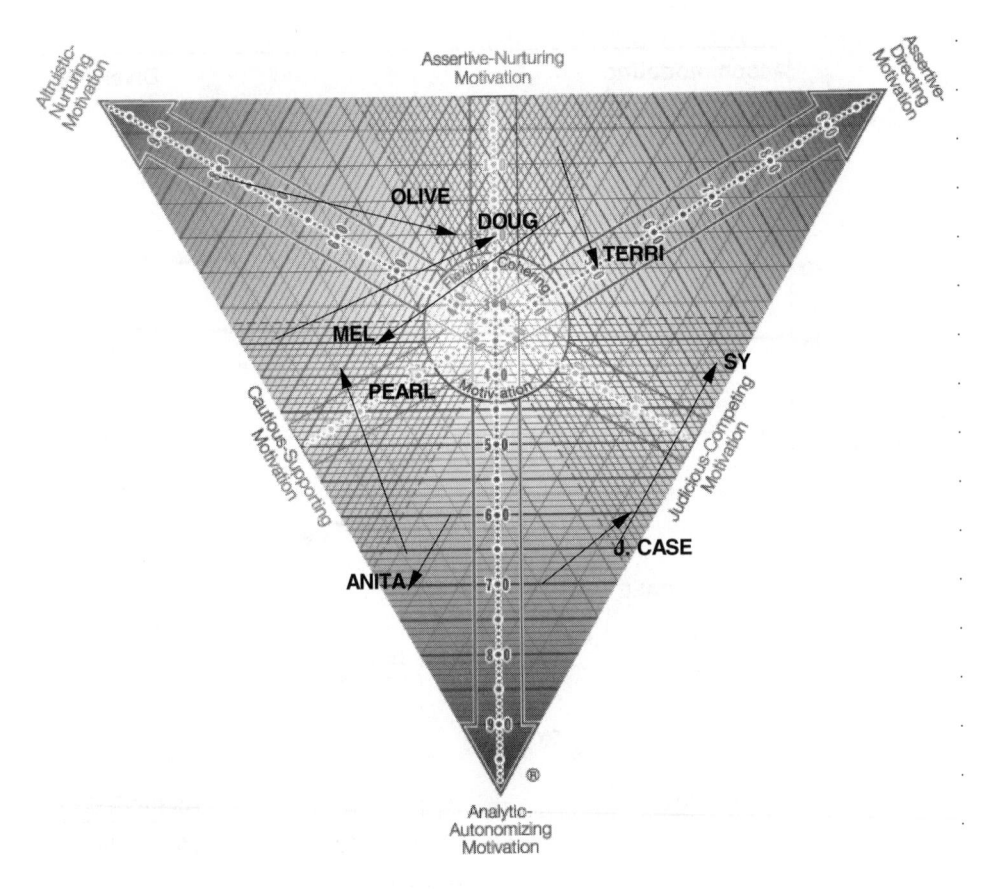

Figure 13.3 SDI profile of the Gold Team.

respect to its problem-solving and decision-making ability. All four quadrants are represented by the team. Pearl and Olive are the only accommodators in the candidate pool, and they are on Team Delta. Doug is the only diverger in the candidate pool, and he is on Team Delta.

Recall from its HBDI kite that the Gold Project had high scores on the A- and B-Quadrants; therefore the project is left-brain. Problems are expected, and the team must be able to solve them effectively. This team should have no difficulty doing that. In practice, the project manager can refer to this profile to decide who should be used in each stage of the problem-solving process. For example, one team member might be charged with formulating the problem while another will have the responsibility of identifying alternative solutions and yet another will have responsibility for building and executing the implementation plan.

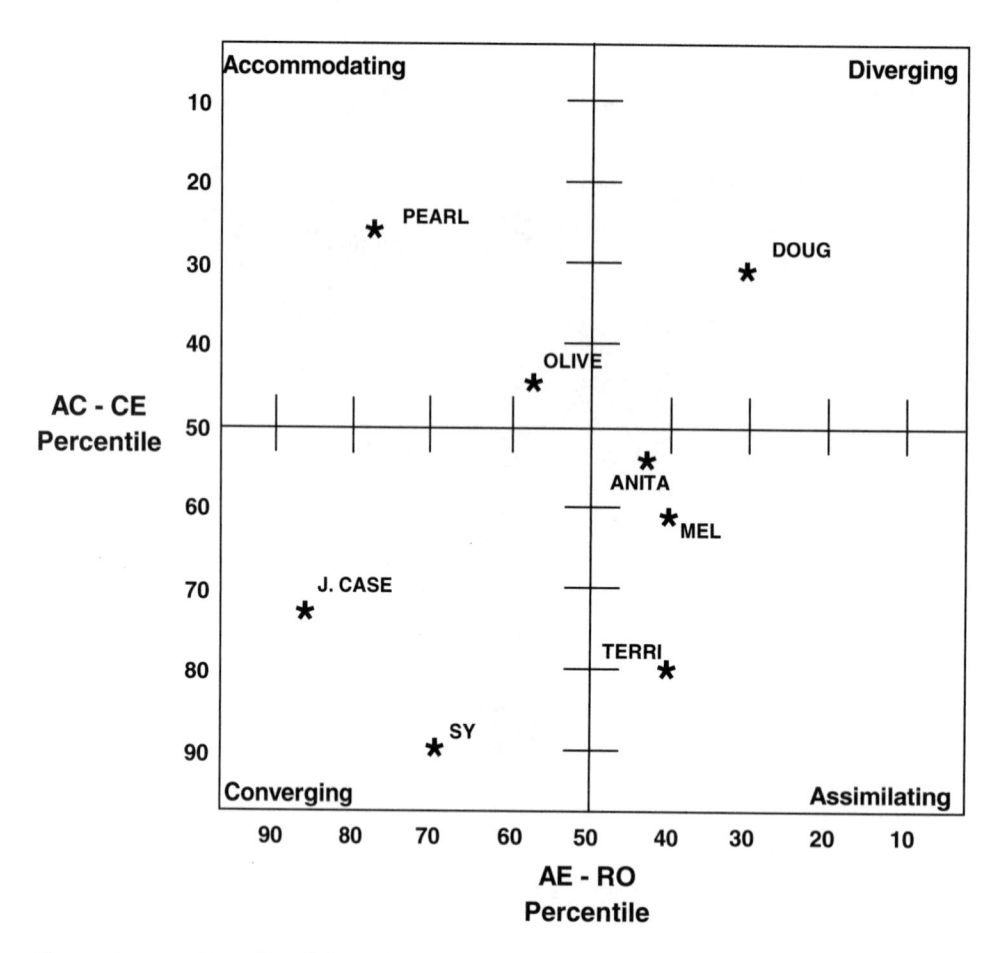

Figure 13.4 LSI profile of the Gold Team.

SWOT Summary

Table 13.2 is a summary of the preceding discussion. I think it is instructive to see how each of the assessment tools relates to the four parts of the SWOT. First note that the team is balanced with respect to the SDI and LSI (strengths are identified, and there are no weaknesses or threats).

The PMSA is the only assessment tool that did not identify any areas of strength but did identify areas of weakness. If the team feels that these weaknesses are serious flaws in the team structure, then they must do something about them. For Team Delta this may mean selected training to remove skill deficiencies. We noted that Pearl was not a leader and resolved that by choosing a shared leadership model. That can be an effective remedy for the team's weak leadership situation.

Table 13.2 SWOT Summary of the Gold Team

	PMSA	PMCA	HBDI	SDI	LSI
Strengths		Pearl's very strong interpersonal skills will help resolve conflicts, both internally and externally. She will be a good moderating factor in all team deliberations.	The composite HBDI profile of the team fairly well represents each of the four quadrants.	All conflict resolution strategies are present on the team, and it should be able to successfully resolve any conflict situation that it faces.	The team has a very well-rounded approach to problem solving and decision making. This should raise its confidence that actions taken are appropriate for the situation.
Weaknesses	• Leadership • Project notebook construction • Implementation • Critical path management • Business assessment	When the team needs a leader, Pearl may not be ready to assert herself in that role, but she will depend on the team to take up the slack.	The team's creative thinking style exceeds the needs of the project.		
Opportunities	The use of a shared leadership model may help form a solid and supportive team environment.	This project may offer Pearl an opportunity to develop some much needed leadership skills.	There is a great diversity of thinking preferences on the team, and these could be productively used if properly focused by the project manager.	Because of the diversity of motivational styles and the balance in conflict resolution styles the team can use conflict in a positive way.	The use of a shared leadership model should add to the team's ability to solve problems and make decisions.
Threats	The lack of a strong leader may get the team bogged down and lengthen the time to make decisions and solve problems.	If the team reaches an impasse, its lack of a strong leader may interfere with progress.	While diversity can be an opportunity it can also be a barrier to team solidarity.		

There are several opportunities that, if exploited, can turn into advantages for the team. For example, shared leadership can be a strengthening factor for the team and can give Pearl a chance to develop new leadership skills by selecting situations that will offer her learning opportunities. The team should look for ways to further capitalize on its balance, as described by the team's HBDI, SDI, and LSI data.

Despite all of this good news there are a few threats that need to be considered as part of the team's risk management. Shared leadership can get the team bogged down in decision making and problem resolution and can cause some loss of momentum. Given the analysis and development and deployment strategies we have discussed, there is a high likelihood that this Gold Team can be successful. We have been able to identify mitigation strategies for each potential problem that the team profile presents. You should have no trouble conducting the same approach for your projects. Understand, however, that this is not just a one-time analysis. It must continue throughout the project. As Figure 13.1 reminds us, a number of changes can be expected. And as we have learned, these changes may suggest changes to development and deployment strategies for the project manager. That is the topic of the next section.

Project Change Management

All of the best-planned strategies for team formation, development and deployment can be easily undone by change. For example, suppose a competitor announces a new product that will compete directly with the one we are currently developing. It has announced that it will be available on July 1. Our plan called for an August 1 announcement. The sales and marketing department has requested a change that would allow for a June 15 rollout of our new product and the addition of two new features that are not in our current plan. The new features have never been part of any of our other products, and to accommodate the requested change the team will have to increase its creative thinking preferences and balance in its problem-solving skills. In other words, that change has changed the project profile, and we have built a balanced team using that profile, so the team may now be seriously out of balance with the new project.

Changes in the project profile can arise because of changes in the market, changes in project priorities, and changes in available staff. Whatever the reason, the project manager has to have a process for responding with further team formation, development, and deployment strategies. There are two major areas of change: project scope and project team.

Project Scope Management

I have been practicing project management for more than 35 years, and I think I am pretty good at planning, but I cannot recall a single project where the project went according to plan. It simply can't happen. I don't care how good you are or how predictable or stable the situation, you simply cannot anticipate everything that will happen or even when it will happen. Be thankful that you can't because if you could, the job of project manager would be boring!

The changes may be significant or relatively uneventful, but they will change the profile of the project. As a precaution, I would suggest that the project scope change be followed immediately by another profiling of the project. If the profile changes are measurable, you will want to assess whether a change in team composition or team member deployment is called for. It may not be, but it is better to be safe than sorry.

Project Team Change Management

Apart from changes in the project profile, the other change that the project manager will also have to cope with is a change in team membership. For our purposes, it doesn't make any difference why the team member has left the team. He or she left the team—accept it and deal with it. Years ago, during that period of time when I was just learning to be a manager, I wondered how I would react to the first time one of my direct reports would resign. Would there be a wringing of hands and admonitions to stay if I gave you . . . I thought about it and tried to put a positive spin on it. Here is what I eventually chose as my strategy. My staff, as good as they might have been, was not perfectly aligned with my needs. If only I had . . . but I didn't have . . . Now that I had that resignation in my hands, all of a sudden I had one new degree of freedom. Yes, there was a brief period of mourning the loss of a trusted and valued member of my staff, but that disappeared quickly as I reveled in the joy of my new-found degree of freedom. I could replace the person with someone who filled the gap that I had earlier identified. I was able to take what some might have seen as a losing situation and turn it into a winning situation. I have remembered that revelation for more than 30 years, and it has never disappointed me. There is always a silver lining, even in the darkest of clouds!

Let's take a brief look at a change in team membership and see what we might do. In this case, Sy Yonara suddenly and unexpectedly disappeared. He simply didn't show up for work one day. No one knows what prompted such unusual behavior. He did, however, leave a note on Anita's desk. It gave her the file names of all the program code he had written to date but contained no documentation or test data results.

Anita has to replace Sy, and her choices are Mack or Mike. She might want to revisit the HBDI, LSI, and SDI data as well as the skill profile of her two choices. In this case, neither option is really very attractive. Mack is a right-brain thinker, and to put him on the team will further extend the team's weakness in analytical thinking preferences. Mike is a very cerebral thinker and the most creative of anyone from the candidate pool. To put him on the team will create further imbalance in the D-Quadrant. Anita has to weigh the consequences of each choice and determine what she might do to mitigate against the additional problems either choice will present to the team.

Putting It All Together

In this chapter we have seen how the PMSA, PMCA, HBDI, SDI, and LSI can be very powerful decision support tools for the project manager and the project team. They may have been used to form the team initially. In many cases, team formation is not a variable in the hands of the project manager. In this case, the tools can be used to assess the team and establish development and deployment strategies to increase team effectiveness. Finally, as an ongoing decision support tool, they can be used to accommodate project scope change and changes in team membership.

Now that you've learned about how to assess and form an effective project team, take a look at your individual projects and think about the following questions:

Where are you with respect to project failure? Are you satisfied with the success rate of your projects? Of course not. I knew the answer without asking the question. Up until now you probably weren't satisfied, but you weren't sure what you could do about it. Now you know that there is something you can do about it. I hope you also know that the benefits of practicing what I have been telling you about TeamArchitect and aligning your project team with the project far outweigh any costs you might attach to that effort. You will probably sleep better at night as well.

Where are you with respect to team formation? If availability and possessing the appropriate technical skills are the only criteria you now use to form your project teams, there is a lot that you can do to improve the effectiveness of your project teams and increase the likelihood of project success. But you know that because you have just read my book. The question is: "Do you have the right stuff to do something about it?"

Do you want to increase team effectiveness and reduce project failure? Of course, you do, but are you willing to pay the price to do it? Maybe, maybe not. I hope I have shown you how easy it can be. It won't be perfect. It won't be optimal, but no one pays for optimal solutions anyway. Your obstacles are clear. You will not have the freedom to adjust team membership as the analyses suggested. There is a rush to get going and to suggest that you take pause, deliberate, and figure out the best course of action may not be consistent with the aggressive schedule under which you are operating. Training for selected team members may be called for, but where will you find the time? Your schedule is already too aggressive. Don't concern yourself too much with these obstacles. Just do the best you can, and remember that the cost of any effort will be far less than the payback you receive.

Where would you like to be with respect to team formation? I leave you with a decision. What do you want to accomplish with team effectiveness, and how much effort are you really committed to put forth? You might be surprised by the return on effort and make team formation, assessment, and development a critical success factor in your project management practices.

How can you get there? Its strategy formation time, and you have a project plan to put in place. You already have a goal statement. It is:

> To implement a process for forming, assessing, and developing effective project teams

I have designed that process for you and given you all the tools you will need to implement it. You just need to put your plan in place and make it happen. It's a project, and you are the project team. You have all the project management skills you need to be successful with this project. Go for it!

Promise me you'll write. I want to hear from you and about your experiences, successes, and suggestions for improvement with TeamArchitect. Contact me at rkw@eiicorp.com.

APPENDIX A

References and Reading List

For the benefit of those who are interested in further readings and study in team effectiveness, I have included an extensive annotated bibliography of books from my library. The list is not exhaustive but does include the major works on team effectiveness. There are 66 titles arranged by major topic to facilitate locating titles of interest to you.

Team Effectiveness Models

The following titles represent the published results of the research that has been done on team effectiveness.

Belbin, R. Meredith. 1981. *Management Teams: Why they succeed or fail.* (Oxford, England: Butterworth-Heinemann). ISBN 0-7506-0253-8.

Belbin, R. Meredith. 1993. *Team Roles at Work.* (Oxford, England: Butterworth-Heinemann). ISBN 0-7506-2675-5.

Belbin, R. Meredith. 1997. *Changing the Way We Work.* (Oxford, England: Butterworth-Heinemann). ISBN 0-7506-4288-2.

Margerison, Charles and Dick McCann. 1995. *Team Management: Practical New Approaches.* (Glucestershire, England: Management Books 2000 Ltd.). ISBN 1-85252-114-7.

Margerison, Charles and Dick McCann. 1995. *Team Reengineering: Using the Language of Teamwork.* (Brisbane, Australia: Team Management Systems). ISBN 0-646-22362-3.

Self-Managed and Self-Directed Teams

Fisher, Kimball. 1993. *Leading Self-Directed Work Teams: A Guide to Developing New Team Leadership Skills.* (New York: McGraw-Hill Inc.). ISBN 0-07-021071-3.

Harper, Ann and Bob Harper. 1991. *Self-Directed Work Teams and Your Organization.* (New York, NY: MW Corporation).

Harper, Bob and Ann Harper. 1991. *Succeeding as a Self-Directed Work Team.* (New York, NY: MW Corpoation).

Harper, Ann and Bob Harper. 1992. *Skill-Building for Self-Directed Team Members.* (New York, NY: MW Corporation). ISBN 1-880859-02-5.

Hicks, Robert F. and Diane Bone. 1990. *Self-Managing Teams: Creating and Maintaining Self-Managed Work Groups.* (Los Altos, CA: Crisp Publications, Inc.). ISBN 1-56052-000-0.

Huszczo, Gregory E. 1996. *Tools for Team Excellence.* (Palo Alto, CA: Davies-Black Publishing). ISBN 0-89106-081-2.

Kelly, Mark. 1991. *The Adventures of a Self-Managing Team.* (San Diego, CA: Pfeiffer & Company). ISBN 0-88390-058-0.

Wellins, Richard S. 1990. *Self-Directed Teams: A Study of Current Practice.* (Pittsburgh, PA: Development Dimensions International).

Wellins, Richard S., William C. Byham, and Jeanne M. Wilson, 1991. *Empowered Teams: Creating Self-Directed Work Groups That Improve Quality, Productivity and Participation.* (San Francisco, CA: Jossey-Bass Publishers). ISBN 1-55542-353-1.

Enterprise Environment

Davidow, William H. and Michael S. Malone. 1992. *The Virtual Corporation.* (New York, NY: HarperCollins Publishers, Inc.). ISBN 0-88730-593-8.

Hackman, J. Richard and Greg R. Oldham. 1980. *Work Redesign.* (Reading, MA: Addison-Wesley Publishing). ISBN 0-201-02779-8.

Helgesen, Sally. 1995. *The Web of Inclusion.* (New York, NY: Currency/Doubleday). ISBN 0-385-42364-0.

Katzenbach, Jon R. and Douglas K. Smith. 1993. *The Wisdom of Teams: Creating the High-Performance Organization.* (Boston, MA: Harvard Business School Press). ISBN 0-87584-367-0.

Lipman-Blumen, Jean and Harold J. Leavitt. 1999. *Hot Groups: Seeding Them, Feeding Them and Using Them to Ignite Your Organization.* (New York, NY: Oxford University Press). ISBN 0-19-512686-6.

Lucas, Henry C., Jr. 1996. *The T-Form Organization: Using Technology to Design Organizations for the 21st Century.* (San Francisco, CA: Jossey-Bass Publishers). ISBN 0-7879-0167-9.

Marshall, Edward M. 1995. *Transforming the Way We Work: The Power of the Collaborative Workplace.* (New York, NY: AMACOM). ISBN 0-8144-0255-0.

Mitroff, Ian I. and Harold A. Linstone. 1993. *The Unbounded Mind: Breaking the Chains of Traditional Business Thinking.* (New York, NY: Oxford University Press). ISBN 0-19-507783-0.

Mohrman, Susan Albers, Susan G. Cohen, and Allan M. Mohrman, Jr. 1995. *Designing Team-Based Organizations: New Forms for Knowledge Work.* (San Francisco, CA: Jossey-Bass Publishers). ISBN 0-7879-0080-X.

Mohrman, Susan Albers and Allan M. Mohrman, Jr. 1997. *Designing and Leading Team-Based Organizations.* (San Francisco, CA: Jossey-Bass Publishers). ISBN 0-7879-0865-7.

Mohrman, Susan Albers and Allan M. Mohrman, Jr. 1997. *Designing and Leading Team-Based Organizations: a workbook for organizational self-design.* (San Francisco, CA: Jossey-Bass Publishers). ISBN 0-7879-0864-9.

O'Connell, Fergus. 1999. *How to Run Successful High-Tech Project-Based Organizations.* (Boston, MA: Artech House). ISBN 1-58053-010-9.

Ostroff, Frank. 1999. *The Horizontal Organization.* (New York, NY: Oxford University Press, Inc.). ISBN 0-19-512138-4.

Plunkett, Lorne C. and Robert Fournier. 1991. *Participative Management: Implementing Empowerment.* (New York, NY: John Wiley & Sons, Inc.). ISBN 0-471-54374-8.

Shonk, James H. 1997. *Team-Based Organizations: Developing a Successful Team Environment.* (Chicago, IL: Irwin Professional Publishing). ISBN 0-7863-1124-X.

Shuster, H. David. 2000. *Teaming for Quality: The Right Way for the Right Reasons.* (Newtown Square, PA: Project Management Institute). ISBN 1-880410-63-X.

Sims, Ronald R. and John G. Veres III (eds.). 1999. *Keys to Employee Success in Coming Decades.* (Westport, CT: Quorum Books). ISBN 1-56720-194-6.

Stacy, Ralph D. 1996. *Complexity and Creativity in Organizations.* (San Francisco, CA: Berrett-Koehler Publishers). ISBN 1-881052-89-3.

Sundstrom, Eric and Associates. 1999. *Supporting Work Team Effectiveness.* (San Francisco, CA: Jossey-Bass Publishers). ISBN 0-7879-4322-3.

Project Environment

Bennis, Warren and Patricia Ward Biederman. 1997. *Organizing Genius: The Secrets of Creative Collaboration.* (Reading, MA: Addison-Wesley Publishing Company). ISBN 0-201-57051-3.

Buchholz, Steve and Thomas Roth. 1987. *Creating the High-Performance Team.* (New York, NY: John Wiley & Sons, Inc.). ISBN 0-471-85674-6.

Cleland, David I. 1996. *Strategic Management of Teams.* (New York, NY: John Wiley & Sons, Inc.). ISBN 0-471-12058-8.

DeMarco, Tom and Timothy Lister. 1987. *Peopleware: Productive Projects and Teams.* (New York, NY: Dorsett House Publishing Co.). ISBN0-932633-05-6.

Duarte, Deborah L. and Nancy Tennant Snyder. 1999. *Mastering Virtual Teams.* (San Francisco, CA: Jossey-Bass Publishers). ISBN 0-7879-4183-2.

Eales-White, Rupert. 1996. *How to Be a Better Teambuilder.* (London, England: Kogan Page Ltd.). ISBN 0-7494-1912-1

Goal/QPC. 1995. *The Team Memory Jogger.* (Salem, NH: QPC and Oriel Inc.).

Hackman, J. Richard (ed.). 1990. *Groups That Work (and Those That Don't).* (San Francisco, CA: Jossey-Bass Publishers). ISBN 1-55542-187-3.

Harrington-Mackin, Deborah. 1994. *The Team Building Tool Kit.* (New York, NY: AMACOM). ISBN 0-8144-7826-3.

Hastings, Colin, Peter Bixby, and Rani Chaudhry-Lawton. 1987. *The Superteam Solution.* (San Diego, CA: University Associates, Inc.). ISBN 0-88390-206-0.

Hayward, Martha. 1998. *Managing Virtual Teams: Practical Techniques for High-Technology Project Managers.* (Boston, MA: Artech House). ISBN 0-89006-913-1.

Isgar, Thomas. 1993. *The Ten Minute Team.* (Boulder, CO: Seluera Press). ISBN 0-9623464-1-1.

Jones, Peter H. 1998. *Handbook of Team Design.* (New York, NY: McGraw-Hill). ISBN 0-07-032880-3.

Lewis, James. 1997. *Team-Based Project Management.* (New York, NY: AMACOM). ISBN 0-8144-0364-6.

Moxon, Peter. 1993. *Building a Better Team.* (Hampshire, England: Gower Publishing). ISBN 0-566-08007-9.

Scholtes, Peter R., Brian L. Joiner, and Barbara J. Streibel. 1996. *The Team Handbook.* (Madison, WI: Joiner Associates Inc.). ISBN 1-884731-11-2.

Smith, Steve. 1997. *Build That Team!* (London, England: Kogan Page Ltd.). ISBN 0-7494-2483-4.

Smith, Karl A. 2000. *Project Management and Teamwork*. (Boston, MA: McGraw-Hill Higher Education). ISBN 0-07-012296-2.

Syer, John and Christopher Connolly. 1996. *How Teamwork Works: The Dynamics of Effective Team Development*. (London, England: The McGraw-Hill Companies). ISBN 0-07-707942-6.

Thompson, Leigh. 2000. *Making the Team*. (Upper Saddle River, NJ: Prentice Hall). ISBN 0-13-014363-4.

Verma, Vijay K. 1997. *Managing the Project Team*. (Upper Darby, PA: Project Management Institute). ISBN 1-880410-42-7.

Leadership

Hersey, Paul. 1984. *The Situational Leader*. (Escondido, CA: Center for Leadership Studies). ISBN 0-446-51342-39.

Martin, Paula K. 1995. *The Buck Stops Here: Accountability and the Empowered Manager*. (Flemington, NJ: Renaissance Educational Services). ISBN 0-943811-02-3.

Peterson, David B. and Mary Dee Hicks. 1996. *Leader as Coach: Strategies for Coaching and Developing Others*. (Minneapolis, MN: Personnel Decisions International). ISBN 0-938529-14-5.

Pinto, Jeffrey K. and Jeffrey W. Trailer (eds.). 1998. *Leadership Skills for Project Managers*. (Newtown Square, PA: Project Management Institute). ISBN 1-880410-49-4.

Verma, Vijay K. 1996. *Human Resource Skills for the Project Manager*. (Newtown Square, PA: Project Management Institute). ISBN 1-880410-41-9.

Skills

Bloom, Benjamin S. 1956. *Taxonomy of Educational Objectives Book I: Cognitive Domain*. (New York, NY: Longman).

Couger, J. Daniel. 1995. *Creative Problem Solving and Opportunity Finding*. (Danvers, MA: Boyd & Fraser Publishing Company). ISBN 0-87709-752-6.

Elbeik, Sam and Mark Thomas. 1998. *Project Skills*. (Oxford, England: Butterworth-Heinemann). ISBN 0-7506-3978-4.

Harris, Jean. 1997. *Sharpen Your Team's Skills in Project Management*. (London, England: The McGraw-Hill Companies). ISBN 0-07-709140-X.

Morris, William C. and M. Sashkin. 1976. *Organization Behavior in Action: Skill Building Experiences*. (St. Paul, MN: West Publishing Company).

Roskin, Rick and R. Stuart Kotze. 1983. *Success Guide to Managerial Achievement*. (Reston, VA: Reston Publishing Company).

Thomas, Kenneth. 1983. "Conflict and Conflict Management," in *The Handbook of Industrial and Organizational Psychology,* edited by Marvin D. Dunynnette. (New York, NY: John Wiley & Sons).

Miscellaneous Cited References

DeBono, Edward. 1992. *Serious Creativity.* (New York, NY: HarperCollins).

Lewis, James P. 2000. *The Project Manager's Desk Reference, 2nd Edition.* (New York, NY: McGraw-Hill). ISBN 0-07-134750-X.

Michalko, Michael. 1991. *Thinkertoys: A Handbook of Business Creativity.* (Berkeley, CA: Ten Speed Press). ISBN 0898-154081.

Porter, Elias H. 1996. Manual of Administration and Interpretation, 9th Edition. (Carlsbad, CA: Personal Strengths Publishing). ISBN 0-9628732-1-7.

Von Oech, Roger. 1983. *A Whack on the Side of the Head.* (New York, NY: Warner Books). ISBN 0-446-38635-9.

Wysocki, Robert K. et al. 2000. *Effective Project Management, 2nd Edition.* (New York, NY: John Wiley & Sons, Inc). ISBN 0-471-36028-7.

Wysocki, Robert K. et al. 2001. *The World-Class Project Manager: A Professional Development Guide.* (Cambridge, MA: Perseus Publishing). ISBN 0-7382-0237-1.

APPENDIX B

Sources of Information

What follows is a list of the companies whose products are mentioned in this book or used in TeamArchitect. I have also included their contact information so that you may buy additional products directly from them. For those who would prefer to buy all of the products used in TeamArchitect from a single source, you may buy directly from Enterprise Information Insights, Inc. Quantity discounts are available from EII, Inc. if you are a registered member of the TeamArchitect User Group.

All of the tools (as well as skill assessments for Accounting, Finance, Marketing, Sales, Information Technology and Executive Management) used in TeamArchitect can be obtained from:

Enterprise Information Insights, Inc.
4 Otsego Road
Worcester, MA 01609
508-791-2062
Web site: www.teamarchitect.com
Web site: www.eiicorp.com

Herrmann Brain Dominance Instrument can be obtained from:
Herrmann International
794 Buffalo Creek Road
Lake Lure, NC 28746

800-432-4234
Web site: www.hbdi.com

Strength Deployment Inventory (SDI), can be obtained from:
Personal Strengths Publishing
P. O. Box 2605
Carlsbad, CA 92018
800-624-7347
Web site: www.personalstrengths.com

Learning Styles Inventory can be obtained from:
Hay McBer Training Resources Group
116 Huntington Avenue
Boston, MA 02116
800-729-8074
Web site: http://trgmcber.haygroup.com

Team Management Systems can be obtained from:
Team Management Systems
1041 Sterling Road
Suite 101
Herndon, VA 20170
800-231-6889
Web site: www.TeamManagementSystems.com

Interplace can be obtained from:
Belbin Associates
3-4 Bennell Court, Comberton
Cambridge, CB3 7DS
United Kingdom
44-(0)1223-264975
Web site: www.belbin.com

DISC can be obtained from:
TTI Performance Systems, Ltd.
16020 North 77th Street
Scottsdale, AZ 85260
Or from:
The Institute For Motivational Living
P. O. Box 925
New Castle, PA 16103
724-658-4361
Web site: www.motivate4u.com

APPENDIX C

How to Get TeamArchitect Tools

All of the tools used by TeamArchitect are available for you to try out on a case study stored on the TeamArchitect Web site. Readers can experience TeamArchitect by visiting www.teamarchitect.com. At the home page click "Login" in the menu across the top of the page. There you will register and choose a username and password. That will establish a password-protected account for you for your use only with the case study data that is stored there. For those who would like to adopt TeamArchitect for use on projects in their companies you will need to have an account on www.teamarchitect.com, which can easily be set up through EII. That account will provide access to the Web-based data collection instruments used in TeamArchitect as well as full use of all analysis and reporting tools. Those instruments and their 2001 list prices are as follows:

Project HBDI Profile	$750.00 per project
Team Member Assessment Kit	$125.00 per person
Herrmann Brain Dominance Instrument (HBDI)	
Strength Deployment Inventory (SDI)	

Learning Styles Inventory (LSI)

Project Management Skill
   Assessment (PMSA)

Project Manager Competency $ 50.00 per person
   Assessment (PMCA)   (includes individual and up
                                              to eight assessors)

Other Skill Assessments (Accounting, Finance, Sales, Marketing, Executive Management, Information Technology) are also available. Contact EII for details and pricing quotes.

Quantity discounts are available, as are password-protected company licenses for high-volume accounts. Request the latest pricing information and account details from sales@teamarchitect.com.

APPENDIX D

The Companion CD-ROM

The companion CD-ROM contains the complete unabridged version of this book—*fully searchable*. Featuring a custom Folio™ infobase using FolioViews 4.2 (included in the install), you can read, search, bookmark, and annotate the text directly in the infobase.

In addition, the Folio infobase contains a "Reports" section at the end of the text, where you'll find links to all the data and reports you need to participate in the O'Neill and Preigh case study, introduced in Chapter 5, as well as the interactive Web site that houses these tools, TeamArchitect, located at www.teamarchitect.com.

All 92 graphic reports for the case study were generated at the TeamArchitect Web site. These reports contain:

- The assessment of the 16-person candidate pool of potential team members
- The assessments of five different teams that were formed from the candidate pool
- The assessment data of each individual in the candidate pool

You'll need to use these reports in order to participate in the evaluation of your potential team in Chapters 6 through 9, and the interpretation of these reports in Chapters 10 through 12.

All of this data is also available for interactive use at a password-protected section of the TeamArchitect site. There, you can navigate the reporting screens to:

- Create new teams
- Generate reports
- Analyze the data
- Make development and deployment decisions

If, after getting a feel for using the tools to help build and manage effective project teams, you decide you'd like to use TeamArchitect for projects in your own company, contact information is also available on the site. Appendix C contains more information on accessing the TeamArchitect tools.

User Assistance and Information

Insert the CD-ROM into your CD-ROM drive and launch the setup.exe to begin the installation process. Follow the instructions on the screens that follow.

The software accompanying this book is being provided as is without warranty or support of any kind. Should you require basic installation assistance, or if your media is defective, please call our product support number at (212) 850-6194 weekdays between 9 AM and 4 PM Eastern Standard Time. Or, we can be reached via e-mail at: **techhelp@wiley.com** or visit **www.wiley.com/techsupport**.

To place additional orders or to request information about other Wiley products, please call (800) 879-4539.

Index

A

A- and B-dominant profile, 93
A- and D-dominant profile, 93
A-, B-, and C-dominant profile, 95
A-, B-, C-, and D-dominant profile, 95
Abstract conceptualization (AC) scores, 192
Abstract conceptualization learning preference, 108
"Accidental teams," 70
Accommodating learning style, 109, 111, 128–129, 137
Accommodators, 110–111, 118, 119, 121, 158, 226
Active experimentation (AE) scores, 192
Active experimentation learning preference, 108
Advising function, 45
Aggressiveness, 135, 136
Alignment. *See* Team alignment
Alignment gap, 219
  interpreting, 219–221
Alternative actions, documenting, 61
Alternative decisions, 16
Altruistic-nurturing style, 130, 223
American Society for Training and Development (ASTD), 169
"Analysis paralysis," 239
Analysis skill level, 150
Analytical-autonomizing style, 130, 193
Analytical thinking, 210, 219, 226, 245
Analyze dimension of a project, 172
Applications development manager
  choosing, 207–210
  Gold Medallion Organ Project, 81–82
Application Service Providers (ASPs), 6
Application skill level, 149
A-Quadrant scores, 186, 205, 223, 245
A-Quadrant thinking, 90, 175, 176
Assertive-directing style, 130, 142, 230
Assertiveness, 137
Assertive-nurturing style, 131, 133, 140, 223
Assessment
  individual, 66–67
  inputs from, 205
  team, 67
Assessment stage, 66–67
Assessor-developer role, 46
Assimilating learning style, 109, 110
Assimilators, 109, 115, 118, 119, 120, 226, 230, 238
Assumptions, risks, obstacles POS section, 178, 179
Avoiding style, 129, 137

B

Balance, 8
  assessing, 217–233
  in conflict management, 16–17
  in decision making, 16
  lack of, 240
  in learning preferences, 112
  need for, 199
  in problem solving, 15
  in skill profile, 17

267

Index

Balanced matrix organization, 30–31, 40
Balanced teams, 17–18
B- and C-dominant profile, 95
B- and D-dominant profile, 93–95
Behavioral characteristics, project-dictated, 55–56
Belbin Team Role Model, 42–44
B-G-R sequence, 135
[BG]-R sequence, 136
"Big picture thinking," 92, 94
Bloom's Taxonomy of Educational Objectives–Cognitive Domain, 145, 149, 231
B-Quadrant gaps, 220
B-Quadrant scores, 99, 99, 100, 186, 206, 223, 238
B-Quadrant thinking, 91, 175, 176
Brainstorming, 110, 114
B-R-G sequence, 134, 137
B-[RG] sequence, 134, 135
[BRG] sequence, 136
[BR]-G sequence, 137
B2B companies, 33
B2B Web site, 175
B2B Web site development, 177
B2C companies, 33
B2C Web site development, 177
Budget management, 36
Build projects, 20, 21
Business assessment, 245
Business competencies, 160, 162, 164, 206, 207
Business environment, 3, 6–7
  changes in, 58
Business functions, division of responsibility by, 27
Business process reengineering projects, 172

Business Skill Profile, 158, 196. *See also* Candidate Pool Business Skill Profile
Business skills, 147–148, 154

C

C- and D-dominant profile, 93
Candidate pool, 183. *See also* Candidate pool members
  analyzing, 184–199
  average profile of, 188
  deficiencies in, 221
  plotting, 185
Candidate Pool Business Skill Profile, 196
Candidate pool data, Gold Medallion Organ Project, 222
Candidate pool HBDI profile, 184–191
Candidate Pool Interpersonal Skill Profile, 196
Candidate pool LSI profile, 191–193
Candidate Pool Management Skill Profile, 197
Candidate pool members
  HBDI profiles for, 97–102
  LSI data for, 120–123
  PMCA of, 161–165
  PMSA of, 155–160
  SDI profiles of, 138–143
Candidate Pool Personal Skill Profile, 195
Candidate Pool Project Management Skill Profile, 195
Candidate pool SDI profile, 193–194
Candidate pool skill percentile profile, 198
Candidate pool skills profile, 194–199
Career development, 201

Case study. *See* O'Neill & Preigh case study
Cautious-supporting style, 131
Center for Project Management, 22, 23
Cerebral thinking, 89, 93, 97
Chairman role, 42
Change, accepting, 6–7
Closed-ended problems, 106
Closing life-cycle phase, 64–65
Cognitive abilities, measuring, 149
Collaborating style, 128, 137
Co-located teams, 39
Command decision style, 116
Commitment
  to process, 5
  shared, 239
Communication plan, 172
Communications
  effective, 12
  inadequate, 9–10
  informal, 36
Communications management, 9
Competence, staff, 13–14
Competencies. *See also* Interpersonal competencies; Project management skills
  business, 160, 162, 164, 206, 207
  interpersonal, 161, 162, 164, 206, 207
  management, 161, 162, 164, 206, 207
  measuring, 145
  personal, 160, 162, 164, 206, 207
Competency areas, 160
Competency survey, 160
Competing style, 128, 137
Competition, 250

Index

Completer/finisher role, 43
Complex adaptive systems development, 7
Complex projects, management of, 59
Compliance (C) personality style, 49
Comprehension, defined, 149
Compromising style, 129, 137
Conceptual thinking, 163
Concluder-producer role, 46
Concrete experience (CE) scores, 192
Concrete experience learning preference, 108
Conferencing calls, 39
Conflict
 choosing behavior in, 130
 pros and cons of, 125
Conflict management, 126–127
 balanced, 16–17
 effective, 126
Conflict management strategies
 Strength Deployment Inventory (SDI) and, 133–137
Conflict management styles, 125–143
 Strength Deployment Inventory (SDI) and, 129–137
Conflict Sequence, 131
Consensus decision style, 116–117
Conservative thinking, 95
Consultation decision style, 116
Contingency planning, 241
Continuous quality improvement, 26
Controller-inspector role, 46

Convergers, 111–112, 118, 119, 121, 226, 230
Converging learning style, 109, 111
Coordinator role, 42
Cost containment, 79
C-Quadrant gaps, 221
C-Quadrant scores, 98, 186–187, 206, 210, 223
C-Quadrant thinking, 91, 175, 181
Crawford Blue Slip technique, 114–115
Creativity, 51, 93, 106, 107
 problem solving and, 112
Creator-innovator role, 46
Critical mission projects, 24, 152
Critical path management, 2456
Critical success factors, 9, 11–14
 project team, 15–18
Critical variables, classification rules based on, 25
Cross-functional project management, 29
Customer
 effective communications with, 12
 needs of, 7

D

Database skills, 53
Decision deployment, planning and, 62
Decision making
 balanced, 16
 Learning Styles Inventory (LSI) and, 115–120
 quick, 35
 six-phase model for, 118–120
 team engagement in, 36
Decisions, alternative, 16
Decision styles, 117

Decision support system (DSS), 59, 170
Deliverables, project, 174, 239, 240
Deployment, gap management and, 71. *See also* Team development/deployment
Deployment stage, 68
Design, as a left-brain activity, 175
Design projects, 20, 21, 51, 172
Detailed planning, 91
Developing function, 45
Development projects, 172, 173
Development stage, 68
Development strategies, 70
DISC System, 47–50
Discussions, open, 12, 14
Dispersed (virtual) teams, 39
Divergers, 109–110, 115, 118, 119, 122
Diverging learning style, 109, 110
Double HBDI profiles, 92–93
D-Quadrant gaps, 221
D-Quadrant scores, 98, 100–101, 187, 210, 221, 223, 238, 245
D-Quadrant thinking, 91–92, 94, 175, 181
Drive (D) personality style, 49

E

E-business applications, 7
E-business companies, 33
Efficiency, improving, 62
Email, 39
Empowerment, of team members, 36
Enterprise environment, 3, 6
Enterprise Information Insights, 179

Enterprises, changes in, 24
Environmental considerations, 37–39
E2E companies, 33
Evaluation, 64
Evaluation skill level, 150
Explorer-promoter role, 46
Extreme projects, 7

F
Failure. *See also* Project failure
  rate of, 252
  reasons for, 8–11
  reducing, 253
Feedback, meaningful, 12
Flexible-cohering style, 130–131
Focus, staff, 14
Formation stage, 67
Functional organizational structures, 27–28

G
Gantt chart scheduling, 22
Gap analysis, 238–239
Gap management, 70–71
G-B-R sequence, 136
G-[BR] sequence, 136–137
Goal POS section, 178, 179
Gold Medallion Organ Project. *See also* Gold Team
  candidate pool data for, 222
  choosing team members for, 202–214
  HBDI profile of, 177–181
  LSI profiles for, 120–123
  Project Overview Statement (POS) for, 178, 179
  project team for, 80–84
  quadrant scores for, 186–187, 189–190
  SWOT summary of, 248–250
Gold Team
  HBDI profile of, 245
  LSI profile of, 246–247
  organizational chart for, 203
  PMSA profile of, 241–245
  SDI profile of, 245–246
  skill deficiency profile for, 242–243
  SWOT analysis of, 241–250
  Team Delta as, 237
  threats to, 250
G-R-B sequence, 137
Group leaders, 35
Groupthink, 16, 125

H
HBDI profiles, 88. *See also* Herrmann Brain Dominance Instrument (HBDI)
  alternative presentations of, 187–191
  Gold Project, 177–181
  Gold team, 245
  interpreting, 97–103
  multiple, 92–95
HBDI Whole Brain Model, 171
Herrmann Brain Dominance Instrument (HBDI), 69, 85, 87, 97. *See also* HBDI entries
  development of, 170
  test-retest reliability of, 96–97
Herrmann International, 179, 180, 189
Hierarchical leadership model, 34–35, 40

I
Ideal project team, establishing the profile of, 69
"Idea people," 91
Ideas
  critiquing, 126
  evaluating and prioritizing, 114
  generating, 114
Implementation
  developing a plan for, 114
  responsibility for, 244–245
Implementation projects, 20, 21, 172, 174
Implementation skills, 197
Implementer role, 42
Individual kite distribution team profile, 189–190
Individuals
  focusing on, 65
  understanding, 205
Influencing (I) personality style, 49
Information, compiling, 114
Information technology (IT), 79
Information technology (IT) industry, 11
Initiating life-cycle phase, 60–61
Innovating function, 45
Inspecting function, 45
Institute for Motivational Learning, 47
Interpersonal competencies, 161, 162, 163, 164, 165, 206, 207. *See also* Competencies
Interpersonal conflict, 126
Interpersonal relations, 95
Interpersonal Skill Profile, 157, 196. *See also* Candidate Pool Interpersonal Skill Profile
Interpersonal skills, 15, 24, 56, 148, 155
  for planning, 13
INTERPLACE software, 43
Interquartile range, 188
IT executive survey, 8–9. *See also* Information technology (IT)

J

Judicious-competing style, 131

K

Kiviatt Chart, 159
Knowledge, defined, 149

L

Launching life-cycle phase, 63
Leadership, shared, 250
Leadership models, 34–37
Leadership skill deficiency, 244
Learning preferences, 108
Learning process, 106–107
Learning Styles Inventory (LSI), 87, 105, 107–112. *See also* LSI entries
  decision making and, 115–120
  problem solving and, 112–115
Learning style types, 109–112
Left-brain activities, 175
Left-brain projects, 210
Left-brain thinking, 89, 91, 92, 93, 226, 226
Limbic thinking styles, 89, 98
Linker role, 47
Linking function, 46
Logic, appeals to, 135, 137
LSI profiles. *See also* Learning Styles Inventory (LSI)
  candidate pool, 191–193, 193–194
  Gold Team, 246–248
  interpreting, 120–123

M

Maintaining function, 45
Management competencies, 161, 162, 164, 206, 207
Management methodologies, 21–22
Management Skill Profile, 158, 195, 197. *See also* Candidate Pool Management Skill Profile
Management skills, 147, 154
Managers, roles of, 5
Manufacturing engineer
  choosing, 210, 213
  Gold Medallion Organ Project, 83
Margerison and McCann team management wheel, 44–47
Matrix organizations, 26–32, 39
  balanced, 30–31
  strong, 31–32
  weak, 29–30
Measurement
  of cognitive abilities, 149
  of skill proficiency level, 148–151
Mechanical engineer
  choosing, 210, 214
  Gold Medallion Organ Project, 83–84
Mergers, 24
Methodology selection, project classes for, 21–22
Moderators, 245
Monitor evaluator role, 42
Monitoring life-cycle phase, 63–64
Morale, boosting, 201
Morris and Sashkin decision-making model, 118
Motivational values, 130–133
Myers-Briggs Temperament Indicator (MBTI), 87

N

Negative alignment gap, 219, 239

O

Objectives, clear, 14
Objectives POS section, 178, 179
O'Neill & Preigh case study, 77–85
  business situation in, 78–79
  Gold Medallion Organ Project, 79–80
  Gold Medallion Organ Project team, 80–84
  team organization, 84
"One size fits all" mentality, 11, 60
Open-ended problems, 106
Opportunity
  delineation of, 113
  making use of, 240
  in SWOT analysis, 238
Organizational chart, Gold Team, 203
Organizationally complex projects, 24, 152
Organizational structures, 26–33
Organize dimension of a project, 172
Organizing function, 45
"Outside of the box" thinking, 15, 110

P

People management, 60, 61–62
People orientation, 210
People preferences, taking into account, 200
People problems, 127
People resources, types of, 62
People skills, 141
Permanent teams, 39
Personal competencies, 160, 162, 164, 165, 206, 207
Personality styles, 49
Personalize dimension of a project, 172

Personal Skill Profile, 157, 195. *See also* Candidate Pool Personal Skill Profile
Personal skills, 56, 148, 155
Personal Strengths Publishing, 239
P4 system, 57–60
Phase profiles, 59
Planning
  implementation, 114
  proper, 12–13
Planning life-cycle phase, 61–63
Plant role, 42
PMCA reports, 205, 217. *See also* Project Manager Competency Assessment (PMCA)
PMSA team profile, 241–245. *See also* Project Manager Skills Assessment (PMSA)
Political environment, 31, 32
Positive alignment gap, 219, 223, 239
Power struggles, 31
Problem definition, 113
Problem/opportunity POS section, 178, 179
Problems
  closed- and open-ended, 106
  pervasiveness of, 15
Problem solving
  balanced, 15
  creativity and, 112
  Learning Styles Inventory and, 112–115
Problem-solving model, 112–115
Problem-solving process, 106
  steps in, 13, 113–114
Problem-solving thinking style, 90
Process, commitment to, 5
Producing function, 45

Professional development, 201
  skills assessments and, 156
Professional staff turnover, 241
Proficiency, measuring, 148–151
Pro forma process, 170, 177
Programmers
  choosing, 210, 211
  Gold Medallion Organ Project, 82
Progress, monitoring, 64
Project administrator, 157
  choosing, 206–207, 208
  Gold Medallion Organ Project, 81
Project change management, 250–252
Project classes, 20–26
  methodology selection and, 21–22
Project classification rules, 25
Project Complexity Model, 22–24, 37
Project deliverables, 174, 239, 240
Project environment, 3, 4–8, 19–40. *See also* Project classes
  considerations for, 37–39
  organizational structures, 26–33
  team leadership models, 34–37
Project evaluation, 64
Project failure, 4, 252
  in functional organizations, 27
  reducing, 253
Projectized organizational structure, 26, 32–33
Project leadership models, characteristics of, 38
Project life cycle, 56
Project management life cycle, 60–65

Project management methodology, 5
Project management process, 59–60
  inappropriate, 11
  type of, 55
Project management skill profile, 156. *See also* Candidate Pool Project Management Skill Profile
Project management skills, 145–165
  list of, 146–147
  of the project manager, 153
Project Manager Competency Assessment (PMCA), 160–161, 203. *See also* PMCA reports
  of candidate pool members, 161–165
Project Manager Skills Assessment (PMSA), 145, 146–160. *See also* PMSA team profile
  of candidate pool members, 155–160
  for five teams, 230–232
Project manager profiles, 95–96
Project managers
  adaptability of, 6
  assigning, 25, 244
  business skills of, 154
  choosing, 204, 205
  for critical mission projects, 24
  Gold Medallion Organ Project, 81
  in the hierarchical leadership model, 34
  interpersonal skills of, 155
  management skills of, 154
  motivational values of, 131

for organizationally complex projects, 24
personal skills of, 155
progressive, 7
progress monitoring by, 64
project management skills of, 153
responsibilities of, 12, 60
for simple projects, 23
strategies of, 3
for technically complex projects, 24
Project needs, changes in, 71
Project notebooks, 64
  construction of, 244
Project Overview Statement (POS), 58, 177
  sections of, 178
Project parameters, 62
Project phases, profiling, 175–177
Project plans, 61–62
  launching, 63
Project portfolio, 199
Project profile, 59, 239
  changes in, 250–252
  defined, 171
  establishing, 69, 169–181
Project Profiling System, 171, 177
Projects
  critical mission, 24
  critical success factors for, 9, 11–14
  differences among, 19, 20, 169
  interpersonal aspects of, 91
  organizationally complex, 24
  simple, 23
  successful, 3–18
  technically complex, 23–24
Project scope, 58, 61
Project scope document, 69

Project scope management, 251
Project success, user involvement and, 11–12. *See also* Success factors
Project support environment, 3, 5, 20
Project team. *See also* Project team formation; Teams
  assessing, 221–232
  building an effective, 201–214
  critical success factors for, 15–18
  dynamic nature of, 71
  forming, 69–70
  improving, 70
  ineffective use of, 10
  successful, 17–18
Project/team alignment, 169
Project/Team Alignment Model, 53–73, 71, 72
  basis of, 54–57
  creating an effective project team, 66–68
  P4 System, 57–60
  phases of, 68–73
  project management life cycle, 60–65
  team life cycle, 65–66
Project team change management, 251–252
Project team development/deployment, 237–253
  general strategies for, 238–241
  SWOT analysis and, 241–250
Project/team environment, 8
Project team formation, steps in, 199–214
Project team members, choosing, 69, 203–214
Project team profile, 55–56, 183–215

candidate pool analysis, 184–199
constancy of, 56
Project team roles, 54–55
Project templates, 26
Project vision, 14
Promoting function, 45
Psychometric tools, 14

Q
Quadruple HBDI profiles, 92–93

R
R-[BG] sequence, 137
R-B-G sequence, 137
Recruiting, of team members, 67
Reengineering projects, 172
Reflective observation (RO) scores, 192
Reflective observation learning preference, 108
Repetitive projects, 26, 28
Reporter-advisor role, 47
Requirements statement, clarity in, 12
Resource investigator role, 42
Resources
  use of, 27
  wasting, 219
Responsibilities
  business functions and, 27
  implementation, 244–245
  project manager, 12, 60
  sharing, 200
[RG]-B sequence, 137
R-G-B sequence, 137
Right-brain thinking, 89, 93
Risk, in SWOT analysis, 238
Risk management, 250
Role preferences, 54–55
  assessment of, 43

S

Scope creep, 12, 61
Scope document, 72
SDI profiles. *See also* Strength Deployment Inventory (SDI)
  Gold Team, 245–246
  interpreting, 138–143
Self-assessment, 161, 163, 165
Self-confidence, 163
Self-image, 164–165
Self-managed teams, 36–37
Senior project managers, 24
Shaper role, 42
Shared leadership, 250
Shared leadership model, 36
Simple projects, 23, 152
  management of, 59
Single HBDI profiles, 92
Skill deficiencies, ranked, 231–232
Skill deficiency profile, Gold Team, 242–243
Skill percentile profile, 159, 198
Skill proficiency level, measuring, 148–151
Skill profiles, 25
  balanced, 17
  candidate profile, 194–199
  information from, 151–155
Skills. *See also* Project Manager Skills Assessment (PMSA)
  business, 147–148
  interpersonal, 148
  management, 147
  measuring, 145
  personal, 148
  project management, 146–147
Skills assessments, professional development and, 156

Specialist role, 43
Staff
  competent, 13–14
  hard-working and focused, 14
  turnover of, 241
Staffing requirements, 5
Standard methodology, enforcement of, 11
Standish Group, 3, 8
Standish Group surveys, 18
Status reporting, 36
Steadiness (S) personality style, 49
Stovepipe organization, 27
Strategic team, 186
Strategize dimension of a project, 172–173
Strength Deployment Inventory (SDI), 125, 127, 129–137. *See also* SDI profiles
  conflict management strategies and, 133–137
Strengths
  in SWOT analysis, 238
  team, 238–239
Strong matrix organization, 31–32
Success, increasing the likelihood of, 3
Success criteria POS section, 178, 179
Success factors, 11–14
  project team, 15–18
Successful project teams, 17–18
Surveys, role-preference, 43
SWOT (Strengths, Weaknesses, Opportunities, Threats) analysis, 238, 241–250
SWOT summary, 248–250
Synthesis skill level, 150
Systems, 5
Systems analyst
  choosing, 210, 212

Gold Medallion Organ Project, 83

T

Task assignments, changing, 56–57
Team alignment
  assessing, 217–233
  focusing on, 65
  project team assessment, 221–232
  team-to-project alignment, 218–221
Team Alpha, 84
Team Alpha assessment, 223
  skill deficiencies in, 231–232
Team Alpha profile, 224
Team analysis, 239
TeamArchitect, 59, 85, 170, 171
  significant feature of, 184
TeamArchitect approach, 52
TeamArchitect classification rule, 171
teamarchitect.com, 85, 215
Team assessment, 67, 218–232
Team average profile, 187–188
Team balance, 45, 103. *See also* Balance; Balanced teams
  determining, 123
Team Beta, 84
Team Beta assessment, 223–226
  skill deficiencies in, 231–232
Team Beta profile, 225
Team characteristics, 8
Team/client coordination, 176
Team coordinator model, 35–36
Team Delta, 84, 237, 247
  LSI scores of, 244

Team Delta Assessment, 226–230
  skill deficiencies in, 231–232
Team Delta profile, 228
Team development/deployment, 10
  strategies for, 238
Team DIC profile, 50
Team effectiveness, 53, 177, 184
  in a balanced matrix structure, 31
  in a matrix organization, 29
  in a strong matrix structure, 32
  in functional organizations, 28
  improving, 170, 253
  organizational structure and, 26
Team Epsilon, 84
Team Epsilon assessment, 230
  skill deficiencies in, 231–232
Team Epsilon profile, 229
Team evolution, 65
Team formation, 252–253
  project classes for, 21
Team Gamma, 84
Team Gamma assessment, 226
  skill deficiencies in, 231–232
Team Gamma profile, 227
Team leadership models, 19, 34–37
  choosing, 37
Team learning style patterns, 191–193
Team life cycle, 65–66
Team Management Index (TMI), 47
Team management wheel, 44–47
Team members
  assessing strengths and weaknesses of, 68
  assignment of, 200–201
  choosing, 183, 218
  diversity among, 15
  reassignment of, 37
  recruiting, 217
  repositioning, 56–57
  selecting, 67
  work preferences of, 200–201
Team membership, changes in, 251–252
Team midrange profile, 188
Team models, 41–52
  Belbin team role model, 42–44
  DISC System, 47–50
  Margerison and McCann team management wheel, 44–47
  shortcomings of, 50–52
Team profile, 55–56, 59, 184. *See also* Candidate pool
  PMSA, 241–245
  understanding, 66
  using individual kite distribution, 189–190
Team role models, comparison of, 48
Team role profiles, 43, 44
Team roles, 42–43
  understanding, 14
Teams
  balanced, 17–18
  competent, 13–14
  defined, 51
  differences among, 21
  dispersed versus co-located, 39
  interpersonal characteristics of, 12
  temporary versus permanent, 39
  understanding, 10
Team size, 51–52, 55
Team skill deficiencies, ranked, 231–232

Team success, premises underlying, 54–56. *See also* Success factors
Team-to-project alignment, 71
Teamworker role, 42
Technically complex projects, 23–24, 152
Technical professionals, demand for, 6
Technical skills, 17
Technology, changes in, 6
Technology infrastructure, 5
Templates
  project, 26
  for simple projects, 23
Temporary teams, 39
Test-retest reliability
  of HDBI, 96–97
  of SDI, 133
Thinking styles, 87–103
  A-Quadrant, 90
  B-Quadrant, 91
  C-Quadrant, 91
  distribution pattern of, 185–186
  D-Quadrant, 91–92
  Herrmann Brain Dominance Instrument (HBDI) and, 97
  mapping, 89
  TeamArchitect and, 184
  variability of, 97–102
Threats
  contingency planning for, 240–241
  to the Gold team, 250
  in SWOT analysis, 238
360-degree assessment tool, 161
Thruster-organizer role, 46
Top-down control, 34
Training, support for, 219
Training management staff, 194
Triple HBDI profiles, 92–93
Turnover, staff, 241

Type I projects, 152, 160
Type II projects, 152, 160
Type III projects, 152, 160
Type IV projects, 152, 160

U

Uncertainty, reducing, 62
Understanding, increasing, 62
Unemployment, 6
Upholder-maintainer role, 47
User involvement, 11–12

V

Value-relating styles, 130, 131, 136
Values, motivational, 130–133
Video conferencing, 37
Virtual teams, 39
Vision
 clarity in, 14
 shared, 239

W

Wants/need gap, 12
Weak matrix organizations, 29–30, 39
Weaknesses
 in SWOT analysis, 238
 team, 239–240
Web-based project/team profiling system, 171
Web-based project tools, 39
Web design projects, 173
Whole-brain approach, 95
Whole Brain Model, 171, 177
Workforce, skilled, 5
Work functions, 45
Work preferences, 47, 201

CUSTOMER NOTE: IF THIS BOOK IS ACCOMPANIED BY SOFTWARE, PLEASE READ THE FOLLOWING BEFORE OPENING THE PACKAGE.

This software contains files to help you utilize the models described in the accompanying book. By opening the package, you are agreeing to be bound by the following agreement:

This software product is protected by copyright and all rights are reserved by the author, John Wiley & Sons, Inc., or their licensors. You are licensed to use this software as described in the software and the accompanying book. Copying the software for any other purpose may be a violation of the U.S. Copyright Law.

This software product is sold as is without warranty of any kind, either express or implied, including but not limited to the implied warranty of merchantability and fitness for a particular purpose. Neither Wiley nor its dealers or distributors assumes any liability for any alleged or actual damages arising from the use of or the inability to use this software. (Some states do not allow the exclusion of implied warranties, so the exclusion may not apply to you.)

System Requirements

- Windows 95, 98, ME, or higher, *or* Windows NT 4.0, 2000, or higher
- IBM-compatible PC with 486 processor or higher (Pentium 233 MHz or higher recommended)
- Minimum 16 MB RAM (32 MB RAM recommended)
- 25 MB free hard drive space available for normal install (recommended)
- 4x or higher CD-ROM drive